AMERICA IN LITERATURE

LITERATURE

The City

AMERICA IN LITERATURE

General Editor, Max Bogart

The Northeast, James Lape, editor
The South, Sara Marshall, editor
The West, Peter Monahan, editor
The Midwest, Ronald Szymanski, editor
The Small Town, Flory Jones Schultheiss, editor
The City, Adele Stern, editor

AMERICA IN LITERATURE
The City

EDITED BY

Adele Stern

Vice Principal and Curriculum Coordinator,
Paramus High School
Paramus, New Jersey

CHARLES SCRIBNER'S SONS • NEW YORK

Library of Congress Cataloging in Publication Data
Main entry under title:
America in Literature: The City.
   Includes index.
   1. American literature—20th century.
2. City and town life—Literary collections.
I. Stern, Adele H.   II. Series.
PS509.C57C5   810'.8'032   79-13292
ISBN 0-684-16139-7

1 3 5 7 9 11 13 15 17 19   V/P   20 18 16 14 12 10 8 6 4 2

Printed in the United States of America

Cover Illustration: *Metropolis No. 2* by Abraham Walkowitz. Courtesy of the Hirshhorn Museum and Sculpture Garden, Smithsonian Institution. Photograph by John Tennant.

Picture Research: Yvonne Freund

ACKNOWLEDGMENTS

ALFRED KAZIN, "The Block and Beyond." From *A Walker in the City,* copyright, 1951, by Alfred Kazin. Reprinted by permission of Harcourt Brace Jovanovich, Inc.
LAWRENCE FERLINGHETTI, "Fortune" and "The pennycandystore beyond the El" from Lawrence Ferlinghetti, *A Coney Island of the Mind.* Copyright 1955, © 1958 by Lawrence Ferlinghetti. Reprinted by permission of New Directions.
LILLIAN MORRISON, "Of Kings and Things" from *The Ghosts of Jersey City* Copyright © 1967 by Lillian Morrison.

Acknowledgments continue on page 243, an extension of the copyright page.

CONTENTS

Contents

AMERICA IN LITERATURE

The City

Introduction

Cities are human inventions—contrived environments of concrete that demonstrate people's compelling need to create an ordered and structured existence. In contrast to the self-replenishing environment of the country—natural, organic—the city's landscape is an artificial world completely dependent upon human activity for its continued growth and prosperity.

Because they are a kaleidoscope of sounds and sights, a melting of rich and poor, a gathering of many people, cities have excited the imaginations of many American writers who have discovered there a rich opportunity for literary expression as well as an abundance of human material on which to comment. In a variety of literary forms, the writer has recreated life in the city, the pace and tempo, the social relationships, the customs and traditions, the conventions and routines, the pervading dynamic atmosphere. Joyce Carol Oates's Detroit has a grayness, a heaviness that is far different from the strident intensity of William Saroyan's San Francisco; E. B. White's New York is a huge, exciting panorama while Edna Ferber's Milwaukee is a true ethnic community with a strong sense of both the old world and the new.

The city's attraction has been no less compelling for writers of verse. A child dancing in front of an open fire hydrant on a hot summer day, the penny candy store beyond the elevated train station where all kinds of sensual treats abound, the workers sitting knee to knee in the hot factory, a scrawny youngster hitting a hard ball with a homemade bat—these are some of the images that have captured the poet's view.

O'Henry said of the New York he loved, "the city is like a mother's knee to many who have strayed far and found the roads rough beneath their uncertain feet. At dusk they come home and sit upon the doorstep." E. B. White called New York a city of "great times and tall deeds, of queer people and events and undertakings." Writers who have left their city homes return

1

A City of Fantasy, American School, Mid-Nineteenth Century

to them on paper: Gerald Green visited his father's house in Brooklyn, Ben Hecht the Chicago of his early days as a reporter; Thomas Wolfe wandered about the city on foot. Alfred Kazin never really left the city block which formed his early experience; so much of what he wrote reached back to that place in Brooklyn and the people he knew there. So it was with James Baldwin, who relived the Harlem experience again and again, even though he may have been doing so from Paris. People create cities, to be sure; but cities also create people. In this volume we shall see how.

Growing Up in the City

Childhood in the city moves quickly because *all* of city life does—and as the following selections show, city children often struggle to make their way in its surging activity. The density of the population, the ceaseless movement and interaction of all who live and work there, and the infinite possibilities for adventure all lead the city child into an awareness of self and environment that is distinctly urban. City children learn early how to deal with danger, how to fall down and get up again, how to stand up and be counted if they are to stand out at all. In the excitement of this enormous campus of sights and sounds, of poverty and riches, of rushing tempos, the growing child must sort out what is personal and immediate from what is beyond the neighborhood of intimacy. Knowledge thus gained marks the beginnings of personal identity, and of maturity.

Alfred Kazin writes of his block in Brownsville, Brooklyn, of the people he knew, of the images and experiences that made up his childhood. All the people—the dedicated shoemaker, the Italian boy and Jewish girl who fell in love and married into a society which rejected such love and marriage; the local madwoman Blumka—all of these nudged the child into early adulthood.

Nancy Hale, a Boston city girl of affluence, measured her youth by the dances she attended at the fashionable Copley-Plaza Hotel. All the trappings of a secure and carefree existence were hers: elegant clothing, rich food, elaborate social gatherings—so different from the experiences of the poor, the immigrant, the black.

At roughly the same time that Hale made her debut into Boston society, Richard Wright was fighting for his existence in the streets of Memphis, his life ultimately dependent on his ability to withstand

Tug of War

the double onslaught of hunger and white hostility. Elva Mangold's portrait of the immigrant's urban plight focuses on the fierce cruelties of poverty.

The process of growing up is universal. It is filled with events and feelings that both ignore and transcend the influences of skin color, or the degree of material advantage. Lillian Morrison's growing child Joey fulfilled his rites of passage with an improvised baseball bat in the game on his block; Ferlinghetti's children marked their experience with visits to the pennycandy store, or gleeful showers provided by the firemen's hoses on hot summer days.

The Block and Beyond*

ALFRED KAZIN

The old drugstore on our corner has been replaced by a second-hand furniture store; the old candy store has been replaced by a second-hand furniture store, the old bakery, the old hardware shop, the old "coffee pot" that was once reached over a dirt road. I was there the day they put a pavement in. That "coffee pot" was the first restaurant I ever sat in, trembling— they served ham and bacon there—over a swiss cheese on rye and coffee in a thick mug without a saucer as I watched the truck drivers kidding the heavily lipsticked girl behind the counter. The whole block is now thick with second-hand furniture stores. The fluttering red canvas signs BARGAINS BARGAINS reach up to the first-floor windows. At every step I have to fight maple love seats bulging out of the doors. It looks as if our old life has been turned out into the street, suddenly reminds me of the nude shamed look furniture on the street always had those terrible first winters of the depression, when we stood around each newly evicted family to give them comfort and the young Communists raged up and down the street calling for volunteers to put the furniture back and crying aloud with their fists lifted to the sky. But on the Chester Street side of the house I make out the letters we carefully pasted there in tar sometime in the fall of either 1924 or 1925:

DAZZY VANCE
WORLDS GREATEST PICHER
262 STRIKEOUTS
BROOKLYN NATIONAL LEAG
GIANTS STINK ON ICE
DAZZY DAZZY DAZZY

The old barbershop is still there. Once it was owned by two brothers, the younger one fat and greasy and with a waxed stiffly pointed mustache of

* Selection from *A Walker in the City.*

9

which he was so proud that he put a photograph of himself in the window with the inscription: "MEN! LOOK AT OUR MUSTACHE AND LOOK AT YOURS!" The older one was dry and sad, the "conscientious" partner. The fat brother had an old fiddle he let me play in the shop when business was bad; he would sprawl in the first barber chair languidly admiring himself in the great mirrors, clicking his teeth over the nudes in the *Police Gazette*, and keep time for me by waving his razor. I never liked him very much; he was what we reproachfully called a "sport," a loud and boastful man; he always smelled of hair lotion. You could see each hair as it ran off the crown of his head so sticky and twisted in lotion that it reflected the light from the bulbs in the ceiling. We were all a little afraid of him. One day he bought a motorcycle on credit, and as he started it from the curb, flew into the window of the delicatessen store. I remember the shiver of the glass as it instantaneously fell out all around him, and as he picked himself up, his face and hands streaming with blood, the sly little smile with which he pointed to the sausages and pickle pots in the street: "Hey you little bastards! Free treat!"

I see the barbershop through the steam from the hot towel fount. The vapor glistened on the unbelievable breasts of the calendar nudes pasted above the mirrors and on the fat bandaged chin of Peaches Browning every day in the *News* and on the great colored drawing all over the front page of the *Graphic* one morning showing Mrs. Ruth Snyder strapped and burning in the electric chair. The smell of hair tonic could never disguise the steaming exhalation of raw female flesh. Everything in that barbershop promised me a first look. On the table, along with the *News* and the *Graphic*, *College Humor* and the *Police Gazette*, lay several volumes of a pictorial history of the World War. I played the barber's violin for him only because I could then get to sit over those volumes by the hour, lost in the gray photographs and drawings of men going into battle, ruined towns in Serbia, Belgium, and France where one chimney still rose from a house destroyed by shell fire, pictures of the victorious French in 1919 dipping their battle standards in the Rhine. There were two photographs I remember particularly: it was really for them that I went back and back to that barbershop. One showed a group of German officers in full uniform, with all their medals, standing outside a brothel in France with the ladies of the house, who were naked to the waist and wore crosses between their enormous breasts. The officers had their arms comfortably draped over the girls' shoulders, and grinned into

10

the camera. GERMAN KULTUR, ran the caption. HOW THE ENEMY AMUSES ITSELF BEHIND THE LINES. The other photograph showed Kaiser Wilhelm with his retinue, inspecting troops. The Kaiser and the generals were walking on wooden planks; the caption noted that the planks had been laid there to keep the distinguished company from walking in the blood that ran over the field.

The shoemaker is still there; the old laundry is now a printing shop. Next to it is the twin of our old house, connected with ours below the intervening stores by a long common cellar. As I look at the iron grillwork over the glass door, I think of the dark-faced girl who used to stand on that stoop night after night watching for her Italian boy friend. Her widowed mother, dressed always in black, a fat meek woman with a clubfoot, was so horrified by the affair that she went to the neighbors for help. The quarrels of mother and daughter could be heard all over the street. "How can you go around with an Italian? How can you think of it? You're unnatural! You're draining the blood straight from my heart!" Night after night she would sit at her window, watching the girl go off with her *Italyéner*—ominous word that contained all her fear of the Gentiles—and weep. The Italian boy was devoted to the daughter and wanted them to marry. Again and again he tried to persuade the mother, but she would lock the door on him and cry out from behind it in Yiddish: "I have harmed you and your family? I interfere with *your* customs? Go away and leave us be! Leave us be! A Jewish girl is not for you, Mister! Go away!" In desperation, he offered "to become a Jew." No one had ever heard of such a thing, and the mother was so astonished that she gave her consent to the marriage. The boy was overjoyed—but waited until the last possible moment before the wedding to undergo circumcision, and as he walked tremblingly to the canopy, the blood dripping down his trouser legs, fainted dead away. The block never stopped talking about it.

Where now is my beautiful Mrs. Baruch, the "chicken lady," who sat smack in the middle of her store on a bloody kitchen chair plucking and plucking the feathers off her chickens with such a raw hearty laugh that you could hear her a block away? I would stop in her doorway on my way back from school just to watch her work, for as she plucked, plucked the feathers off her chickens with one grimly impatient pull along her right elbow, she seemed instantaneously to draw out of their bellies a great coiling mass of

11

intestines and blood vessels, and—never for a moment letting up in her unending hoarse cackle—scolded and gossiped with the women standing around her. Whenever she looked up and saw me standing in the doorway, she would hold up her hands in mock dismay, feathers sticking to each finger, and her hairy chin trembling with laughter, would call out—"Hey, studént! My Alfred! Come give me a big kiss! Is all right! Your mother left here an hour ago!"

And where is Blumka, our local madwoman, who every Friday afternoon just before the Sabbath began, icy pale under her sleek black pompadour, made the rounds of the block dragging a child's cart behind her and wearing a long satin dress? She often sat on the stoop of our house with her head resting against the glass in the door, gossiping with the neighbors or talking to herself, and never budged until the cart was heaped with charcoal, chicory, the long white Sabbath *khalleh*, and fruit. It was on our steps particularly that she liked to take her rest. Perhaps she enjoyed embarrassing us; perhaps, I used to think, she stopped there because she knew how much I loved watching her, for she would smile and smile at me with a fixed and shameless grin. Shamless was our word for her—a Jewish woman to beg in the streets! She had a brutal directness in the way she did everything—flopped around the streets all Friday long with her cart ignoring everyone with a dreamy contempt unless she wanted to talk; openly demanded her living of us; sat herself down on a stoop whenever she liked, mumbling to herself or jeering at the children; and when she liked, lay flat on the steps singing old Yiddish ditties to herself. Always in the same long black satin dress that came down to her high button shoes, always dragging that battered children's cart behind her, she would sometimes lie there against the glass, her tightly coiled mass of dead-looking hair splitting the light where she lay, her long straight nose and fierce jaw jutting into the air with a kind of insolent defiance. She seemed always to be jeering, but it was hard to find out what she meant by it, for she said everything that came into her mind in the same gruff oddly disdainful tone of voice, her icy pale cheeks moving tensely up and down as she chewed at a piece of bread.

The block: *my* block. It was on the Chester Street side of our house, between the grocery and the back wall of the old drugstore, that I was hammered into the shape of the streets. Everything beginning at Blake Avenue would always wear for me some delightful strangeness and mildness, simply because it was not of my block, *the* block, where the clang of your head sounded against the pavement when you fell in a fist fight, and the rows of storelights on each side were pitiless, watching you. Anything away from the block was good: even a school you never went to, two blocks away: there were vegetable gardens in the park across the street. Returning from "New York," I would take the longest routes home from the subway, get off a station ahead of our own, only for the unexpectedness of walking through Betsy Head Park and hearing the gravel crunch under my feet as I went beyond the vegetable gardens, smelling the sweaty sweet dampness from the pool in summer and the dust on the leaves as I passed under the ailanthus trees. On the block itself everything rose up only to test me.

We worked every inch of it, from the cellars and the backyards to the sickening space between the roofs. Any wall, any stoop, any curving metal edge on a billboard sign made a place against which to knock a ball; any bottom rung of a fire escape ladder a goal in basketball; any sewer cover a base; any crack in the pavement a "net" for the tense sharp tennis that we played by beating a soft ball back and forth with our hands between the squares. Betsy Head Park two blocks away would always feel slightly foreign, for it belonged to the Amboys and the Bristols and the Hopkinsons as much as it did to us. *Our* life every day was fought out on the pavement and in the gutter, up against the walls of the houses and the glass fronts of the drugstore and the grocery, in and out of the fresh steaming piles of horse manure, the wheels of passing carts and automobiles, along the iron spikes of the stairway to the cellar, the jagged edge of the open garbage cans, the crumbly steps of the old farmhouses still left on one side of the street.

As I go back to the block now, and for a moment fold my body up again in its narrow arena—there, just there, between the black of the asphalt and the old women in their kerchiefs and flowered housedresses sitting on the tawny kitchen chairs—the back wall of the drugstore still rises up to test me. Every day we smashed a small black viciously hard regulation handball against it with fanatical cuts and drives and slams, beating and slashing at it almost in hatred for the blind strength of the wall itself. I was never good enough at handball, was always practicing some trick shot that might earn me esteem, and when I was weary of trying, would often bat a ball down Chester Street just to get myself to Blake Avenue. I have this memory of playing one-o'-cat by myself in the sleepy twilight, at a moment when everyone else had left the block. The sparrows floated down from the telephone wires to peck at every fresh pile of horse manure, and there was a smell of brine from the delicatessen store, of egg creates and of the milk scum left in the great metal cans outside the grocery, of the thick white paste oozing out from behind the fresh Hecker's Flour ad on the metal signboard. I would throw the ball in the air, hit it with my bat, then with perfect satisfaction drop the bat to the ground and run to the next sewer cover. Over and over I did this, from sewer cover to sewer cover, until I had worked my way to Blake Avenue and could see the park.

With each clean triumphant ring of my bat against the gutter leading me on, I did the whole length of our block up and down, and never knew how happy I was just watching the asphalt rise and fall, the curve of the steps up to an old farmhouse. The farmhouses themselves were streaked red on one side, brown on the other, but the steps themselves were always gray. There was a tremor of pleasure at one place; I held my breath in nausea at another. As I ran after my ball with the bat heavy in my hand, the odd successiveness of things in myself almost choked me, the world was so full as I ran—past the cobblestoned yards into the old farmhouses, where stray chickens still waddled along the stones; past the little candy store where we went only if the big one on our side of the block was out of Eskimo Pies; past the three neighboring tenements where the last of the old women sat on their kitchen chairs yawning before they went up to make supper. Then came Mrs. Rosenwasser's house, the place on the block I first identified with what was farthest from home, and strangest, because it was a "private" house; then the fences around the monument works, where black cranes rose up above the yard and you could see the smooth gray slabs that would be cut and carved into tombstones, some of them already engraved with the names and dates and family virtues of the dead.

Beyond Blake Avenue was the pool parlor outside which we waited all through the tense September afternoons of the World's Series to hear the latest scores called off the ticker tape—and where as we waited, banging a ball against the bottom of the wall and drinking water out of empty coke bottles, I breathed the chalk off the cues and listened to the clocks ringing in the fire station across the street. There was an old warehouse next to the pool parlor; the oil on the barrels and the iron staves had the same rusty smell. A block away was the park, thick with the dusty gravel I liked to hear my shoes crunch in as I ran round and round the track; then a great open pavilion, the inside mysteriously dark, chill even in summer; there I would wait in the sweaty coolness before pushing on to the wading ring where they put up a shower on the hottest days.

14

Beyond the park the "fields" began, all those still unused lots where we could still play hard ball in perfect peace—first shooing away the goats and then tearing up goldenrod before laying our bases. The smell and touch of those "fields," with their wild compost under the billboards of weeds, goldenrod, bricks, goat droppings, rusty cans, empty beer bottles, fresh new lumber, and damp cement, lives in my mind as Brownsville's great open door, the wastes that took us through to the west. I used to go round them in summer with my cousins selling near-beer to the carpenters, but always in a daze, would stare so long at the fibrous stalks of the goldenrod as I felt their harshness in my hand that I would forget to make a sale, and usually go off sick on the beer I drank up myself. Beyond! Beyond! Only to see something new, to get away from each day's narrow battleground between the grocery and the back wall of the drugstore! Even the other end of our block, when you got to Mrs. Rosenwasser's house and the monument works, was dear to me for the contrast. On summer nights, when we played Indian trail, running away from each other on prearranged signals, the greatest moment came when I could plunge into the darkness down the block for myself and hide behind the slabs in the monument works. I remember the air whistling around me as I ran, the panicky thud of my bones in my sneakers, and then the slabs rising in the light from the street lamps as I sped past the little candy store and crept under the fence.

In the darkness you could never see where the crane began. We liked to trap the enemy between the slabs and sometimes jumped them from great mounds of rocks just in from the quarry. A boy once fell to his death that way, and they put a watchman there to keep us out. This made the slabs all the more impressive to me, and I always aimed first for that yard whenever we played follow-the-leader. Day after day the monument works became oppressively more mysterious and remote, though it was only just down the block; I stood in front of it every afternoon on my way back from school, filling it with my fears. It was not death I felt there—the slabs were usually faceless. It was the darkness itself, and the wind howling around me whenever I stood poised on the edge of a high slab waiting to jump. Then I would take in, along with the fear, some amazement of joy that I had found my way out that far.

Beyond! Beyond! *Beyond* was "the city," connected only by interminable subway lines and some old Brooklyn-Manhattan trolley car rattling across Manhattan Bridge. At night, as the trolley ground its way home in the rain though miles of unknown streets from some meeting in the Jewish Daily *Forward* building on the East Side to which my father had taken me, I saw the flickering light bulbs in the car, the hard yellow benches on which we sat half asleep, the motorman's figure bulging the green curtain he had drawn against the lights in the car, as a rickety cart stumbling through infinite space—the driver taking us where? *Beyond* was the wheeze of an accordion on the Staten Island ferry boat—the music rocking in such unison with the vibration of the engines as the old man walked in and out of the cars on the lower deck squeezing the tunes out of the pleats that never after would I be able to take a ferry from South Ferry, from Christopher Street, from 23rd, from Dyckman, from 125th, without expecting that same man to come round with his silver-backed accordion and his hat in his hand as he jangled a few coins in a metal plate. *Beyond* was the long shivering blast of the ferry starting out from the Battery in sight of the big Colgate ad across the river in Jersey; the depth of peace as the sun warmed the panels of the doors sliding out to the observation deck; the old Italian shoeshine men walking round and round with their boxes between all those suddenly relaxed New Yorkers comfortably staring at each other in the high wind on the top deck; a garbage scow burning in the upper bay just under Liberty's right arm; the minarets on Ellis Island; the old prison walls under the trees of Governor's Island; then, floating back in the cold dusk toward the diamond-lighted wall of Manhattan skyscrapers, the way we huddled in the great wooden varnish-smelling cabin inside as if we were all getting under the same quilt on a cold night.

Beyond was the canvas awnings over an El station in summer. Inside, the florid red windows had curlicues running up and down their borders. I had never seen anything like them in all the gritty I.R.T. stations below. Those windows were richer than all my present. The long march of snails up and down and around the borders of those windows, the cursive scrolls in the middle patch forever turning back on themselves, promised to lead me straight into the old New York of gaslight and police stations I always looked for in the lower city. And of a winter afternoon—the time for which I most lovingly remember the El, for the color of the winter dusk as it fell through those painted windows, and the beauty of the snow on the black cars and iron rails and tar roofs we saw somewhere off Brooklyn Bridge—when the country stove next to the change booth blazed and blazed as some crusty old woman with a pince-nez gave out change, and the heavy turnstiles crashed with a roar inside the wooden shed—then, among the darkly huddled crowds waiting to go out to the train, looking out on Brooklyn Bridge all dark sweeping cable lines under drifts of snow, I pretended those were gaslights I saw in the streets below, that all old New Yorkers were my fathers, and that the train we waited for could finally take me back—back and back to that old New York of wood and brownstones and iron, where Theodore Roosevelt as Police Commissioner had walked every night.

Beyond was anything old and American—the name *Fraunces Tavern* repeated to us on a school excursion; the eighteenth-century muskets and glazed oil paintings on the wall; the very streets, the deeper you got into Brooklyn, named after generals of the Revolutionary War—Putnam, Gates, Kosciusko, DeKalb, Lafayette, Pulaski. *Beyond* was the sound of *Desbrosses* Street that steaming July morning we crossed back on a Jersey ferry, and the smell of the salt air in the rotting planks floating on the green scummy waters of the Hudson. *Beyond* was the watery floor of the Aquarium that smelled of the eternally wet skins of the seals in the great tank; the curve of lower Broadway around Bowling Green Park when you went up to Wall Street; the yellow wicker seats facing each other in the middle of the El car; the dome of the Manhattan Savings Bank over Chinatown at the entrance to Manhattan Bridge, and then in Brooklyn again, after we had traveled from light into dark, dark into light, along the shuddering shadowy criss-cross of the bridge's pillars, the miles and miles of Gentile cemeteries where crosses toppled up and down endless slopes. *Beyond* was that autumn morning in New Haven when I walked up and down two *red* broken paving stones, smelled the leaves burning in the yard, and played with black battered poker chips near the country stove in an aunt's kitchen; it was the speckles on the bananas hanging in the window of the grocery store another aunt owned in the Negro streets just behind Union Station in Washington; the outrageously warm taste of milk fresh from a cow that summer my mother cooked with a dozen others in the same Catskill boarding house; it was the open trolley cars going to Coney Island, the conductor swinging from bar to bar as he came around the ledge collecting fares; it was the *Robert Fulton* going up the Hudson to Indian Point, the ventilators on the upper deck smelling of soup.

Beyond, even in Brownsville, was the summer sound of *flax* when my mother talked of *der heym.* It was the Negroes singing as they passed under our windows late at night on their way back to Livonia Avenue. It was the Children's Library on Stone Avenue, because they had an awning over the front door; in the long peaceful reading room there were storybook tiles over the fireplace and covered deep wooden benches on each side of it where I read my way year after year from every story of King Alfred the Great to *Twenty Thousand Leagues Under the Sea. Beyond* was the burly Jewish truckers from the wholesale fruit markets on Osborne Street sitting in their dark smoky "Odessa" and "Roumanian" tearooms, where each table had its own teapot, and where the men sat over mounds of saucers smoking Turkish cigarettes and beating time to the balalaíka. *Beyond* was the way to the other end of Sutter Avenue, past a store I often went into to buy buttons and thread for my mother, and where the light simmered on the thin upturned curves of the pearl buttons in the window. *Beyond* was the roar in the Pennsylvania freight yards on the way to East New York; even the snow houses we built in the backyard of a cousin's house on Herzl Street waiting to ambush those thieves from Bristol Street. It was the knife grinder's horse and wagon when he stopped on our block, and an "American" voice called up to every window, *Sharpen knives! Sharpen knives!*—that man had obviously come from a long way off.

Fortune

LAWRENCE FERLINGHETTI

Fortune
       has its cookies to give out

which is a good thing

          since it's been a long time since

     that summer in Brooklyn
   when they closed off the street
       one hot day
       and the

       FIREMEN

          turned on their hoses
and all the kids ran out in it

    in the middle of the street

   and there were

      maybe a couple dozen of us

          out there

Growing Up in the City

with the water squirting up
                          to the

                    sky

                                and all over
                                        us

there was maybe only six of us
                          kids altogether
        running around in our
                          barefeet and birthday
            suits
                and I remember Molly but then

        the firemen stopped squirting their hoses
            all of a sudden and went
                    back in
                their firehouse
                    and
            started playing pinochle again
                just as if nothing
                    had ever
                          happened
    while I remember Molly
                    looked at me and

        ran in

    because I guess really we were the only ones there

The pennycandystore beyond the El

LAWRENCE FERLINGHETTI

The pennycandystore beyond the El
is where I first
                    fell in love
                            with unreality
Jellybeans glowed in the semi-gloom
of that September afternoon
A cat upon the counter moved among
                            the licorice sticks
                and tootsie rolls
            and Oh Boy Gum

Outside the leaves were falling as they died

A wind had blown away the sun

A girl ran in
Her hair was rainy
Her breasts were breathless in the little room

Outside the leaves were falling
                    and they cried
                            Too soon! too soon!

Of Kings and Things

LILLIAN MORRISON

What happened to Joey on our block
Who could hit a spaldeen four sewers
And wore his invisible crown
With easy grace, leaning, body-haloed
In the street-lamp night?

He was better than Babe Ruth
Because we could actually see him hit
Every Saturday morning,
With a mop handle thinner than any baseball bat,
that small ball which flew forever.
Whack! straight out at first, then
Rising, rising unbelievably soaring in a
Tremendous heart-bursting trajectory
To come down finally, blocks away,
Bouncing off a parked car's
Fender, eluding the lone outfielder.

Did he get a good job?
Is he married now, with kids?
Is he famous in another constellation?
I saw him with my own eyes in those days
The God of stickball
Disappearing down the street
Skinny and shining in the nightfall light.

Chalk Games

The Land of Room Enough

ELVA MANGOLD

Manuel looked at the dilapidated brownstone house with its chipped cement steps. He was disappointed. Manuel had been filled with hope and excitement when the man in the grocery store told him of the fine home near Central Park where one could go boating and play baseball. It even had a magic address—Columbus Avenue. But this building held no magic, except the miracle of its continued existence.

"Since we are here," said Mama, "we look!"

Pulling her good black crepe dress down over her portly frame, still holding a suitcase in one hand and Marzo in the other, she climbed the stairs, a grim look marring her usually placid features. Papa Jorge following with the other children, all six of them.

A wiry, mustached man with steel-gray hair stood at the entrance.

"What can I do for you folks?" he asked.

Manuel disliked him instinctively. He was Puerto Rican, same as they, but, thought Manuel to himself, "he's trying to act bold like American cowboy."

"We come to see the rooms," Papa explained, stepping forward with a slip of paper which he presented.

"Just off the boat?" asked the man.

"The airplane," snapped Manuel. "Last week we come to La Guardia airport from San Juan. The Welfare Society gave us a room way up Madison Avenue but we want to change. Man in the grocery gave me this address. He said it was beautiful place!" He glanced about disdainfully. "Is not beautiful!" he said bitterly.

Papa smiled with embarrassment. "He expect too much. He was told there were four rooms here. Big apartment. As you can see, we need big apartment." He laughed nervously and pointed to his wide-eyed children standing uncomfortably in their best and only suits.

24

Mullen's Alley, ca. 1888–9.

"You've come to the right place," said the man, "My name's Jesepo. There's one apartment left, but . . ."

Papa's body tightened with anxiety. "We have to have place, Mr. Jesepo. I got good job with my sister-in-law. Her husband die and I take over his photography business with her. I don't go back to Manati. I stay here and make good Americans of my children. Mama, we forget to introduce our children. The man must think we have no manners."

A flicker of a smile passed over Mama's face. With the wisdom of forty-five years of hardships she understood what Mr. Jesepo was trying to do. Nevertheless, there were formalities. She pointed to each child with a curt, stiff gesture.

"Rosa—thirteen, Eduardo eleven, Dolores ten, Enero eight, Febrero six, Marzo four."

Mr. Jesepo's exaggerated grin vanished. "You joke with me!" he said, "I speak Spanish, too! Who would be stupid enough to name their children after the months?"

Papa's body tightened with anxiety. "We have to have humor. She have so many children she run out of names!"

Mr. Jesepo grunted and changed the subject. "And the big one—what's his name?"

"Manuel. He is fourteen," answered Mama proudly, looking into her son's flashing brown eyes. Manuel turned to Jesepo and blurted, "Let's see the rooms!"

Jesepo gave him a shrewd look. "You can pay seventy-five dollars a month perhaps?" he asked in a testy voice. For a moment all was silent. Papa shook his head in dismay.

"To think we give up farm at twelve dollars a month to pay many times that for nothing."

Mama protested. "You never make fifty dollars a week before, Jorge. You can pay more, but not seventy-five dollars. Besides, we haven't seen the rooms yet."

Mr. Jesepo became flustered and excited.

"Sixty-five dollars then! In advance! There isn't another apartment in all New York!"

"Is true," said Mama firmly. "We must take it, Jorge, no matter. Tomorrow's another working day and you have no time to look around."

Manuel gave Mr. Jesepo a shrewd look and said, "If you don't like it here, Papa, I can go look some more."

Mr. Jesepo led them into the dark halls. He gripped Manuel's shoulder, digging his fingers into the bony shoulder blades. "I can see you're green about this country, boy," he whispered, "You can't get another room here if you saw the President!"

"*No me molestes!*" hissed Manuel as he pulled himself away.

Mr. Jesepo unlocked the apartment door. The metal number hung by one screw as if it had already given up the struggle. They entered a long hallway. On one side were four rooms arranged like a pullman train. The living room, the same as the other rooms, all lined with sagging cots, was only distinguishable by the final vestiges of a beige marble fireplace. The fourth room was empty. All that could be said in its defense was that it was quite large, had three windows, and was a corner room.

"This is your room!" Mr. Jesepo announced.

"You mean," asked Papa, "only this one room?"

"The others are already occupied," replied Jesepo, "You are lucky to find anything."

"Lucky?" sobbed Dolores sitting down on the suitcase in the middle of the floor. "This is no better than the room we left."

Manuel attempted to justify the money and hope which his eagerness had cost them. "We're near the park," he said, "The fine houses are only a few blocks away. We can play baseball in the big fields, Eduardo, and you, Dolores, can walk with Enero to the zoo. The apartment will do until I find a better one."

Mama laughed and rumpled Manuel's black hair as Mr. Jesepo looked at him with annoyance. "He is the real man of the family, my Manuel!" she said.

Manuel, proud but shy, knew that she loved Papa none the less for saying this. Mama was the housekeeper and protector. Papa was the bread-winner but he, by the Holy Virgin, *he* was the man of the house!

By the time a week had passed Manuel could see that such close quarters were nervewracking. Mama ignored the problem with deliberate evasiveness, busying herself with the cooking and washing. Papa was hard at work. Manuel and the children, except for Marzo, were enrolled in school. In the rooms meant for one family there were four families. Twenty-two people huddled together, fighting and crying and loving together. Manuel strode through the hall to his room, smelling with eager appetite the familiar aroma of his mother's cooking. *Asapio* for dinner—and rice—and—. Then another odor struck him. One of the other women was cooking *pescado!* Fish! What a combination of odors! Fish and chicken. There just had to be some way to get more room—a little privacy.

The nights were sweltering although it was almost October. Even Manuel's dreams were cramped for space as he lay awake during the night hearing the varied snores of his family and smelling the musty odors of bodies covered by sweat and cheap powder. *Mama mia*, who could sleep? There was Dolores' whimpering and Eduardo's coughing, Enero's sniffling, and Febrero's endless visits to the bathroom. It seemed that the night was filled with a thousand small violences. When would it stop?

Each day Manuel strode through the dark hallway hating the faded, blotched yellow daisies on the wallpaper. One day he heard, from across the hall, a young plaintive voice singing "La Casita." It was one of his favorite songs. "Home" was a magic word to Manuel. There were many reasons why he wished never to return to Puerto Rico. Reasons only valid to an idealistic fourteen-year-old boy. A worshiping perhaps. A worshiping of baseball players; an awe of large buildings; the ecstasy of living in the same city with the Empire State building; with its gigantic boats on the nearby piers; the excitement he felt when he strolled through the amusement galleries and saw the lights of Broadway; the mixture of different peoples—Chinese, Spanish, Italian, all living together in this wonderful country. Yet he knew it was impossible to live as they did. To whom could he go for help?

As Manuel listened to the singing he got an idea. The singer was Enrique Dias, a small boy of twelve. Enrique lived with his father, a waiter, who seemed to know all about everything. There seemed to be nothing he could not discuss. Manuel visited often, despite Mr. Dias sitting him at the dining table and making him listen to opinions on world situations. Sometimes what Mr. Dias said really interested him. Manuel decided to ask Mr. Dias what he should do.

Mr. Dias was sitting with his body bulging over one chair and his short, hairy feet on another. He was smoking a pipe and laughing.

"Your family are really fools," he said. "You let that Mr. Jesepo lead you into a hole like a mouse after cheese. Look at our apartment. Three rooms. Is it not nice?"

28

Manuel had to agree that it was. He would give a great deal for three such rooms. Even his pictures of the baseball players. Even the Ted Williams one.

"And do you know what I pay?" asked Mr. Dias, edging over and shaking his fat finger before Manuel's nose. "Same as you, that's what! A sweet racket that Jesepo has. I would like to have the money and the nerve to do such a thing."

"What is a racket?" Manuel asked.

"Mr. Jesepo is getting sixty dollars from each family and keeping it all."

Manuel's eyes narrowed as he asked quietly, "What do you mean, keeping it all? He's the landlord isn't he?"

Mr. Dias' fat rippled as he laughed. "I told you, Enrique, he fools them all!" Then, seriously, he looked at Manuel. "Mr. Jesepo is a tenant, even as you. Only a rich one. Rich enough to have two apartments and rent them all out."

Manuel flushed with anger. "But I thought Mr. Jesepo was the landlord."

"Did he ever say he was?" asked Mr. Dias.

"Well, no . . ."

"No is right. He isn't, and he isn't supposed to sublease his apartments either. But who's to complain? Would you want to be kicked out on the streets? Would that suit you better?"

Manuel clenched his fists and remained silent.

"There must be someone who could make him stop," said Enrique, protecting his friend.

"Sure," jeered his father, "go fight City Hall!"

Noting Manuel's confused look he added, "That's just an expression."

"No," said Manuel, shaking his head. "That is exactly what I will do. I'll go fight City Hall. Who would you go to, Mr. Dias, if you wanted someone to help you?"

Mr. Dias realized that Manuel was serious. He pondered for a moment and then asnwered:

"You are American citizen, you know. So go to the political club in this district. Tell them about this. Maybe they help."

"Certainly, I will do just that," Manuel cried, "and now!"

"Now?" asked Enrique, as he lifted his guitar from the table. "We were supposed to sing heel beely songs tonight."

"Tomorrow I'll have more to sing about!" Manuel said and marched from the apartment. As he ran down the front steps he could hear his friend playing "El Jibarito"—the Hillbilly. He kept humming it as he skipped down the street.

Manuel walked up a steel flight of stairs to the clubroom. It was smoky and there was a great deal of noise. Most of it was laughter. He walked timidly, edging his way through the crowd of coatless men until he faced a man sitting at a table.

"Excuse it, sir," he stammered, "where can I find the leader?"

"The leader?" the man asked, smiling, "What is your name?" He took a pad and pencil from the drawer.

"Manuel Ricoco, but . . ."

"What's your address?" Manuel told him with impatience. The man pointed through the haze of smoke to a younger man who was surrounded by several confidants.

"That's your block captain," the man at the desk explained. "Go to him with your problem."

Manuel stopped, ashamed of his rudeness. He bowed and thanked the man and walked over to the captain, who was not pleased to stop his jokes and listen to a small, shabby boy who probably didn't know what he was talking about. But finally he listened. Manuel explained very earnestly how his family were all crowded into one room and how Mr. Jesepo was on ogre and had no right to crowd everyone together that way. The man wasn't sure if Manuel was telling the truth.

"Besides," he said, "we don't go into matters of this sort."

"You don't?" said Manuel; stunned, "but I was told . . ."

"I'm sorry, sonny," the man said, "you'll have to see your assembly-man."

"What's that?" asked Manuel, thinking the man was joking. The man obviously wasn't. He too took out a pad and pencil. He scribbled an address on it.

"Just in case something comes up, I'll put your name on our list. However, go to this address. Just take the subway downtown. It's near City Hall."

Manuel nodded. Mixed with his disappointment was determination and a growing hatred for Mr. Jesepo, the cause of all his difficulties.

The following day Manuel skipped his afternoon classes. He wanted to give himself plenty of time in case he got lost on the subway. Every hour was important. Manuel could see how irritable and unhappy his father had become. Who could blame him? A man needed peace and sleep after a long day's work. In the one room there was neither—only crying and complaining and the everlasting smell of cooking and dirty wash.

So Manuel went to the assemblyman. After waiting and waiting he was given only a moment of attention and then the businesslike retort, "Sorry. Can't help you. That's a Federal matter." What, wondered Manuel, meant "federal"? He would have to go back to Mr. Dias for some additional advice.

When Manuel entered the apartment the excited jabberings of the other families clapped like thunder against his ears. He saw a strange face, too. A small man with a black leather case. The medico!

"Who is sick?" ask Manuel, pulling at the doctor's sleeve. The doctor sighed, shaking his head with pity and distress.

"What can you expect in a pigpen like this? Some day . . ." Mrs. Rodriguez from the next room spat Spanish profanities in the doctor's ear. It had something to do with work. Manuel rushed into his home. There was Mama, sitting on the floor, her large body rocking as she sobbed. Papa was lying on the bed. He was very pale. Eduardo, excited with the importance of his news, blurted out, "Papa, he has the scarlet fever!"

"Scarlet fever!"

"Oh, he'll be all right but, we're not supposed to go to school for awhile. The doctor from the Board of Health said so. See the sign on the door?"

Manuel glanced at the door. There was a big sign tacked onto it saying "Quarantined." Manuel was concerned about his father, but the matter of another apartment seemed even more important now. He hurried over to the doctor and tugged the sleeve again.

"You are right, Doctor," he said. "We want to get out of this place but we don't know who to ask about it. Could you tell me, kind doctor, how we can do this?"

The doctor looked down at the intense, undernourished youngster.

"Let your father worry about that. When he goes back to work, he can take care of it. You should be more concerned about a good tonic, young man. I'd prescribe something for you, but I know you people. Tortillas and rice and you wouldn't spend the money on the prescription."

"Please, Doctor," begged Manuel, "who should I see to complain about this apartment?"

"Well, the Welfare Department, I suppose. For all the good it will do you. But you're going no place for awhile. You're quarantined!"

Manuel nodded glumly, but he knew he wouldn't wait. How could they stand it, huddled together all day and all night? The other families were already cursing Mama and Papa, as if it were Papa's fault he was sick. Their men couldn't afford to stay home from work and the doctor knew it, but, just the same, it was his duty to warn them.

Papa was very sick. All night Mama tended to him. The suffocating room was made worse by the heavy smell of medication. There was a great need in Manuel to prove, now more than ever, that he was head of the family. He was really needed now, for more important things than helping Mama with the dishes or lacing Marzo's shoes. He prayed to his Virgin that he would prove capable. The next day Papa was feeling no better. Mama was moaning her prayers and lighting a candle to the Virgin.

"Papa," Manuel said, "we never should have come here. I tried to find us a bigger place. I couldn't. Maybe we should go home." Already his dreams seemed too big for him to handle. He hated to leave. He turned so his father wouldn't notice his tears. He wasn't sure why he felt this way. Surely matters had been better at home. They were often hungry, yes, but they had a little farm where they grew beet sugar. Yet, how dull life was there! In America life seemed full and exciting. Only the poem Mr. Dias quoted all the time wasn't quite true. The poem called America the "Blessed land of room enough." Surely that poem must have been written years ago!

Mama now shook her head tearfully, "Yes, Jorge, why don't we go home?"

Papa, sick as he was, managed to rouse himself, leaning on one elbow. He whispered,

"No. We stay! Someday that store will be mine. It is good store. I never get chance like this again."

"But this room," sobbed Mama. "This is no place to raise family. I would like to go home!"

Manuel couldn't remember Papa ever crossing Mama but this time there was a sure, decisive look in his eyes.

"This," Papa said, "is home. Home is not a place. Home is you, Mama, and you, Eduardo, and you, Dolores." As he said this he rumpled each head tenderly. His children huddled around him, scarcely breathing.

"Home," continued Papa, "is where we're all together. No matter where. In time I'll be able to take off and look around. That can wait. But I don't want to hear any more talk of leaving. We stay!"

Mama wiped his brow. She would stay, if that's what he wanted.

Manuel knew that he positively must find another place. Papa was right, but tempers worn down by days and nights of cramped proximity could change the strongest of minds. And Papa's mind was never stronger than his heart.

Manuel ignored the quarantine and left the house. He went to Broadway and Duane streets where the telephone directory told him the Department of Welfare was located. This time they listened. The man in the gray suit gave Manuel all his attention. He didn't seem to mind Manuel's shabby shoes and uncut hair, nor the nervous rubbing of his hands against his trousers.

"You know," he said kindly, "it's just a little unusual that a young boy like you should come here with a housing problem. Why doesn't your father come? What's your name?"

Manuel sat, wide-eyed and suspicious. He could lie about his father perhaps, but not if he had to give the correct name. And he certainly would have to if something was to be done! But then the man would discover that his father was sick and that Manuel disregarded the quarantine. Surely something terrible would happen to him for that!

Manuel jumped up. He bowed, said several amiabilities in Spanish and ran out. The man arose and called, "Come back here!" but Manuel scampered down the stairs, not even waiting for the elevator.

Then he wandered, for a half hour, cursing himself in Spanish. What a coward he was! What if he were even put in jail! If it would help Papa and the children get a bright apartment, it would be worth it. Still he hesitated about going back to the curious man at the Welfare Department. Why did he not do what he had originally intended doing? Why did he not go straight to the mayor? Wasn't that what mayors were for? Why, in his country, the mayors knew everyone! On the day of the *Fiestos Patronales* he shook hands with everyone in the whole town. From daybreak till dark the band played in the municipal square and announced the day's festivities. It was the biggest day of the year, the Festival of the Patron Saints. Everyone met everyone and work was forgotten. The mayor knew everyone by name. Surely it would be the same here! Why, the mayor would be glad to help!

Manuel was confused and awed by the many rooms in City Hall. Finally his request was interpreted and he was sent to the right section. A man there kindly assured Manuel that he was one of the mayor's assistants, but Manuel was not reassured. This man had been referred to as Assistant for Minority Affairs. Manuel knew what "minority" meant and he assured the man that his was a big, important problem—to be attended to at once! The man smiled understandingly and gave Manuel a slip of paper.

"Another paper?" asked Manuel, exasperated. "Always another place, another building! Always they put me on a list. The problem, it is so simple! Can't anyone help me?" The man was quiet and firm.

"This is where you should have gone in the first place. The Legal Aid Society. Ask for Mr. Frederic Sinclair. He's very close to the housing authorities and his pet peeve is injustice!" He looked at his watch. "He leaves his office at five. You'll just have time to make it." Manuel thanked him profusely and rushed over to the other building. What a wonderful thing it would be if he could bring good news to his family tonight!

Mr. Sinclair wasn't at all what Manuel expected. He was young and scrubbed-looking and too friendly to seem important. Manuel doubted if he could help. But the man listened intently and nodded while Manuel recounted the story of his problem and the attempts he'd made to solve it.

"And you really went to all those places for help?" asked Sinclair.

"By the Virgin!" swore Manuel, raising his right hand.

"You must need help very badly."

"Oh, I do! I do!"

"Do you know," Mr. Sinclair asked, "how many people have the same problem as you? How do you imagine we can find places for all these people?"

Manuel stared at him. "There is no place?"

"No place," said Mr. Sinclair, "but there's something I can fix. This Mr. Jesepo is illegally renting that apartment and taking money that's not his. His game is finished." The young man stood up, tucked his shirt further into his trousers and picked up his coat. "And we'll finish this right now!"

"What do you mean?" Manuel exclaimed.

"I'm going to drive you home."

Manuel's face lit up. "You'll take me home in a real car?"

"Of course. I live just a few blocks away from you."

Manuel smiled, feeling warm towards this tall, sure, young man.

"In our town you make good mayor," he said. "Everybody like you."

"Some day," said Mr. Sinclair, putting on his hat and locking his desk, "that mightn't be such a bad idea. Only this," he said, gesturing to the streets, "is our town, and don't you forget it."

Manuel was so excited, sitting in the front seat beside a man who wanted to be mayor that he almost forgot his fear. But then he remembered. He turned to Mr. Sinclair, who was patiently steering his car through the heavy traffic.

"I forgot to tell you," said Manuel, softly and humbly, "I escaped!"

"You what?"

Looking straight ahead and speaking quickly, Manuel told him.

"My father has the scarlet fever. I wasn't supposed to leave the house, but I had to. You can see how I had to, can't you?" he pleaded.

Mr. Sinclair shook his head with amusement. "Now I've heard everything!"

Mr. Sinclair stopped in front of a large building where he said he lived. Manuel screwed his eyes upwards, trying to see the top of it. It looked important. There was a large blue awning all the way to the street and a man with a red uniform bowed as they pulled up.

"Go ahead," the young man said to Manuel, letting him out of the car. "I'll be there in a minute. I must call my office." Manuel was hesitant. "It's all right," he was assured, "I've got your address. Now go ahead, but don't mention I'm coming!"

Manuel ran the rest of the way. He felt six feet tall, even taller than his father. He had done a man's job, so wasn't he a man?"

Suddenly he shrank to size. On the steps of the old brownstone stood three men. Mr. Jesepo was one of them. He was tapping his feet repeatedly on the steps. His arms crossed and he almost growled as he watched Manuel approach.

"That's the rascal," he snapped. "We've been waiting for you! He's caused me more trouble than a nest of hornets."

Manuel's cheerfulness vanished.

"What have you got to say for youself, devil?"

Manuel twisted out of his clutches.

"Déjame en paz! Déjame en paz!"

"Yes, let him go," said the other man. He was a stranger in a tweed suit. Manuel realized that the third man was the doctor.

"Is anything wrong with my father?" he asked.

"He's doing all right," the doctor answered curtly, "but you weren't supposed to go out of the house. Don't you know you could spread the disease? Don't you people have any sense?"

"I told you," said Mr. Jesepo, "this boy's been nothing but trouble. He goes sneaking around trying to find out bad things about me. Just because I'm entitled to more rent than his stingy, big family can pay. If they don't like it, there's plenty others . . ."

"All right," said the stranger, "but what I want to know is, what have you been doing with yourself when you were not in school?"

Manuel looked puzzled. Mr. Jesepo pointed a bony finger.

"The truant officer, smart boy. You think you can not go to school and get away with it? In this country we want educated children. If you're too lazy to learn, then go home . . ."

"Go home! Go home!" shouted Manuel. "This is my home! Why you tell me to go home?"

"You can be sent back, smart boy, or put in reformatory school. In this country you're not allowed to leave school and break quarantines. That's the law. If you don't like our laws, get out of here!"

"That's enough!" said the truant officer. "I want to hear what the boy has to say. Why weren't you in school?"

Manuel shuffled his feet awkwardly.

"I just did some odd jobs to earn a few cents—just enough to get subway money to look for a new apartment!" He glared at Mr. Jesepo. "There's no sin in that, is there?"

Mr. Jesepo's face reddened as he tried to control his anger.

"I think, smart boy, you and your family had better leave. You don't like it here, you go!"

"Go?" said Manuel, in horror. "Where would we go to?"

"That's your problem," answered Jesepo. "I hear you've been to every organization in New York City. Let them get you someplace!"

Manuel looked at the three of them. He forgot his impending triumph. It was all too much for him. He broke down and cried, sitting on the steps, his head leaning on his bony knees.

"Humph!" snorted Mr. Jesepo. "When they don't know what to do, they always cry. That won't save you, smart boy. Tonight your family gets out and stays out!"

"Not so fast! The quarantine. Ten days," reminded the doctor.

"Then there's a week left. After that"—Jesepo made a swift gesture across his throat—"Out!"

Just then, as Manual blinked through his tears, he saw Mr. Sinclair walking toward him.

"Which one of you is Mr. Jesepo?" asked Sinclair. Mr. Jesepo swallowed hard and muttered that it was he.

"Are you the landlord of this building?"

Mr. Jesepo flushed and his eyes fell to his worn shoes. Before the officer and the doctor he could hardly lie about it.

"No. I live here like everyone else," he said. The doctor looked astonished and Manuel sprang up.

"He's been saying he's the landlord! He's been taking our money!"

"Calm down, Manuel," said Mr. Sinclair. "You told me your story."

"It's a lie!" bellowed Mr. Jesepo.

"Never mind that. I'm from the Legal Aid Society and I've checked. The real owner of this building tells me that he rented two apartments to a Mr. Jesepo and his cousin, also named Jesepo. They each bring in sixty dollars a month."

"I pay every month on the dot!" said Jesepo.

"What about the second apartment? Do you live in one alone?"

"Yes."

"Four rooms, all to yourself?"

"Yes."

"But in the other apartment there are twenty-two people in four rooms. Is that right?" Manuel could scarcely hear Mr. Jesepo's affirmation. Mr. Sinclair took out a pad and pencil and did some figuring.

"You've worked this setup for two years now. That makes roughly forty-three hundred dollars that you owe the government taxes on."

Jesepo breathed heavily, "Does that mean I go to jail?"

"That means you give it back. If not, you go to jail. How long did you think this would work?"

"If it weren't for that damned boy!" said Jesepo angrily.

Suddenly Manuel's eyes filled again with tears and a terrible truth tugged at his heart. Victory was not sweet. There seemed an urgent necessity to find out why.

"We're your people, Mr. Jesepo. Why do you do this to us? Why you hurt us?"

"I came here, same as you, Manuel, full of hopes and dreams," Jesepo replied bitterly. "In America the streets would be paved with gold!" He laughed cynically. "Nothing's paved with gold, boy, only the jewelry in the store windows. Only, here it's worse than home because every day you see it near you—near enough to reach out and touch—the fine clothes in the department stores; the fancy cars on the streets. It's all here—but not for you!" His face twisted with emotion. "How long can you watch and want and not touch, boy? How long?"

Mr. Jesepo turned and trudged wearily up the steps. Manuel's eyes followed him and then again, before them all, Manuel began to cry. He was ashamed but he couldn't help himself. He was crying because, suddenly he had grown up and, oh God in Heaven—how it hurt!

Mr. Sinclair put a comforting arm around Manuel's shoulders and walked with him to his apartment.

"It's going to be all right," he promised. "Everything's going to be all right."

Mama opened the door and, seeing the strange man and her weeping son, said,

"What you do to my boy? Why you make him cry?" Her fatigue was evident. Sticky wisps of black hair hung over her brow.

"Don't worry, Mama," Manuel said, "I cry for happiness. Mr. Sinclair is going to get us a new home."

Mr. Sinclair remonstrated, "Not so fast, young man. I can't work miracles. There are thousands of people and not enough room."

"That's like the poem!" Manuel explained. "Only the poem says there's plenty of room in America." He said angrily, "Is a lie!"

Mr. Sinclair nodded in reminiscence.

> It's home again and home again—America for me.
> I want a ship that's Westward bound to plough the rolling sea.
> To the blessed land of room enough, beyond the ocean bars,
> Where the air is full of sunlight and the flag is full of stars.

"That's it!" Manuel proclaimed. "Mr. Dias' poem!"

"No—not his—but a very famous one. If you believe in America, you can make these things true." He gently pushed aside the frayed net curtains and pointed to the street below. "Manuel—the flag *is* full of stars and there's sunlight here and it *is* playing on your sidewalk. So—part of the poem *is* true, Manuel. Me—and you—and others like us—can make it *all* true. Will you help?"

38

Mr. Sinclair laid a friendly arm across Manuel's slim shoulders as Mama blew her nose lustily. Happily Manuel asked,

"When did you learn that poem, Mr. Sinclair?"

"I know a lot of poems. I learned them when I was a young boy like you. I had some time on my hands one winter . . ."

Mr. Sinclair opened the apartment door and thumped his finger on the notice posted there. His face broke out into a preposterous smile as he replied,

"That was the winter I had scarlet fever. . . ."

*Hunger**

RICHARD WRIGHT

Hunger stole upon me so slowly that at first I was not aware of what hunger really meant. Hunger had always been more or less at my elbow when I played, but now I began to wake up at night to find hunger standing at my bedside, staring at me gauntly. The hunger I had known before this had been no grim, hostile stranger; it had been a normal hunger that had made me beg constantly for bread, and when I ate a crust or two I was satisfied. But this new hunger baffled me, scared me, made me angry and insistent. Whenever I begged for food now my mother would pour me a cup of tea which would still the clamor in my stomach for a moment or two; but a little later I would feel hunger nudging my ribs, twisting my empty guts until they ached. I would grow dizzy and my vision would dim. I became less active in my play, and for the first time in my life I had to pause and think of what was happening to me.

"Mama, I'm hungry," I complained one afternoon.

"Jump up and catch a kungry," she said, trying to make me laugh and forget.

"What's a *kungry?*"

"It's what little boys eat when they get hungry," she said.

"What does it taste like?"

"I don't know."

"Then why do you tell me to catch one?"

"Because you said that you were hungry," she said smiling.

I sensed that she was teasing me and it made me angry.

"But I'm hungry. I want to eat."

"You'll have to wait."

"But I want to eat now."

"But there's nothing to eat," she told me.

---

* Selection from *Black Boy.*

"Why?"

"Just because there's none," she explained.

"But I want to eat," I said, beginning to cry.

"You'll just have to wait," she said again.

"But why?"

"For God to send some food."

"When is He going to send it?"

"I don't know."

"But I'm hungry!"

She was ironing and she paused and looked at me with tears in her eyes.

"Where's your father?" she asked me.

I stared in bewilderment. Yes, it was true that my father had not come home to sleep for many days now and I could make as much noise as I wanted. Though I had not known why he was absent, I had been glad that he was not there to shout his restrictions at me. But it had never occurred to me that his absence would mean that there would be no food.

"I don't know," I said.

"Who brings food into the house?" my mother asked me.

"Papa," I said. "He always brought food."

"Well, your father isn't here now," she said.

"Where is he?"

"I don't know," she said.

"But I'm hungry," I whimpered, stomping my feet.

"You'll have to wait until I get a job and buy food," she said.

As the days slid past the image of my father became associated with my pangs of hunger, and whenever I felt hunger I thought of him with a deep biological bitterness.

My mother finally went to work as a cook and left me and my brother alone in the flat each day with a loaf of bread and a pot of tea. When she returned at evening she would be tired and dispirited and would cry a lot. Sometimes, when she was in despair, she would call us to her and talk to us for hours, telling us that we now had no father, that our lives would be different from those of other children, that we must learn as soon as possible to take care of ourselves, to prepare our own food, that we must take upon ourselves the responsibility of the flat while she worked. Half frightened, we would promise solemnly. We did not understand what had happened between our father and our mother and the most that these long talks did to us was to make us feel a vague dread. Whenever we asked why father had left, she would tell us that we were too young to know.

One evening my mother told me that thereafter I would have to do the shopping for food. She took me to the corner store to show me the way. I was proud; I felt like a grown-up. The next afternoon I looped the basket over my arm and went down the pavement toward the store. When I reached the corner, a gang of boys grabbed me, knocked me down, snatched the basket, took the money, and sent me running home in panic. That evening I told my mother what had happened, but she made no comment; she sat down at once, wrote another note, gave me more money, and sent me out to the grocery again. I crept down the steps and saw the same gang of boys playing down the street, I ran back into the house.

"What's the matter?" my mother asked.

"It's those same boys," I said. "They'll beat me."

"You've got to get over that," she said. "Now, go on."

"I'm scared," I said.

"Go on and don't pay any attention to them," she said.

I went out the door and walked briskly down the sidewalk, praying that the gang would not molest me. But when I came abreast of them someone shouted.

"There he is!"

They came toward me and I broke into a wild run toward home. They overtook me and flung me to the pavement. I yelled, pleaded, kicked, but they wrenched the money out of my hand. They yanked me to my feet, gave me a few slaps, and sent me home sobbing. My mother met me at the door.

"They b-beat m-me," I gasped. "They t-t-took the m-money."

I started up the steps, seeking the shelter of the house.

"Don't you come in here," my mother warned me.

I froze in my tracks and stared at her.

"But they're coming after me," I said.

"You just stay right where you are," she said in a deadly tone. "I'm going to teach you this night to stand up and fight for yourself."

She went into the house and I waited, terrified, wondering what she was about. Presently she returned with more money and another note, she also had a long heavy stick.

42

"Take this money, this note, and this stick," she said. "Go to the store and buy those groceries. If those boys bother you, then fight."

I was baffled. My mother was telling me to fight, a thing that she had never done before.

"But I'm scared," I said.

"Don't you come into this house until you've gotten those groceries," she said.

"They'll beat me; they'll beat me," I said.

"Then stay in the streets; don't come back here!"

I ran up the steps and tried to force my way past her in the house. A stinging slap came on my jaw. I stood on the sidewalk, crying.

"Please, let me wait until tomorrow," I begged.

"No," she said. "Go now! If you come back into this house without those groceries, I'll whip you!"

She slammed the door and I heard the key turn in the lock. I shook with fright. I was alone upon the dark, hostile streets and gangs were after me. I had the choice of being beaten at home or away from home. I clutched the stick, crying, trying to reason. If I were beaten at home, there was absolutely nothing that I could do about it; but if I were beaten in the streets, I had a chance to fight and defend myself. I walked slowly down the sidewalk, coming closer to the gang of boys, holding the stick tightly. I was so full of fear that I could scarcely breathe. I was almost upon them now.

"There he is again!" the cry went up.

They surrounded me quickly and began to grab for my hand.

"I'll kill you!" I threatened.

They closed in. In blind fear I let the stick fly, feeling it crack against a boy's skull. I swung again, lamming another skull, then another. Realizing that they would retaliate if I let up for but a second, I fought to lay them low, to knock them cold, to kill them so that they could not strike back at me. I flayed with tears in my eyes, teeth clenched, stark fear making me throw every ounce of my strength behind each blow. I hit again and again, dropping the money and the grocery list. The boys scattered, yelling, nursing their heads, staring at me in utter disbelief. They had never seen such frenzy. I stood panting, egging them on, taunting them to come on and fight. When they refused, I ran after them and they tore out for their homes, screaming. The parents of the boys rushed into the streets and threatened me, and for the first time in my life I shouted at grown-ups, telling them that I would give them the same if they bothered me. I finally found my grocery list and the money and went to the store. On my way back I kept my stick poised for instant use, but there was not a single boy in sight. That night I won the right to the streets of Memphis.

The Copley-Plaza*

NANCY HALE

I see by an advertisement in a year-old magazine I came across cleaning out my Virginia cellar that a big hotel chain has bought the old Copley-Plaza in Boston and renamed it the Sheraton-Plaza. This seems to me absurd. It was called the Copley-Plaza because it is on Copley Square. My own early life was so bound up with the Copley-Plaza that I feel now very much as if someone insisted that I call my mother Mrs. Sheraton.

My earliest Copley-Plaza memory is, I think, of Miss Macomber's dancing class, to which I went when I was about twelve. No, from even before that there are echoes; whispers of the small stringed orchestra playing among the palms as I sit with my feet dangling above the marble floor and am treated to an ice—raspberry or orange—and something called *petits fours*. I have been taken to a matinée to see, from a box, John Craig and Mary Young do *Romeo and Juliet* at the Arlington Street Theatre. The orchestra is playing a waltz called "Les Patineurs," and the *petits fours* are beautiful—green, pink, and white; diamond-shaped and square—but why "fours"? Because there are four corners, or what? I sit comfortably munching, and looking with favor at the palmy scene before me: this, then, is the great world, and very nice.

But by the time I began to go to Miss Macomber's some faint glaze of social comparisons had obscured my consciousness, and I was aware that Miss Macomber's was not the last word in Boston dancing classes. The last word was Foster's classes, held at the Somerset, out on Commonwealth Avenue.

Was it this that lent such a poignant, somehow heartbreaking quality to those late afternoons? Outside, the street lights are being turned on in the early-falling dusk along Dartmouth Street, Huntington Avenue, St. James Avenue. Inside the vast, marble, worldly Copley-Plaza, the little girls are

* Selection from *The Emperor's Ring*.

45

having their pink taffeta and blue satin sashes retied in the dressing room down the corridor from the ballroom. The moment comes, and we edge out into the corridor, where the boys wait in their blue serge suits. With somebody (who?) directing us, we form couples to march up the steps and into the smaller ballroom, where Miss Macomber stands awaiting us in a peacock-blue taffeta dress and bronze kid slippers. The lady at the piano is playing "Won't You Wait Till the Cows Come Home?" We mince or shamble across the shining parquet; the boys bow, the girls curtsy, and then we hurry, with relief, away to reassemble strictly according to sex on the gilt chairs along the wall, until Miss Macomber gives the order "Boys, choose partners for the Slide Polka." At one end of the room, a few mothers sit—my mother among them—in their furs, their dark-blue suits neatly fitted over the bust, their plumed hats. Because of the tragic, romantic air of the whole thing, it is a relief to me when it is over and I am taken across Dartmouth Street, on our way home, to S. S. Pierce's, its lights blazing out in the Back Bay twilight, where I can walk round and round the circular display counter covered with party favors while my mother sits ordering California pea beans and a five-pound stone crock of strawberry jam at the grocery counter.

But the memories of that dancing class are not all tragic in atmosphere. There was the afternoon that I won the Elimination Prize with, as partner, a boy named Sidney Shurtleff (who is now a landscape architect and has changed *his* name to Shurcliff). The Elimination Contest was a part of the cotillion that marked the last dancing class of the season. Favors were given out, to be handed, grudgingly, to the girls by the boys; I think the last figure in the cotillion was the Elimination Contest. In principle, it was like musical chairs. Each couple was given a number, and we all danced—the fox trot, the one-step, the slide polka—and then abruptly the music would cease, and Miss Macomber would call out a few numbers drawn from a hat and the couples holding those numbers sat down. The last couple left dancing won. Sidney and I were the last couple left dancing, and side by side we marched the length of the small ballroom to receive our prizes. I do not remember what the prizes were. I remember the tune the lady at the piano was playing as we danced all alone the full circuit of the ballroom, as victors—a tune from the First World War called "Babes in the Wood." That last clumsily danced circuit—for we had not won our prize because of any talent, any superiority whatsoever, only by chance—was the high point of my life up to then. I tasted triumph.

The next set of memories I bear of the Copley-Plaza are very different from these in mood. I must have been fourteen. I had begun going to Miss Winsor's School, out in Longwood, and I found it hard to make friends; as far as I could figure at that age, my total inability to play basketball or field hockey was the cause of my unpopularity. Some sort of instinct, right or wrong, caused me to begin stopping in at the Copley-Plaza on my way home from school, in seach of a kind of comfort, in seach of a kind of distraction.

For here I would sit, in the main lobby, opposite to the huge marble desk, dressed in my thick, untidy school clothes, my galoshes, with my plaid schoolbag huddled into the thronelike chair with me, and watch what seemed to me the worldly and wealthy conducting their fascinating lives at the Copley-Plaza. In from the Dartmouth Street entrance would hurry a bellboy, or two bellboys, laden down with expensive luggage, followed by a blond woman in a fur coat, or a close-shaven man in a check waistcoat, or a dark, romantic-looking lady all in black and attended by what seemed to be a governess with two or three rich, well-dressed children—important children, children with lives.

Occasionally I would get up and go down the corridor to the ladies' room, not so much because I needed to as that there I found myself not two feet away from beautiful, expensively dressed women who talked to each other busily about their approaching engagements. I would wash my hands, taking a long time about it, and listen to some lovely girl saying, "We're going to Paris Friday, on the *Ile*. . . ." Then I would go back to my throne in the lobby to watch some more people make their entrances. All the time, the stringed orchestra would be playing waltzes, behind in the palm court— fast and sweet and queerly nostalgic. It was almost as if this were the only life I had.

The final stage of my relationship with the Copley-Plaza takes up where "Babes in the Wood" left off—on a note of triumph. I am a Boston débutante—a *popular* Boston débutante—going to those larger balls which are held here, and which, compared with the dances at the Somerset, somehow never seem quite quite. The Somerset is definitely quite quite. But now I go to all those dances, too. My triumph is almost complete; I have not had to *do* anything to achieve it, it just came, as I grew older and had my hair shingled and began being told I danced well and that I looked like Greta Garbo. I feel a little superior toward balls at the Copley-Plaza.

Back in the old dressing room again. Now it is thronged with girls; girls in knee-length evening dresses, girls with rigid gold slave necklaces around their slender, immature throats, girls in silver kid slippers and ostrich *leis* and Chanel bracelets and pearls—pearls twisted once close around the neck and left swinging down almost to the waist. The most beautiful girl of our year is in black velvet, with a flesh chiffon bosom; she gazes as though sightlessly into the big mirror as she applies eyeshadow to those fabulous eyelids. Someone says, "I hear you made the Vincent. Congrats."

Mixed through the crowd, as though for their own protection, are the pills—the girls with glasses, the girls in pink taffeta dresses, the girls who played field hockey so terribly well as Miss Winsor's. Later in the evening they will retire here to the dressing room after a few too many circlings of the ballroom in the same man's arms, to wait alone until they summon courage to issue forth once more. And here, like birds of a feather, chattering together of Sherry's and the Meadowbrook, are the New York girls—a little taller than anyone else, more glamorous, more unattainable, because they come from New York. They all make the same joke—"The best thing about Beantown is the Merchants Limited going home." New York! It is the as yet unconquered, the next world.

We drift out, dégagé, a little blasé, to find the Harvard men with whom we came. Tails, they wore in those days. The small ballroom and the big ballroom are thrown open together to me now, and Billy Lossez's orchestra is playing. He has a banjo man who is supposed to be hot stuff and who has written a song, called "Afraid of You," that is rumored to have been inspired by one of the débutantes. *Which?* But the great Lossez specialty is "J'ai Pas Su Y Faire," delicate, a little melancholy; you sing it, in your best low, hoarse voice, into your partner's ear in the moment before the next man cuts in. "Do you belong to the Spee or the A.D.?" "Isn't Hope divine?" "How about coming tea dancing with me here tomorrow?" Tea dancing at the Copley-Plaza—that was another facet of this coming-out diamond. But tonight is a ball, given by one of the hunting people out at Myopia for their lumpy daughter. The great thing is to be able to dance in a corner, with your own private stag line. The New York boys are the best dancers—they are snaky. But you are nice to everybody; it pays. One dismal, damp-palmed pipsqueak always says the same thing as he cuts in—"Greetings!" My friends and I call him Greetings.

This is a really smooth dance, they are serving supper *throughout*, with champagne continuously. We débutantes are only allowed to drink champagne. But some of the boys carry hip flasks, and the girls who are wild accept a sip from the flask when they go to sit out. That is another category of girl—the girls who go the limit. There are only a few of them and they are mentioned with bated breath.

I have met a new man. He is tall and rather an awkward dancer, but I know all about him; he is a big man in the Porcellian. After cutting back several times, he asks me if I would like to sit out, and I am delighted to.

We go to one of the small writing rooms; the girls with their beaux wander in and out. "Hello, Sarah." "Uh, hello." "Hello, Lily, Joe."

The hour is timeless. Outside, the Back Bay is fast asleep. Down the street, Childs is drowsing, we will go there for pancakes later. Only here is life going on, to the tune of "J'ai Pas Su Y Faire." "Darling, are you coming to my dance the twelfth?" "I wouldn't miss it." There are three dances on the twelfth—at the Somerset, here, and at the Women's Republican Club.

My new beau says, "Have you ever seen a loof?"

I say, "Never actually, but I've always imagined what one must look like."

"There must be hundreds of them," he says. "So many people seem to be aloof."

At one of the writing desks, we take turns, there in the sitting-out room at half-past two in the morning, at drawing a loof. It has three eyes, a pointed head; its tongue sticks out permanently.

"Aren't you ever going to come back on the floor?" some man passing asks me, but I say "I'm busy drawing a loof." "A *what?*" We laugh, and here my memories fade away, and end.

It is these memories that make the Copley-Plaza seem to me like a showy, faintly second-rate, meretricious mother that nonetheless did give me a kind of life. You can't make my mother into somebody different by suddenly beginning to call her Mrs. Sheraton.

But, if I know the Bostonians, they will keep right on calling the old hotel the Copley-Plaza anyway.

Working in the City

And who made 'em? Who made the skyscrapers?
Man made 'em, the little two-legged joker, Man.
Out of his head, out of his dreaming, scheming skypiece,
Out of proud little diagrams that danced softly in his head—
Man made the skyscrapers.
FROM "GOOD MORNING, AMERICA"—CARL SANDBURG

Leave the farm. Go to the city. There is work for everyone—these exhortations have sounded in the ears of countless ambitious young men and women for whom urban life holds the key to human happiness: success. The city offers seemingly infinite possibilities for achievement and advancement, both personal and professional—and its legendary attractions rest precisely in this belief that its opportunities are endless.

Theodore Dreiser writes of the young woman Carrie Meeker, fresh from the farm, newly arrived in turn-of-the-century Chicago—whose idealism and ambition are matched only by the city's starkness and enormity. In spite of her exhausting search for a job and her acceptance of miniscule reward, she still feels the excitement of possibility as she goes cautiously from one factory or shop to another. "It's a beginning," Dreiser seems to be saying about the young who come to seek fortunes. "Tomorrow will be better."

Not so for Tommy Castelli in Bernard Malamud's short story, "The Prison." Work is dull and exhausting and the prospects for advancement are minimal. He works long hours for a meagre living, and yearns for a change from the tedium—so much so that the

51

discovery of a young thief in his candy store offers him a welcome change from the monotony of his days.

Two young journalists, Edna Ferber and Ben Hecht, find the openendedness and adventure of city life exhilarating. For Ferber, stimulated by the challenges of life in German Milwaukee, work was a daily drama of frenetic activity either in the city room of the *Milwaukee Journal* or on the site of a story. Although she was a woman in a man's world, her experience was not so different from Ben Hecht's, who started his career as a novice writer in Chicago, where he was, he says, in addition to being a reporter, "a playwright, novelist, short story writer, propagandist, publisher," among other things.

The city itself is a worksite: for the builder, the teacher, the taxi driver, the doctor, news vendor. People use the city for sustenance, and the city uses people, and everywhere there is demonstration of work.

Good Morning, America

CARL SANDBURG

In the evening there is a sunset sonata comes to the cities.
There is a march of little armies to the dwindling of drums.
The skyscrapers throw their tall lengths of walls into black
    bastions on the red west.
The skyscrapers fasten their perpendicular alphabets far
    across the changing silver triangles of stars and streets.

And who made 'em? Who made the skyscrapers?
Man made 'em, the little two-legged joker, Man.
Out of his head, out of his dreaming, scheming skypiece,
Out of proud little diagrams that danced softly in his
    head—Man made the skyscrapers.
With his two hands, with shovels, hammers, wheelbarrows, with
    engines, conveyors, signal whistles, with girders, molds,
      steel, concrete
Climbing on scaffolds and falsework with blueprints, riding the
    beams and dangling in mid-air to call, Come on, boys—
    Man made the skyscrapers.

When one tall skyscraper is torn down
To make room for a taller one to go up,
Who takes down and puts up those two skyscrapers?
Man . . . the little two-legged joker . . . Man.

FROM *A Peculiar Treasure*

EDNA FERBER

They put me on the Schandein case there on the Milwaukee Journal. A good deal of the time I didn't know what they were talking about. But I sat in the courtroom with Cook, the Journal court and police reporter, taking it all down and telephoning it in, for it was hot stuff, and the Milwaukee papers were getting out special editions on it. The Schandein case had started, innocently enough, seemingly, as a private squabble about a will in one of the wealthy Milwaukee beer-brewing families. But in turning over these legal matters they were found to give off a frightful stench. Medical, clinical, sexual terms rose like a miasma from the witness stand. I was being initiated into big-town reporting with a vengeance. That was why they had so hurriedly sent for me. The regular woman reporter, who wrote under the name of Jean Airlie, was away on vacation when the Schandein case broke. Campbell, the managing editor, had liked my stuff as Appleton correspondent. I was put in as an emergency stop-gap to get what was known as the woman's angle. If they were taken aback at the appearance of a wide-eyed kid they said nothing but hurled me into the nauseating mess and I waded through it. Milwaukee's aristocracy was made up of brewing families. They lived in vast stone or brick houses on Grand Avenue, the lawns decorated with iron deer, with pergolas, gazebos, and painted dwarfs patterned after those we now know in Snow White. The social gathering place for these clans was the old Germania Club. Names such as Pabst, Schlitz, Uhlein, Schandein were Milwaukee's Royal Family titles, and some of these were present in the courtroom or were pulled into the case. The Milwaukee papers were delirious with joy.

The Milwaukee of that time was as German as Germany. There actually were to be seen signs in the windows of shops on the almost solid German South Side which read, "Hier wird Englisch gesprochen." Of the four hundred thousand population, surely three fourths were German or Polish. There was a distinctly foreign flavor about the city—its architecture, its tempo, the faces of its people, its food, its solid dowdy matrons. Victor Berger, the Socialist, was a growing influence. When you were sent to interview him he was given to mild attempts at cheek-pinching, but then, mine was a plump pink cheek and politics is a dusty business. I didn't resent it.

Arrived, I made straight for a boarding house that had been recommended to me as cheap, clean, good. On fifteen dollars a week I couldn't be too luxurious. Kahlo's turned out to be a gold mine, for I used it, complete, in my first novel, Dawn O'Hara, written four years later. Kahlo's was a decent three-story brick house directly across from the pleasant Courthouse Square. I never have seen anyone work with such a fury of energy as the lean gaunt Mrs. Kahlo. She cooked, cleaned, showed rooms, managed the place. Her hair was skewered in a tight knob that seemed to pull the skin away from her eyes. She wore clean gingham, and I never saw her without an apron and rolled-up sleeves. Herr Kahlo, true to the tradition of boarding-house ladies' husbands, was the ornamental end of the partnership. I never saw him work, except that occasionally you might behold him setting a very special dish—an Apfel Pfannkuchen or an extra wienerschnitzel—before a favored guest, with a flourish. He wore bright blue suits, sported a waxed Kaiser Wilhelm mustache, ushered the guests to their places in the dining room or sat chatting with them at table, a sociable glass of beer at his elbow. Perhaps he did the marketing. Certainly the food was excellent and plentiful enough to have been bought by one who liked good living and easy going.

Except for an occasional trip to Chicago I never had been away from home alone over a period of more than a few days. I wasn't lonely or apprehensive for a moment. I was enormously exhilarated. Every move was adventure. My first room at Kahlo's seemed fabulously luxurious, but my grandeur was only temporary. My permanent room, commensurate with my purse, was unavailable for the moment, and I was therefore regally lodged in temporary quarters. It turned out that my permanent bedroom, much lower-priced, could be reached only by passing through the kitchen. I didn't mind. It was a clean-scoured kitchen, full of fine smells. This room of mine boasted a fireplace in which I rather furtively took to burning bits of wood, old magazines and newspapers, lolling romantically before the brief blaze, until the fire-engine company dashed up and I discovered that I was about to burn the house down, the fireplace and chimney being intended more for ornament than use. I made up my mind that if ever I built a house I'd have a fireplace in practically every room. (The house is just built. And there they are. Life is truly a wonderful thing.) I never had had a bedroom to myself. This first one looked like a ballroom. My scant wardrobe was lost in the vast clothes closet with its forest of bristling hooks. This, I felt, was Life. This was the Girl Reporter in her proper setting.

At Kahlo's, as at home in Appleton, dinner was served at noon, supper at night. That held true in most Milwaukee households. Milwaukee businessmen, other than those owning the big department stores on Grand Avenue and Wisconsin Street, locked their shops at noon, went home to a huge hot dinner, then composed themselves for an hour's nap on the sofa, the open sheets of the day's Germania spread over their faces to keep the flies away.

Kahlo's dining room might have been a pension in Berlin or Munich. I put on a fresh shirtwaist and went down to supper. A roar of guttural conversation stopped as I entered the dining room. It was not that the Kahlo boarders were struck dumb by my beauty. It was their disconcerting way of taking stock of a newcomer. In silence Herr Kahlo ushered me to my solitary table. Forks were suspended in mid-air, spectacles turned like searchlights upon me, knobby foreheads glistened in my direction.

"Wer ist das?"

"Nichts schönes."

"Hm. Neues Mädchen. Hi, Karl! Etwas neues!"

I understand German. Not flattering.

They were, for the most part, engineers imported from Germany, employed in the huge works of the Allis Chalmers Company in South Milwaukee; in the Cutler-Hammer Company, or any of a dozen big steel works or engineering plants in and about Milwaukee. They had bulging foreheads, their hair was shaved or worn en brosse, many of them wore beards and thick spectacles, their neckties were echt Deutsch, they were brilliant technicians, they were the worst-mannered lot I'd ever encountered. An occasional engineering wife was meek, deferential and frumpy. Supper was buttery, German and good. Kalter aufschnitt with kartoffel salat, or wienerschnitzel with Germanfried. The floor was carpetless and clean, there was a stand of hardy potted plants in the bay window, the walls were ornamented with colored pictures showing plump bare-armed serving girls being chucked under the chin by mustached lieutenants in splendid uniforms. The men drank beer with their meals and read the Milwaukee Staats-Zeitung and the Germania.

One heard practically no English spoken. Herr Kahlo had assured me that, while he spoke English very well, still, in Milwaukee, "it gives meistens German." It did give mostly German, indeed.

After supper I went upstairs and wrote home a ten-page letter bursting with description.

That first glimpse of the Milwaukee Journal office was disillusioning. They were even then erecting a new building on Fourth Street, just off Grand Avenue. The present building was a ramshackle dirty brick affair on Michigan and Milwaukee streets. As at the Crescent office we were here jumbled together in a heap. The city room was dark, dusty, crowded. The city editor, the sporting editor, reporters, stenographers worked amidst incredible racket and seeming confusion. I thought it was wonderful.

At that time the Milwaukee Journal was a very yellow bulletin afternoon paper. Edition after edition rolled off the presses from eleven in the morning until three in the afternoon. When something enormous broke in the way of news there were later editions. To this day my brain is freshest between the hours of eight and three. After three it seems to click off as though extinguished by an electric switch. That comes of working during my formative years on an afternoon paper. A fiction writer trained on a morning paper usually finds his mind keenest at night.

It was a good training course, that paper, but brutal. My fifteen a week did not come unearned. Three or four of the staff stood out as definite characters. Campbell, the managing editor, turned out to be not only Scotch, but dour. His name was Henry, but I always spoke of him as Haggis (behind his back). Lou Simonds, the city editor, could have gone on in a play just as he was, complete. He was young, massive, powerful; a slave driver. He wore a green eyeshade, a blue shirt with no collar, his sleeves were rolled above his great elbows, his pink face was always smeared with ink or lead. In one mighty fist he usually carried a wad of copy paper, his pants were inadequately sustained by a leather belt out of whose precarious clutch they appeared always on the verge of slipping. This, together with his rather portly stomach, gave his costume a vaguely Egyptian effect.

He swore fluently, but not offensively. Nothing he did was offensive, for he was a really superb fellow and a great newspaperman. His method was nerve-racking. When you came in with a hot story he would stand over your typewriter with a huge pair of desk scissors in his hand, and as you wrote he snipped the typed bits off your machine and thrust them at the waiting copy boy to be rushed to the composing room. If you delayed a split second he yelled, "Hell, what d'you think this is—a weekly! Come on, now. Get it out!"

The paper was a miracle of condensation. It used the bulletin method. Most stories were worth a stick or two only. A stick is a printer's metal frame holding type. There is a saying in the Journal office that a murder rated one stick, a massacre two. By noon, when the city room was crackling with typewriters at which the reporters sat turning out their morning's grist, you would hear Simonds' bellow above the din: "Keep it down now, fellas! . . . Boil it! . . . Shave it! Na-a-a, Cook, don't get fancy. . . . Heh, waddy yuh think this is—a weekly!"

On the copy desk Distelhorst's blue pencil slashed like a Turk's scimitar. You learned to make one word do duty for ten. You began to search your very vitals for the right first word for that first paragraph. It was a city-room rule that the gist of your story must be packed into that first paragraph, and the paragraph must be brief. When I ceased to be a reporter and became a writer of fiction I found the habit of condensation so fixed that fifteen hundred or two thousand words covered any short-story idea I might have. The stories contained in my first book of short stories, Buttered Side Down, could only have been written by an ex-newspaper reporter.

By far the most picturesque and altogether engaging person about the Journal office was the little sports editor, Wallie Rowland. Wallie was much more than sports editor—he was a sort of unofficial general guiding spirit, though he would have denied this fact. He knew every inch of the newspaper business from the delivery alley to the office of Niemann, the proprietor of the Journal. He signed his stuff Brownie, and he was known all over Wisconsin. Thin, small-boned, swarthy, of Welsh descent, curly black hair, enormous black eyes in a sallow pointed face. His face was somber until he smiled his peculiarly winning smile, which transformed him. The women in the office all cooed over Wallie, but he played no favorites. Even Edith Crombie, the society editor, an old society gal herself, who came in daily at the elegant hour of eleven wafting a delicate scent into the gritty city room and wearing always the most immaculate of lemon chamois gloves, condescended to Wallie, though she spoke to no one else. Wallie called her Edie and slapped her English tweed shoulders and she beamed frostily. At the age of six Wallie had sold papers on a downtown corner. Then he got a Journal job as office boy. Half the time he had slept at night on a pile of old papers and sacks in a warm corner of the pressroom. Occasionally he would be sent out with the photographer to carry the tripod and pretty soon he himself was staff photographer. He knew more ball players, fighters and horsemen than the sports editor himself. He never went out of the building that he didn't come back with a story. He used to take a hand in the sports department on rush days. He became sports editor. He could operate a linotype, he could act as managing editor in Campbell's absence, and did. His conversation was droll, wise, witty, laconic. He was partial to gaudy habiliments. His shirts, ties, socks and shoes bordered on the fantastic, but in the office he wore a disreputable out-at-elbows coat that was little more than a ragged bundle of tobacco burns, mucilage spots and ink. His office visitors were likely to be battered gentlemen with cauliflower ears, husky voices, brown derbies, and noses that swerved in odd directions, unexpectedly. Also ladies very bright as to hair and general color effect. He kept a revolver, loaded, in his desk drawer and had a disconcerting way of twirling it absent-mindedly on one forefinger as he sat back in his swivel chair, his feet propped high. No one knew what risky devious paths intersected little Wallie's life that he should have this grim weapon of defense; but it wasn't there for fun.

When we collected dimes and quarters for a devil's-food cake sent round from the Princess Restaurant it always was cut in Wallie's office, the portions firmly dissected with a piece of string held taut. He never drank. He smoked a virulent pipe whose bowl was shaped like a miniature automobile. There came to me more knowledge, warmth and companionship from my association with Wallie Rowland than from anyone I had ever known until that time. In my first novel, Dawn O'Hara, he appears in the romantic (I hope) character of Blackie.

Fortunately the Journal office was within walking distance of Kahlo's. By eight or eight-thirty I was at work. I stayed almost four years on the paper, doing a man-size job which, at the end, pretty well wrecked my health for a year, and which certainly has affected it in all the years thereafter. I loved every minute of it, and I'd do it all over again.

It was part of my duties to cover the morning nine-o'clock police court with Cook, when the dirt of the streets was swept in from the night before. In the foul-smelling room off the courtroom there always was huddled a

motley pitiable crew of petty criminals, prostitutes, drunks, pickpockets, vagrants; all the flotsam and jetsam of the night streets in a town of four or five hundred thousand.

Thirty days. Thirty days. Thirty days. The judge rapped it out, monotonously. The bedraggled girls had the paint and mascara of the night before on their unwashed faces and stale cheap perfume emanated from the crushed finery. The faces of the men had the blank and secret look of those who have learned the prison lesson of keeping their mouths shut and their sensibilities from registering anything but sullen resentment. Outside corridors and courtroom benches were usually crowded with weeping or voluble relatives or hangers-on, or shyster lawyers. I was not yet nineteen, I had lived most of my life in the small-town atmosphere, mine was an intelligent middle-class family of taste. My year and a half on the Appleton Crescent had been a kindergarten. Now I was smack up against the real school of life.

That daily morning police court was—and is—a terrible indictment of civilized society. Vaguely I sensed this. Once, in the very beginning, when I spoke a word of pity or remonstrance a tobacco-chewing bailiff said, "Aw, don't worry yourself about them there. They earn it easy."

"They do not!" I snapped, feeling very superior. He laughed.

Juvenile court was another assignment. In these stories we were, humanely enough, forbidden to use the names of first-offense minors. The phrase "sob sister" to describe a newspaper woman feature writer had come in. Juvenile court stories were sob-sister stuff. About an old courtroom in daily use there is a distinctive smell that, to one accustomed to it, cannot be mistaken. It is an odor of unwashed bodies, unaired garments, tobacco, dust, and despair or fright. For the human body gives off certain odors under various emotions, as the glands function. The courtroom smell is the smell of the underprivileged; the worried poor folks smell.

It was a fine breaking-in for me—the Schandein case. After that anything to which I was assigned seemed mild and fragrant. In those first days Cook and I covered the case turn and turn about; he would be out in the corridor telephoning his stuff into the waiting office while I held the fort. When he returned I dashed to the telephone to dictate my story to the waiting stenographer. I had to make a reasonably coherent and smooth-running story out of my hastily scribbled notes. I was blithely ignorant of the meaning of much of the testimony.

Today city newspapers pool their stories. There is practically no such thing as a scoop. The Richard Harding Davis days when reporters beat or scooped one another have vanished before a central news office from which a story is dealt out to each paper, all of one cut. But in my Journal days it was every man for himself. It made newspaper life exciting and newspaper jobs precarious. Underpaid, overworked, it was (and perhaps still is) one of the most exhilarating occupations in the world.

Strangely enough, though Milwaukee was full of beer gardens, ranging all the way from the famous Schlitz's Palm Garden to any little saloon backroom, none of these was the favorite rendezvous of Milwaukee's newspaper fraternity. After the Press Club (men only) it was Martini's that claimed their patronage. Though the name has a racy sound, Martini's was nothing more than a little German bakery and coffee house over on East Water Street. I described it at length in Dawn O'Hara. It was a part of the newspaper life of my Milwaukee. The shop occupied the front, facing the street. The café was behind this. Before noon the pastry trays began to come up. No real meals were served. One could have only cakes and coffee or chocolate. The newspaper and theatrical people began to drop in at four in the afternoon or thereabouts. Milwaukee had clung to the old-country custom of coffee and cakes in midafternoon. Mr. and Mrs. Martini were Alsatians. That flaky confection, custard or cream-filled, known the world over as a Napoleon, was called a Bismarck at Martini's. There were acres of cakes and kuchens—coffee rings, bund-kuchen, apple, plum, apricot kuchens, cream-filled horns (hörnchen, in German; similar in shape to the French croissant, but richer). Practically every edible thing in Milwaukee was filled or ornamented with whipped cream. They put cream in the marinated herring, cream in the sauerkraut, in the soup. Their figures were frightful. In the back room were small marble-topped tables, a huge stove glowed in the middle of the room in winter, on the wall were racks holding German newspapers and magazines: Jugend, Die Woche, Fliegende Blätter. Chess games went on indefinitely. Oceans of coffee and rich chocolate topped with whipped cream were consumed, together with tons of buttery cakes. Here you found the afternoon newspapermen when their day's grist was in, and the morning newspapermen fortifying themselves for the night's work. The actors and actresses from the Pabst Theater German stock company had tables sacred to their use. These were a vivacious and picturesque crew, frumpy, voluble, self-absorbed.

Your coffee or chocolate was served you, but you armed yourself with plate and fork and foraged for your own pastries. Here at Martini's I spent many a late afternoon hour with Wallie. The reporters on the German newspapers seemed to live there.

Martini's has gone grand. The massive crockery (you could just manage to get your lips over the thick cup edge) has become china, the old East Water Street stand (even that is now North Water) has been abandoned. Like many pleasant institutions, it went with the war.

Somehow, I made out on my fifteen a week. Free theater tickets often came my way through the office. My clothes were made in Appleton. My room with board came to about eight dollars a week. I simply did without most things. What I could not afford—and what could I not afford!—I simply ignored. About every two or three weeks I went home to Appleton by train, a distance of over one hundred miles. Sometimes I had enough money for this trip; sometimes I hadn't. But I had to see my invalid father; he counted on my coming. At such times I committed the only deliberately dishonest act of which I have been consciously guilty. I would buy a twenty-five-cent parlor-car seat ticket on the five-o'clock train and take my place grandly in green plush luxury. When the conductor came round I would hand him the parlor-car ticket with a dollar bill neatly folded beneath. Years later I sent the Northwestern Railroad what I thought I owed them. But perhaps they still can put me in jail. It was pleasant to be with my father, my mother and sister for twenty-four hours, but it was good to be back at work on Monday. I liked my new independence. Appleton, outside my own family, had lost much interest for me.

After Anacreon

LEW WELCH

When I drive cab
    I am moved by strange whistles and wear a hat.

When I drive cab
    I am the hunter. My prey leaps out from where it
    hid, beguiling me with gestures.

When I drive cab
    All may command me, yet I am in command of all who do.

When I drive cab
    I am guided by voices descending from the naked air.

When I drive cab
    A revelation of movement comes to me: They wake now.
    Now they want to work or look around. Now they want
    drunkenness and heavy food. Now they contrive to love.

When I drive cab
    I bring the sailor home from the sea. In the back of
    my car he fingers the pelt of his maiden.

When I drive cab
    I watch for stragglers in the urban order of things.

When I drive cab
    I end the only lit and waitful thing in miles of
    darkened houses.

We Question of Fortune: Four-fifty a Week*

THEODORE DREISER

Once across the river and into the wholesale district, she glanced about her for some likely door at which to apply. As she contemplated the wide windows and imposing signs, she became conscious of being gazed upon and understood for what she was—a wage-seeker. She had never done this thing before, and lacked courage. To avoid a certain indefinable shame she felt at being caught spying about for a position, she quickened her steps and assumed an air of indifference supposedly common to one upon an errand. In this way she passed many manufacturing and wholesale houses without once glancing in. At last, after several blocks of walking, she felt that this would not do, and began to look about again, though without relaxing her pace. A little way on she saw a great door which, for some reason, attracted her attention. It was ornamented by a small brass sign, and seemed to be the entrance to a vast hive of six or seven floors. "Perhaps," she thought, "they may want some one," and crossed over to enter. When she came within a score of feet of the desired goal, she saw through the window a young man in a grey checked suit. That he had anything to do with the concern, she could not tell, but because he happened to be looking in her direction her weakening heart misgave her and she hurried by, too overcome with shame to enter. Over the way stood a great six-story structure, labelled Storm and King, which she viewed with rising hope. It was a wholesale dry goods concern and employed women. She could see them moving about now and then upon the upper floors. This place she decided to enter, no matter what. She crossed over and walked directly toward the entrance. As she did so, two men came out and paused in the door. A telegraph messenger in blue dashed past her and up the few steps that led to the entrance and disappeared. Several pedestrians out of the hurrying throng which filled the sidewalks passed about her as she paused, hesitat-

* Selection from *Sister Carrie.*

65

ing. She looked helplessly around, and then, seeing herself observed, re-treated. It was too difficult a task. She could not go past them.

So severe a defeat told sadly upon her nerves. Her feet carried her mechanically forward, every foot of her progress being a satisfactory portion of a flight which she gladly made. Block after block passed by. Upon street-lamps at the various corners she read names such as Madison, Monroe, La Salle, Clark, Dearborn, State, and still she went, her feet beginning to tire upon the broad stone flagging. She was pleased in part that the streets were bright and clean. The morning sun, shining down with steadily increasing warmth, made the shady side of the streets pleasantly cool. She looked at the blue sky overhead with more realisation of its charm than had ever come to her before.

Her cowardice began to trouble her in a way. She turned back, resolv-ing to hunt up Storm and King and enter. On the way she encountered a great wholesale shoe company, through the broad plate windows of which she saw an enclosed executive department, hidden by frosted glass. With-out this enclosure, but just within the street entrance, sat a grey-haired gentleman at a small table, with a large open ledger before him. She walked by this institution several times hesitating, but, finding herself unobserved, faltered past the screen door and stood humbly waiting.

"Well, young lady," observed the old gentleman, looking at her some-what kindly, "what is it you wish?"

"I am, that is, do you—I mean, do you need any help?" she stammered.

"Not just at present," he answered smiling. "Not just at present. Come in some time next week. Occasionally we need some one."

She received the answer in silence and backed awkwardly out. The pleasant nature of her reception rather astonished her. She had expected that it would be more difficult, that something cold and harsh would be said—she knew not what. That she had not been put to shame and made to feel her unfortunate position, seemed remarkable.

Somewhat encouraged, she ventured into another large structure. It was a clothing company, and more people were in evidence—well-dressed men of forty and more, surrounded by brass railings.

An office boy approached her.

"Who is it you wish to see?" he asked.

"I want to see the manager," she said.

Hester Street from Clinton Street,
New York, Late Nineteenth Century

He ran away and spoke to one of a group of three man who were conferring together. One of these came towards her.

"Well?" he said coldly. The greeting drove all courage from her at once.

"Do you need any help?" she stammered.

"No," he replied abruptly, and turned upon his heel.

She went foolishly out, the office boy deferentially swinging the door for her, and gladly sank into the obscuring crowd. It was a severe setback to her recently pleased mental state.

Now she walked quite aimlessly for a time, turning here and there, seeing one great company after another, but finding no courage to prosecute her single inquiry. High noon came, and with it hunger. She hunted out an unassuming restaurant and entered, but was disturbed to find that the prices were exorbitant for the size of her purse. A bowl of soup was all that she could afford, and, with this quickly eaten, she went out again. It restored her strength somewhat and made her moderately bold to pursue the search.

In walking a few blocks to fix upon some probable place, she again encountered the firm of Storm and King, and this time managed to get in. Some gentlemen were conferring close at hand, but took no notice of her. She was left standing, gazing nervously upon the floor. When the limit of her distress had been nearly reached, she was beckoned to by a man at one of the many desks within the near-by railing.

"Who is it you wish to see?" he inquired.

"Why, any one, if you please," she answered. "I am looking for something to do."

"Oh, you want to see Mr. McManus," he returned. "Sit down," and he pointed to a chair against the neighbouring wall. He went on leisurely writing, until after a time a short, stout gentleman came in from the street.

"Mr. McManus," called the man at the desk, "this young woman wants to see you."

The short gentleman turned about towards Carrie, and she arose and came forward.

"What can I do for you, miss?" he inquired, surveying her curiously.

"I want to know if I can get a position," she inquired.

"As what?" he asked.

"Not as anything in particular," she faltered.

"Have you ever had any experience in the wholesale dry goods business?" he questioned.

"No, sir," she replied.

"Are you a stenographer or typewriter?"

"No, sir."

"Well, we haven't anything here," he said. "We employ only experienced help."

She began to step backward toward the door, when something about her plaintive face attracted him.

"Have you ever worked at anything before?" he inquired.

"No, sir," she said.

"Well, now, it's hardly possible that you would get anything to do in a wholesale house of this kind. Have you tried the department stores?"

She acknowledged that she had not.

"Well, if I were you," he said, looking at her rather genially, "I would try the department stores. They often need young women as clerks."

"Thank you," she said, her whole nature relieved by this spark of friendly interest.

"Yes," he said, as she moved toward the door, "you try the department stores," and off he went.

At that time the department store was in its earliest form of successful operation, and there were not many. The first three in the United States, established about 1884, were in Chicago. Carrie was familiar with the names of several through the advertisements in the "Daily News," and now proceeded to seek them. The words of Mr. McManus had somehow managed to restore her courage, which had fallen low, and she dared to hope that this new line would offer her something. Some time she spent in wandering up and down, thinking to encounter the buildings by chance, so readily is the mind, bent upon prosecuting a hard but needful errand, eased by that self-deception which the semblance of search, without the reality, gives. At last she inquired of a police officer, and was directed to proceed "two blocks up," where she would find "The Fair."

The nature of these vast retail combinations, should they ever permanently disappear, will form an interesting chapter in the commercial history of our nation. Such a flowering out of a modest trade principle the world had never witnessed up to that time. They were along the line of the most effective retail organisation, with hundreds of stores coördinated into one and laid out upon the most imposing and economic basis. They were handsome, bustling, successful affairs, with a host of clerks and a swarm of patrons. Carrie passed along the busy aisles, much affected by the remarkable displays of trinkets, dress goods, stationery, and jewelry. Each separate counter was a show place of dazzling interest and attraction. She could not help feeling the claim of each trinket and valuable upon her personally, and yet she did not stop. There was nothing there which she could not have used—nothing which she did not long to own. The dainty slippers and stockings, the delicately frilled skirts and petticoats, the laces, ribbons, haircombs, purses, all touched her with individual desire, and she felt keenly the fact that not any of these things were in the range of her purchase. She was a work-seeker, an outcast without employment, one whom the average employee could tell at a glance was poor and in need of a situation.

It must not be thought that any one could have mistaken her for a nervous, sensitive, high-strung nature, cast unduly upon a cold, calculating, and unpoetic world. Such certainly she was not. But women are peculiarly sensitive to their adornment.

Not only did Carrie feel the drag of desire for all which was new and pleasing in apparel for women, but she noticed too, with a touch at the heart, the fine ladies who elbowed and ignored her, brushing past in utter disregard of her presence, themselves eagerly enlisted in the materials which the store contained. Carrie was not familiar with the appearance of her more fortunate sisters of the city. Neither had she before known the nature and appearance of the shop girls with whom she now compared poorly. They were pretty in the main, some even handsome, with an air of independence and indifference which added, in the case of the more favoured, a certain piquancy. Their clothes were neat, in many instances fine, and wherever she encountered the eye of one it was only to recognise in it a keen analysis of her own position—her individual shortcomings of dress and that shadow of *manner* which she thought must hang about her and make clear to all who and what she was. A flame of envy lighted in her heart. She realised in a dim way how much the city held—wealth, fashion, ease—every adornment for women, and she longed for dress and beauty with a whole heart.

On the second floor were the managerial offices, to which, after some inquiry, she was now directed. There she found other girls ahead of her, applicants like herself, but with more of that self-satisfied and independent air which experience of the city lends; girls who scrutinised her in a painful manner. After a wait of perhaps three-quarters of an hour, she was called in turn.

"Now," said a sharp, quick-mannered Jew, who was sitting at a roll-top desk near the window, "have you ever worked in any other store?"

"No, sir," said Carrie.

"Oh, you haven't," he said, eyeing her keenly.

"No, sir," she replied.

"Well, we prefer young women just now with some experience. I guess we can't use you."

Carrie stood waiting a moment, hardly certain whether the interview had terminated.

"Don't wait!" he exclaimed. "Remember we are very busy here."

Carrie began to move quickly to the door.

"Hold on," he said, calling her back. "Give me your name and address. We want girls occasionally."

When she had gotten safely into the street, she could scarcely restrain the tears. It was not so much the particular rebuff which she had just experienced, but the whole abashing trend of the day. She was tired and nervous. She abandoned the thought of appealing to the other department stores and now wandered on, feeling a certain safety and relief in mingling with the crowd.

In her indifferent wandering she turned into Jackson Street, not far from the river, and was keeping her way along the south side of that imposing thoroughfare, when a piece of wrapping paper, written on with marking ink and tacked up on the door, attracted her attention. It read, "Girls wanted— wrappers & stichers." She hesitated a moment, then entered.

The firm of Speigelheim & Co., makers of boys' caps, occupied one floor of the building, fifty feet in width and some eighty feet in depth. It was a place rather dingily lighted, the darkest portions having incandescent lights, filled with machines and work benches. At the latter laboured quite a company of girls and some men. The former were drabby-looking creatures, stained in face with oil and dust, clad in thin, shapeless, cotton dresses and shod with more or less worn shoes. Many of them had their sleeves rolled up, revealing bare arms, and in some cases, owing to the heat, their dresses were open at the neck. They were a fair type of nearly the lowest order of

71

shop-girls—careless, slouchy, and more or less pale from confinement. They were not timid, however; were rich in curiosity, and strong in daring and slang.

Carrie looked about her, very much disturbed and quite sure that she did not want to work here. Aside from making her uncomfortable by side-long glances, no one paid her the least attention. She waited until the whole department was aware of her presence. Then some word was sent around, and a foreman, in an apron and shirt sleeves, the latter rolled up to his shoulders, approached.

"Do you want to see me?" he asked.

"Do you need any help?" said Carrie, already learning directness of address.

"Do you know how to stitch caps?" he returned.

"No, sir," she replied.

"Have you ever had any experience at this kind of work?" he inquired.

She answered that she had not.

"Well," said the foreman, scratching his ear meditatively, "we do need a stitcher. We like experienced help, though. We've hardly got time to break people in." He paused and looked away out of the window. "We might, though, put you at finishing," he concluded reflectively.

"How much do you pay a week?" ventured Carrie, emboldened by a certain softness in the man's manner and his simplicity of address.

"Three and a half," he answered.

"Oh," she was about to exclaim, but checked herself and allowed her thoughts to die without expression.

"We're not exactly in need of anybody," he went on vaguely, looking her over as one would a package. "You can come on Monday morning, though," he added, "and I'll put you to work."

"Thank you," said Carrie weakly.

"If you come, bring an apron," he added.

He walked away and left her standing by the elevator, never so much as inquiring her name.

While the appearance of the shop and the announcement of the price paid per week operated very much as a blow to Carrie's fancy, the fact that work of any kind was offered after so rude a round of experience was gratifying. She could not begin to believe that she would take the place, modest as her aspirations were. She had been used to better than that. Her mere experience and the free out-of-door life of the country caused her nature to revolt at such confinement. Dirt had never been her share. Her sister's flat was clean. This place was grimy and low, the girls were careless and hardened. They must be bad-minded and hearted, she imagined. Still, a place had been offered her. Surely Chicago was not so bad if she could find one place in one day. She might find another and better later.

Her subsequent experiences were not of a reassuring nature, however. From all the more pleasing or imposing places she was turned away abruptly with the most chilling formality. In others where she applied only the experienced were required. She met with painful rebuffs, the most trying of which had been in a manufacturing cloak house, where she had gone to the fourth floor to inquire.

"No, no," said the foreman, a rough, heavily built individual, who looked after a miserably lighted workshop, "we don't want any one. Don't come here."

With the wane of the afternoon went her hopes, her courage, and her strength. She had been astonishingly persistent. So earnest an effort was well deserving of a better reward. On every hand, to her fatigued senses, the great business portion grew larger, harder, more stolid in its indifference. It seemed as if it was all closed to her, that the struggle was too fierce for her to hope to do anything at all. Men and women hurried by in long, shifting lines. She felt the flow of the tide of effort and interest—felt her own helplessness without quite realising the wisp on the tide that she was. She cast about vainly for some possible place to apply, but found no door which she had the courage to enter. It would be the same thing all over. The old humiliation of her plea, rewarded by curt denial. Sick at heart and in body, she turned to the west, the direction of Minnie's flat, which she had now fixed in mind, and began that wearisome, baffled retreat which the seeker for employment at nightfall too often makes. In passing through Fifth Avenue, south towards Van Buren Street, where she intended to take a car, she passed the door of a large wholesale shoe house, through the plate-glass window of which she could see a middle-aged gentleman sitting at a small desk. One of those forlorn impulses which often grow out of a fixed sense of defeat, the last sprouting of a baffled and uprooted growth of ideas, seized upon her. She walked deliberately through the door and up to the gentleman, who looked at her weary face with partially awakened interest.

"What is it?" he said.

"Can you give me something to do?" said Carrie.

"Now, I really don't know," he said kindly. "What kind of work is it you want—you're not a typewriter, are you?"

"Oh, no," answered Carrie.

"Well, we only employ book-keepers and typewriters here. You might go around to the side and inquire upstairs. They did want some help upstairs a few days ago. Ask for Mr. Brown."

She hastened around to the side entrance and was taken up by the elevator to the fourth floor.

"Call Mr. Brown, Willie," said the elevator man to a boy near by.

Willie went off and presently returned with the information that Mr. Brown said she should sit down and that he would be around in a little while.

It was a portion of the stock room which gave no idea of the general character of the place, and Carrie could form no opinion of the nature of the work.

"So you want something to do," said Mr. Brown, after he inquired concerning the nature of her errand. "Have you ever been employed in a shoe factory before?"

"No, sir," said Carrie.

"What is your name?" he inquired, and being informed, "Well, I don't know as I have anything for you. Would you work for four and a half a week?"

Carrie was too worn by defeat not to feel that it was considerable. She had not expected that he would offer her less than six. She acquiesced, however, and he took her name and address.

"Well," he said, finally, "you report here at eight o'clock Monday morning. I think I can find something for you to do."

He left her revived by the possibilities, sure that she had found something at last. Instantly the blood crept warmly over her body. Her nervous tension relaxed. She walked out into the busy street and discovered a new atmosphere. Behold, the throng was moving with a lightsome step. She noticed that men and women were smiling. Scraps of conversation and notes of laughter floated to her. The air was light. People were already pouring out of the buildings, their labour ended for the day. She noticed that they were pleased, and thoughts of her sister's home and the meal that would be awaiting her quickened her steps. She hurried on, tired perhaps, but no longer weary of foot. What would not Minnie say! Ah, the long winter in Chicago—the lights, the crowd, the amusement! This was a great, pleasing metropolis after all. Her new firm was a goodly institution. Its windows were of huge plate glass. She could probably do well there. Thoughts of Drouet returned—of the things he had told her. She now felt that life was better, that it was livelier, sprightlier. She boarded a car in the best of spirits, feeling her blood still flowing pleasantly. She would live in Chicago, her mind kept saying to itself. She would have a better time than she had ever had before—she would be happy.

The News Stand

DANIEL BERRIGAN

In cold November
the old man stood
like a stone man, all day
in a flimsy canvas box
of struts and patches; a lung, a world
billowing with big portentous names.
And the stone man stood;
eighty years, voice drumming like a god
wars, death, time's bloodletting and getting.

At sundown the world came apart,
a shack of cloth and board, roped, hefted.

Last, rolled up his pages; the leonine faces
snuffed without a cry, dead as all day.

The Prison

BERNARD MALAMUD

Though he tried never to think of it, at 29 Tommy Castelli's life was a screaming bore. It was not just Rosa or the store they tended for profits counted in pennies, or the unendurably slow hours and endless drivel that went with dispensing candy, cigarettes, and soda water; it was this sick-in-the-stomach feeling of being trapped in old mistakes, even those he had made before Rosa changed Tony into Tommy. He had been, as Tony, a kid of many ideas and schemes, especially for getting out of this thickly tenemented, kid-squawking neighborhood, with its lousy poverty, but everything had fouled up against him before he could.

When he was 16 he quit the vocational school where they were making him into a shoemaker and began to hang out with the gray-hatted, thick-soled-shoe boys who had the spare time and the mazuma* and displayed it in fat wonderful rolls down in the cellar clubs to all who would look, and everyone did, popeyed. They were the ones who had bought the silver *caffè expresso* urn and later the television, and they arranged the pizza parties and had the girls down; but it was getting in with them and their cars, leading to the holdup of a liquor store, that had started all the present trouble. Lucky for him their landlord knew the district leader and they arranged something so nobody bothered him after that.

Then before he knew what was going on—he had been frightened sick by the whole business—there was his father cooking up a deal with Rosa's old man that Tony would marry her and the father-in-law would, out of his savings, open a candy store for him to make an honest living. He wouldn't spit on a candy store, and Rosa was too plain and lank a chick for his personal taste, so he beat it off to Texas and bummed around for three months in too much space, and when he came back everyone said it was for Rosa

* Money.

and the candy store, and it was all arranged again and he, without saying no, was in it.

That was how he had landed on Prince Street in the Village, working from eight in the morning to almost midnight every day, except for an hour each afternoon when he went upstairs to sleep, and on Tuesdays, when the store was closed and he slept some more and went at night alone to the movies. He was too tired, always, for schemes now, but once he tried to make a little cash on the side by secretly taking in punchboards a syndicate had distributed in the neighborhood, on which he collected a nice cut and saved 55 bucks that Rosa didn't know about; but then the syndicate was exposed by a newspaper; the punchboards stopped.

Another time, when Rosa was at her mother's house, he took a chance and let them put in a slot machine that could guarantee a nice piece of change if he kept it long enough. He knew of course he couldn't hide it from her, so when she came home and screamed when she saw it, he was ready and patient, for once not yelling back when she yelled, and he explained it was not the same as gambling because anyone who played it got a roll of mints every time he put in a nickel. Also the machine would supply them a few extra dollars cash they could use to buy a television so he could see the fights without going to a bar; but Rosa wouldn't let up screaming, and later her father came in shouting he was a criminal and chopped the machine apart with a hammer. The next day the cops raided for slot machines and gave out summonses wherever they found them, and though Tommy's place was the only candy store in the neighborhood that didn't have one, he felt bad about the machine.

Mornings had been his best time of day because Rosa stayed upstairs cleaning, and since few people came into the store till noon, he could sit around alone, a toothpick between his teeth, looking over the *News* and *Mirror* on the fountain counter, or maybe chin with one of the old cellar-club guys who had happened to come by for a pack of cigarettes; or just sit there drinking coffee and thinking how far away he could get on the 55 he had stashed away in the cellar. Generally the mornings were this way, but after the slot machine usually the whole day was rotten and he along with it. Time moldered in his heart and all he could think of all morning was going to sleep in the afternoon, and he would wake up with the sour remembrance of the long night in the store ahead of him while everybody else was doing as he pleased. He cursed the place and Rosa, and cursed, from its beginning, his unhappy life.

It was one of these bad mornings that a ten-year-old girl from around the block came in and asked for two rolls of colored tissue paper, one red and one yellow. He wanted to say go away and stop bothering, but instead went with bad grace to the rear, where Rosa, whose bright idea it was to handle the stuff, kept it. He went from force of habit, for the girl had been coming in every Monday since the summer for the same thing, because her rock-faced mother, who looked as if she had arranged her own widowhood, took care of some small kids after school and gave them the paper to cut out dolls and such things. The girl, whose name he didn't know, had very light skin with dark eyes; but she was a plain kid and would be more so at 20.

He had noticed, when he went to get the paper, that she always hung back as if afraid to go where it was dark, though he kept the comics there and most of the other kids had to be slapped away from them; and that when he brought her the tissue her skin seemed to grow whiter and her eyes shone. She always handed him two hot dimes and went out without glancing back.

It happened that Rosa, who trusted nobody, had just hung a mirror on the back wall, and as Tommy opened the drawer to get the girl her paper, he looked up and saw in the glass something that made it seem as if he were dreaming. The girl had disappeared, but he saw a white hand reach into the candy case for a chocolate bar and for another, then she glided forth from behind the counter and stood there, innocently waiting for him. At first he felt like grabbing her by the neck and smacking her, but then he had begun to think, as he often did, how his Uncle Dom, years ago before he went away, used to take him with him when he went crabbing to Sheepshead Bay, Tony alone of all the kids. Once they went at night and threw the baited traps into the water and after awhile pulled them up and they had this green lobster in one, and just then this fat-faced cop came along and said they had to throw it back unless it was nine inches. Dom said it was nine inches all right, but the cop said not to be a wise guy so Dom measured it and it was 10 inches, and they laughed about the lobster all night. Then he remembered how he had felt after Dom was gone, and tears filled his eyes and he found himself thinking about the way his life had turned out, and then about this girl, sorry that she was a thief. He felt he should do

79

something for her, warn her to cut it out before she got into a jam and fouled up her whole life. The urge to do so was strong, but when he went forward she glanced up frightened because he had taken so long. The way the fear showed in her eyes bothered him and he did not attempt to say anything. Then she thrust out the dimes, grabbed at the tissue rolls, and ran out.

He had to sit down. He kept trying to make the urge to speak to her go away but it came stronger than ever. He asked himself what difference does it make if she swipes candy—so she swipes it; and the role of reformer was strange and distasteful to him, yet he could not convince himself that what he felt he must do was unimportant. But he worried he would not know what to say to her. Always he had trouble speaking, stumbled over words, especially in new situations. He was afraid he would make a sap of himself, and she would not take him seriously. He had to tell her in a sure way so that even if it scared her some, she would understand he had done it to set her straight.

He mentioned it to no one but often thought about her, always looking around whenever he went outside to raise the awning, or wash the window, to see if any of the girls playing in the street was her, but they never were.

The following Monday in an hour after opening the store he had smoked a full pack of butts. He thought he had what he wanted to say but was afraid for some reason she wouldn't come in, or if she did, this time she wouldn't take the candy. He was not sure he wanted that until he said what he had to say. But at about 11, while he was reading the *News*, she appeared, asking as usual for tissue paper, her eyes shining so she had to look away. He knew then she meant to steal. Going to the rear he slowly opened the drawer, keeping his head lowered as he sneaked a look into the glass and saw her slide behind the counter. His heart beat hard and his feet felt nailed to the floor. He ransacked his mind to recall what he had intended to do but it was like an empty room so he let her slip away and stood with the dimes burning his palm.

Afterwards he explained it to himself that he hadn't spoken to her because it was while she had the candy on her and she would have been more scared than he wanted. When he went upstairs, instead of sleeping, he sat at the kitchen window, looking out into the backyard. He blamed himself for being too soft, too much chicken, but then he thought, no, there was a better way to do it. He would do it indirectly, slip her a hint that he knew, and he was pretty sure that would stop her, and then sometime after, he would explain to her why it was a good thing she had stopped.

So next time he cleaned out the particular candy platter she helped herself from, thinking she would get wise he was on to her, but she seemed not to, only hesitated with her hand before she took two candy bars from the next plate and dropped them into the black patent leather purse she always had with her. The time after that he cleaned out the whole top shelf, and still she was not suspicious, and reached down to the next and took something different.

One Monday he put some loose change, nickels and dimes, on the candy plate but she left them there, only taking the candy, which bothered him a little. Rosa asked him what he was moaning about and why he had all of a sudden taken to eating chocolate bars. He didn't answer, and she began to look suspiciously at the women who came in, and he would gladly have rapped her in the teeth, but it didn't matter as long as she didn't know what was what. At the same time he figured he would have to do something decisive soon or it would get harder for the girl to stop stealing. He felt he had to be strong about it. Then he thought of a plan. He would leave just two chocolate bars in the plate and insert under the wrapper on one a note she could read when she was alone. He experimented on paper, printing many messages to her, and the one that seemed best he cleanly copied on a strip of cardboard and slipped it under the wrapper of one chocolate bar. It said, "Don't do this any more or you will suffer your whole life." He puzzled over whether to sign it A Friend or Your Friend and finally chose Your.

This was on Friday, and he could not contain his impatience for Monday. But on Monday she did not appear. He waited for a long time, until Rosa came down, then he had to go up and the girl still hadn't come and he was intensely disappointed because she had never failed to come. He lay on the bed with his shoes on and stared at the ceiling. He felt hurt, disillusioned, the sucker she had played him for and was now finished with because she probably had another. The more he thought about it the worse he felt. He worked up a splitting headache that kept him from sleeping, then he suddenly slept and woke without it. But he had awakened depressed, saddened. He thought about Dom getting out of jail and going away. He wondered whether he would ever meet him somewhere if he took the 55 dollars and left. Then he remembered Dom was a pretty old guy now and he might not know him even if they did meet. He thought about life. You never really got what you wanted. No matter how you tried you made mistakes and could never get past them. You could never see the sky and the ocean because you were locked in a prison, except that nobody called it a prison, and if you did, nobody knew what you were talking about, or they said they didn't.

But when he finally went downstairs, ironically amused that Rosa had permitted him so long a period of grace, there were people in the store and he could hear her screeching at the top of her lungs. Shoving his way through the crowd he saw in one sickening look that she had trapped the girl with the candy bars and was shaking her in such fury that the kid's head bounced back and forth like a balloon on a stick. With a curse he tore her away from the girl, whose sickly face showed her terrible fright.

"Whatsamatter," he shouted at Rosa, "you want blood?"

"She's a thief!" Rosa screamed.

"Shut your filthy mouth."

"A dirty rotten thief!"

To stop her yowling he slapped her, hard, but it was a harder blow than he had intended. Rosa fell back with a gasp. She did not cry but looked dazedly around at the people and tried to smile, and everyone could see her lip was flecked with blood.

"Go home," Tommy ordered the girl, but then there was a commotion near the door and her mother came in.

"What happened?" she said.

"She stole my candy," Rosa shrieked.

"I let her take it," Tommy said.

Rosa stared at him as if she had been hit again, then with mouth distorted began to sob.

"One was for you, Mother," said the girl.

Her mother socked her hard across the face. "You little thief, this time you'll get your hands burned good."

She pawed at the girl, grabbed her arm and yanked her out. The girl, like a grotesque ballerina, half ran, half fell forward, but at the door she managed to turn her white face and thrust out at him her red tongue.

Chicago *

BEN HECHT

I return to Chicago, the tall marching town shouldering its sky-scraper spearheads.

I come back with almost the same mood I brought to it more than thirty years ago—to look on wonders.

Wonders to be; and now wonders that were. I once looked forward and I now look back, and between these two looks is most of my life.

So one might watch a speeding automobile approaching and vanishing and remain standing on a lonely corner with the thought in one's head, "My God, that was me in that car! I have come, I have gone."

I encountered many things in the city of my first manhood. I met torrents that spun me around, tides that drowned me and comets that pulled me across the sky. I had many adventures. I found there also a first understanding of myself—that I was in love with life. The child's joy I had first felt watching the symmetry and colors of sky, day, night, remained to delight me in the city.

This delight has never left me, and it has altered little. It is the only thing of continuity in me, that I have been always in love with the pulse of existence. Now after long immersion in the brutishness and lunacy of events and with the vision in me that tomorrow is a hammer swinging at the skull of man, I still glow with this first love. I have only to look at the sky, to see people in the streets, to see oceans, trees, roads, houses, to feel and smell snow and rain, and listen to wind—I have only to open my senses and I am again as I was in my boyhood—and in my Chicago time—delighted to be present.

My years in Chicago were full of this mothlike avidity that kept me beating around the days as if they were shining lamps. When I look back to that time I see the city as I saw it then, all at once; no separate streets, neigh-

---

* Selection from *A Child of the Century*.

Chicago

borhoods or buildings, but a great gathering of life, an army encamped behind windows.

At sixteen, the windows of buildings became a new poetry in my mind. Their sameness, numerousness and metronomic sweep excited me. I thought of windows as if they were in the heads of people rather than in the walls of buildings.

The walls of the city, the buildings that slid off into space; the rooftops of houses like a tangle of decks of ships at anchor; the smoke of chimneys making awning stripes across the sky; the porcelain-lettered names on windows telling the story of trades and crafts and people behind counters; the Noah's Ark streetcars and the taxicabs like tattered couriers and the firecracker signs that hung in the air in a continuous explosion—all these things gave me a similar elation.

Most fascinating of all that I met in the city was the crowd. I had read no books about it yet, nor heard of its bad repute. Watching it flow like a river, wriggle like a serpent, scatter like a disturbed ant-hill, I had no thought of its mindlessness. I saw only life in its face and the valor of survival in its movement. The feet of this crowd had come walking out of endless yesterdays. My heart applauded the long unbroken march.

I used to stand glued to the sides of buildings watching the crowd more avidly than I have watched any performance on the stage. And some such thoughts as these would come to me, "As it moves now it has always moved, wave on wave of humans thrusting their legs forward, their secrets draped in immemorial cloths. The great thing called survival hovers over the bobbing fedoras and jiggling breasts and gives them a dramatic look, as if their little walk from doorway to doorway were the winning of a glamorous battle."

My instinct never looked on the crowd as a history-figure. It did not come marching out of the events of history but out of the caves of existence. Watching it, I thought of a seed that could not be stamped out by glaciers, drowned out by floods or devoured by saber-toothed tigers.

There were no Governments in my crowd and no Philosophies. It carried no scar of Time on it. It was my family grown too big to embrace and too numerous to count.

CONFERENCE BETWEEN GHOSTS

My years in Chicago were a bright time spent in the glow of new worlds. I was newspaper reporter, playwright, novelist, short-story writer, propagandist, publisher and crony of wild hearts and fabulous gullets. I haunted streets, studios, whore houses, police stations, courtrooms, theater stages, jails, saloons, slums, mad houses, fires, murders, riots, banquet halls and bookshops. I ran everywhere in the city like a fly buzzing in the works of a clock, tasted more than any fly belly could hold, learned not to sleep (an accomplishment that still clings to me) and buried myself in a tick-tock of whirling hours that still echo in me.

But before I begin the tale of these antic years, my curiosity makes me pause to look at two people, the one of whom I write and the one who writes. I have boasted I am unchanged. I withdraw the boast. The young man of whom I write inhabited a world that was unthinkable without him. Tomorrow never existed for him. He felt a childish immortality within the day he occupied.

He saw people shot, run over, hanged, burned alive, dead of poison and crumpled by age; he attended deathbeds, executions, autopsies; he counted corpses in disasters, he even haunted the county morgue in quest of data and tidbits, and still there was no knowledge of death in his hours, no whisper of it anywhere in the word "future." Neither literature nor reality awoke his sense of being mortal. His relatives began dying, friends collapsed and were shoveled into the earth, and he continued as unaware of death as if it were a language no teacher could bring to his tongue.

Put beside that young man whose name and the remains of whose face I bear, I am quite a ghostly fellow. Not he who is long gone but I who still exist am more the spook. For his activities were solely part of living, mine are divided between living and dying. What he could not imagine, I think of a great deal of the time, and when it is not in my head it settles in my mood, and I can even feel it as a sudden brake on my laughter—the world without me—that strange, busy and eerie activity from which I shall be absent. The sky will be in place, the automobiles will run, the crowds will move in and out of buildings, the great problems will blow like threatening winds through the mind of man, and I shall not be there.

I can recall the hour in which I lost my immortality, in which I tried on my shroud for the first time and saw how it became me. This is a queer thing to be writing about, having promised exuberantly the tale of my youth in Chicago. But the tale must wait on the teller. My youth speaks to me, and I see myself not as I was but as I am.

The knowledge of my dying came to me when my mother died. There was more than sorrow involved. I felt grief enough, and my heart felt the rip of a dear one dying. I carried her image in my eyes, seeing her when she was no longer seeable. Her vanished voice echoed in my head and the love she bore me struggled painfully to stay alive around me. But my heart did not claw at the emptied space where she had stood and demand her return. I accepted death for both of us.

I went and returned dry-eyed from the burial, but I brought death back with me. I had been to the edge of the world and looked over its last foot of territory into nothingness. I had seen mortality and it remained in me like a disease. It changed my knowledge of life. Its delights were never quite able to fool me again. The secret of death appeared in all the faces around me. I knew they were citizens of two worlds, of the small vanishing one of light and noise, and of the vast endless one of darkness and silence.

The passing of time, which had once been a happy and unimportant thing, became a matter of meaning. There was a plot to the rising and setting of the sun. Life was passing. The days were dropping from me as if I were shedding my life. Time was my blood ebbing.

THE GOOD-FAIRY LIQUOR SALESMAN

It was the third of July, 1910. I stood before the box-office window of the Majestic Vaudeville Theater waiting to buy a ticket for the matinee. I had run away from Madison, Wisconsin, the day before. I had slept on a bench in the Chicago railroad station until morning, walking all morning through the coffee-smelling Loop, bought a new tie and debated with myself whether I should notify my mother of my decision against further education. I had won the debate. I intended to notify her after a few days. I had fifty dollars in my pocket, my university budget for July. After the money was spent (although how to spend fifty dollars far away from the needs of boats, huts and Indian warfare was a mystery to me), I would return to Racine with a fine crop of lies concerning mishaps at the university—pickpockets, desperate gamblers who cheated. I was certain the right story would occur to me. A university was an institution so far removed from my mother's experience that she was sure to believe anything I told of it.

A voice called my name as I was paying for my theater ticket, and terror almost sent me flying. But at sixteen, one does not yield too quickly to panic. One has dignity and the beginnings of courage toward one's guilts. I turned with pounding heart but unbroken ranks and saw a man with a large red nose beaming at me. Logic told me it was a relative, for who else would know me?

It was an uncle distantly related, a penumbra uncle who might never see my parents for the rest of his life. Hope came to me. Not only was this uncle's nose red, but his belly was big, his eyes were bloodshot and he did not look as if he would live long.

"I recognized you by your eyes," the uncle said. "They're like your mother's. How is she?"

"Fine," I said.

"And your father?"

"Fine."

I thought of darting into the theater and trusting to luck that this vague uncle would forget so brief an encounter.

"And what are you doing here?"

"I'm going to a show."

"So I see." The red nose beamed. "I mean what are you doing in Chicago?"

A sudden lie occurred to me, one that would do service not only now but later when I faced my parents.

"I'm looking for a job," I said.

"Any particular kind of a job?"

"Not exactly."

"Come on with me. Maybe I can fix you up with something."

"I just bought a ticket to the show. I'll see you afterwards."

"Afterwards is no good." The bloodshot eyes smiled. "Get your money back for the ticket and come along."

I turned in the ticket and walked off reluctantly beside the big belly and the red nose. A conversation drifts out of a long-ago street.

"Do you know my name, young man?"

"It's Mr. Moyses."

"That's right. Manny Moyses. You don't drink, do you?"

"You mean whisky?"

"Yes, that's what I was referring to, young man."

"No, I don't drink that."

"Is that so? And you came to Chicago in this heat to hunt for a job?"

"Yes, sir."

"What would you like to be?"

"That depends on the offer, I think."

"Well, have you been trained for anything—like a bookkeeper or salesman?"

"I've been trained to be an acrobat."

"You don't say so! A tumbler, eh?"

"No, on the trapeze."

"That's crazy."

"If necessary I can play the violin."

"That's kid stuff. It's not practical. Come on. I've got something better for you."

"Are we going anywhere in particular?"

"Yes. We're going to call on one of my best customers. You've got to be smart, boy. Now I'm in a business where people are always glad to see me. I'm a liquor salesman."

Fifteen minutes later he said, "Here we are."

I looked up at a gray stone building with extra large windows. One of the windows was lettered in gold, "Chicago Daily Journal."

I hesitated. The smell of the near-by river came to my nose.

"I'd like to do something on a boat," I said.

"That's no good, working on a boat. Come on, now. Don't be scared. And let me do the talking."

"Certainly. I'll be exceedingly glad to."

We rode up a large elevator into a urinous smell of ink. A door read, "John C. Eastman, Publisher." We entered.

A man with a mat of gray hair, a large red nose like my uncle's and almost the same sort of bloodshot eyes, sat at a desk. He said, "Hello, Manny, what have you got today?"

"Something special, John," said my uncle. "I've brought you a hundred-and-twenty proof genius. Just the thing your great newspaper needs. This is my nephew, Bennie Hecht."

"How do you do, Mr. Hecht." The bloodshot eyes peered at me. "What kind of a genius are you?"

I was left dumb by my first "mister."

"He's a writer," Uncle Moyses answered, and a greater lie I had never heard.

"Can you write poetry?" the other red nose demanded.

"He can write anything," my genie uncle answered recklessly.

"I'm giving a party," Mr. Eastman confided, "and I want a poem written about a bull who is nibbling some God-damn grass in a pasture and swallows a God-damn bumblebee by mistake. The bee goes down his throat into his stomach and after two days of hardship comes out of his ass in a big load of bull shit. Mad as hell, this God-damn bumblebee crawls out, dusts himself off, jumps on the bull, and stings the be-Jesus out of him. I want that written in a poem. Think you can do it, Mr. Hecht?"

"Give him a pencil," Uncle Moyses answered proudly.

"I want a moral on the end," Mr. Eastman explained, "about not keeping a good man down."

Both red noses left. I heard them laughing in the hall, and I sat at the publisher's desk writing a poem. I was nervous about using dirty words but decided to utilize Mr. Eastman's vocabulary.

When he came back an hour later the poem was finished. It was six verses long with a *"L'Envoi."* He read it slowly.

"That's all right," he said. "I can use it at the party. Come along, Mr. Hecht."

I followed beside him to the second floor. We entered a large barnlike room full of desks and long tables, piled with typewriters and crumpled newspapers. There were many men in shirt sleeves. Some of them were bellowing, others sprawled in chairs asleep, with their hats down over their eyes. The smell of ink was sharper here.

Mr. Eastman took me to the largest roll-top desk I had ever seen. There was an awesome railing enclosing it. At this desk sat a man with a mat of gray hair, a red nose and another pair of bloodshot eyes. I was introduced to Mr. Martin Hutchens, the managing editor. Mr. Eastman said, "I hope you can find a place for Mr. Hecht on your staff, Mr. Hutchens."

Mr. Hutchens took a long look at me. I wondered what had become of my uncle.

"Journalism is a high calling," announced Mr. Hutchens in a loud growl. "I ask chiefly of a newspaperman that he devote himself to his craft, which is one of the finest in the world."

He stood up. Mr. Eastman had disappeared like my uncle. Mr. Hutchens led me to a flat-topped desk that swarmed with telephones, baskets, spikes and smeared paper streamers. A tall man with an imperious face was standing at this desk. He had an eagle beak and the look of a captain running a ship.

"Mr. Ballard Dunne, this is Mr. Ben Hecht," said Mr. Hutchens, "a new journalist who will assist you."

Mr. Dunne turned a look on me like a searchlight.

"Mr. Dunne will be your city editor," Mr. Hutchens added. He stood for a moment regarding me with a sort of increasing surprise. Then he walked abruptly away.

"Have you had any experience on a newspaper?" Mr. Dunne asked.

"Only today," I said.

"Indeed! What did you do today?"

"I wrote a poem for Mr. Eastman about a bull," I said.

"As a rule we prefer prose in our columns," Mr. Dunne muttered. He turned and frowned at the distant desk behind which Mr. Hutchens already sat glaring at a newspaper. After a moody silence Mr. Dunne addressed a handsome black-haired man sitting on the other side of his table. I had not noticed him before.

"Mr. Finnegan, this is Mr. Hecht," said Mr. Dunne, and the searchlight eyes played on me again. "Mr. Finnegan is our assistant city editor. You will report to him at six o'clock tomorrow morning."

I was amazed that so omnipotent a man could make so great a mistake. Tomorrow was the Fourth of July, a day sacred to torpedoes on streetcar tracks, cannon crackers and hundreds of little explosives. I sought to correct Mr. Dunne's lapse.

"Tomorrow is the Fourth of July, a holiday," I said.

"Allow me to contradict you, Mr. Hecht," replied Mr. Dunne. "There are no holidays in this dreadful profession you have chosen."

I nodded and waited for something more to be said. But I seemed to have vanished. I stood for several minutes staring out of limbo. Then I walked away. Mr. Finnegan had smiled at me, and I left quickly to keep from bursting into tears.

ROBINSON CRUSOE IN A NEWSPAPER OFFICE

There will be no end to this book if I continue unreeling memory spools. For I have come to a part of my life that is as vivid still in me as if it were happening. I have forgotten whole months and years, almost whole lives. But of this time I remember minutes and words, smells, grimaces, the quality of air I breathed, the expression of faces and every move and turn I made. And I do not lament this time as one does a lost love. I enjoy it as one of the few proofs of my existence. Whatever I have become, that youth who sat breathlessly in the *Journal* local room was what I was meant to be.

Many habits were formed by those days, and points of view which I have never outgrown or improved upon came to roost in my head. I shall write of these later. I would like now only to relive that swift time without adding present ornament to it.

I had been dropped willy-nilly into a world that fitted me as water fits a fish. It was a world that offered no discipline, that demanded no alteration in me. It bade me go out and look at life, devour it, enjoy it, report it. There were no responsibilities beyond enthusiasm. I needed nothing else than to remain as I always had been—excited, careless, bouncing through rain, snow, hot sun and vivid streets. I have never seen my Pumblechookian Uncle Moyses again to this day. But I stare at his big belly and red nose with never-ending gratitude.

City People

City dwellers come in all shapes, sizes, colors, races, ages, and income levels. Some are long-standing members of the community, like Konrad Bercovici's Goldstein family, who find the patterns and traditions of their lives disrupted by unaccustomed prosperity. Others, like those in Langston Hughes' "Ballad of the Landlord," will never manage to break out of their vicious cycle of poverty and oppression. Still others, newly arrived in the city like those in Karl Shapiro's "D.C.," have the aura of all transplanted people who yearn to feel at home in their new environment but who must endure the pangs of dislocation for long periods of time. And in Mark Helprin's "Back Bay Conservatory," we see the lives of two people who are learning how to come to terms with city life by coming to terms with each other.

Thomas Wolfe wandered about Brooklyn with his ear sharply attuned to the rich complexity of the much-parodied Brooklyn accent. His short story, (which should, for maximum enjoyment, be read aloud) is a hilarious tribute to the versatility of the human voicebox.

Willa Cather and Joyce Carol Oates have written disturbing portraits of urban adolescence. Cather's story "Paul's Case" takes place in Pittsburgh and New York; Detroit is Carol Oates's city—she knows its smells, its feelings, its people. Both writers have written suspenseful tales of affluent teenagers struggling to make an impact on smug, unresponsive environments—environments that include home, family, city, and self. In reading these two stories, one has the sense that something has gone very wrong—the individual's inability to feel a part of the community is in itself a stinging indictment of communal life.

The Newly-Rich Goldsteins

KONRAD BERCOVICI

The Goldsteins were destined for light work and comfort. "Middle Class" was stamped on their faces and radiated from their speech and movements. Every stitch of clothing proclaimed that they belonged to the happy, contented-with-what-God-gives middle class.

"H. Goldstein & Co., Embroidery," occupied the first floor of a dilapidated building on St. Mark's Place near Third Avenue. The two daughters, Sophy and Leah, were the working force of the firm. H. Goldstein himself was the salesman, bookkeeper, deliverer, collector and buyer. Four sewing machines near the rear windows, a table, an assortment of cardboard boxes and a few shelves in a corner were all the machinery of the factory.

But the Goldsteins were a contented lot. They lived in a five-room apartment on Tenth Street, had good old soft chairs to sit on; Mrs. Goldstein prepared fine meals, and on Saturday as the factory was closed each one of the family had his own private joys. H. Goldstein went to the synagogue to meet his old friends and discuss the Talmud. Mrs. Goldstein visited all her relatives on the Sabbath. Sophy was out with her beau, Joseph Katz; and Leah strolled on Second Avenue on the arm of Maurice Feldman.

The factory just covered house expenses and a small dollar or two for a rainy day saved by Mrs. Goldstein from table money. But they were independent, in business for themselves, as befits the Goldsteins the whole world over, and not hired workers. At the synagogue, Hirsh Goldstein was respected for his learning and piety; and though his contributions were not very large, still they were never beggarly.

When America entered the war the embroidery business took a jump. The Goldsteins obtained orders for shoulder straps, epaulets, chevrons, hat bands and a lot of other paraphernalia absolutely necessary to soldiers and officers to go over the top. The Goldsteins added four more machines and hired half a dozen Italian girls for the work. Soon even this

95

enlarged force could not cope with the orders. Another floor was hired, six more machines fixed up, and Joseph Katz, Sophy's beau, became the book-keeper. Three months later the factory moved to a Bond Street loft and sixty machines power driven and of the latest model, were installed. Little by little the Sabbath was neglected. The rush orders forced them to work seven days a week, seven days and seven nights. Maurice Feldman, Leah's beau, was engaged as assistant bookkeeper.

"Reb Goldstein, we missed you last Saturday," friends questioned him at the synagogue.

"The Talmud says, 'The welfare of the country you live in stands higher than your own rites,'" was all he answered.

Though people knew that his translation of the passage was a bit loose, they did not interfere.

After the factory had moved over to Bond Street, Sophy and Leah remained at home. Their presence in the factory was no longer needed.

Mother Goldstein argued that it ill-befitted the daughters of so big a manufacturer to be working. Goldstein was making money faster than he could count it. The girls were flattered and adulated wherever they went, and they began to think the Tenth Street apartment and the district they lived in entirely out of keeping with their new station in life. They had rich clothing now, and thought themselves too good for their former friends.

A large contribution to a charitable undertaking brought the young ladies an invitation to a party given by some wealthy people on Riverside Drive. It was the first time they had seen such living quarters. It sharpened their appetites to the pomps and vanities of the world. It made them feel the people living downtown were dust or dross.

Maurice Feldman and Joseph Katz were the first to feel the changed attitude. Sure enough! The young ladies were not going to marry their father's bookkeepers!

Riverside Drive became the ideal of the two sisters. At first the father refused even to hear of it. But when fortune had favored him and he made a lump sum in some side speculation, he half gave his consent.

At the synagogue he was seldom seen, and if he happened to come once in a while he was not as warmly greeted as formerly. He had offended several members of the congregation, had humbled them, by giving a donation of a hundred dollars when they had only given ten.

When the two sisters had won over their mother to the Riverside Drive plan the father could no longer resist. Soon an interior decorator was busy garnishing the nine-room two-bath apartment, with brand-new highly polished furniture. Gold-tinted hangings and gold-painted chairs, bookcases filled with deluxe sets in red and blue, an Oriental room, a Louis XV piano, and "real" oil paintings. Sophy and Leah were all the time buying new things. The visits to the great stores did not improve taste, but it pricked ambition. When the bustle ended, the Goldsteins had spent a young fortune on the Riverside apartment. The rooms were well filled with whatever could be bought, with all the Goldsteins could afford; and they could afford a good deal, because Hirsh Goldstein was making more money then he had ever dared to dream.

The war had to be won, and it could not be done without the assistance of "H. Goldstein & Co."

The first few days the Goldsteins enjoyed their acquisitions so much they had no time to think of anything else. Then they joined a fashionable temple. The daughters became members of charitable societies, the membership of which was composed of older parvenues. The downtown crowd and old associations were forgotten in the whirl. When some of the relatives came to visit the Goldsteins, they felt so outclassed and outdistanced that they never returned again.

But after the girls had wearied somewhat of their furniture and things, they began to notice that the new acquaintances made no friendly overtures. A feeling stole over them that their new friends laughed behind their backs. Whenever they happened to be in the company of the new aristocracy, the others spoke of things they knew nothing about. The others, college-bred most of them, mentioned names of authors and artists the Goldsteins had never heard of before. The others had tapering fine fingernails, slender wrists, thin ankles, and wore the simplest clothes with distinction.

Sophy and Leah felt that the young men of the new set avoided them. They were always courteous, but cold—cold to the invaders. But of course they could not think of marrying the firm's bookkeepers—twenty-five-dollar-a-week men! Yet they despaired ever to find mates from amongst those other people.

Once a collection was made to cover some minor expense of a children's party. Sophy gave a hundred dollars. She surprised the others laughing, and never knew whether she had given too much or too little. Hirsh Goldstein did not fare any better. The German Jews he met at the synagogue were nice and polite, but patronizing to an exasperating degree. Though they accepted his gifts for the synagogue and other charities, they looked down upon him. When he gave a small amount he was critized as a miser, when he gave a big sum he was a parvenu. He missed his old cronies. He had no chance to exhibit learning to those "new people."

Mrs. Goldstein wandered about the rooms, as if in prison. It was seldom that anybody ever visited the family now. They were reputed to be so rich! Joseph and Maurice came once to Sophy's birthday party, but they found there other guests, and felt lonesome. The Goldsteins had not learned how to be idling busily.

The two sisters now lacked a certain freedom of movement, surety of action. Sophy began to long for the firm grasp of Maurice's hand. Leah longed to hear Joseph's simple songs. The house with all its new wealth was not their home. It was too cold, too new, too clean. The men and women they met were not of their kind. The Goldsteins felt daily that they were only tolerated by them.

This situation lasted six months.

Then Hirsh Goldstein returned to his old synagogue on Hester Street. He went there in his old coat. To make up with his old friends he gave only five dollars when he was called to read from the holy book.

"Hirsh is down from his high horse," they whispered, when he returned the next week bringing his wife also to the synagogue. She too came in her second-best wraps.

A few weeks later the news spread that the Goldsteins had lost most of their fortune or all of it. Sophy and Leah came downtown to a party to which former friends invited them, just to show that it mattered not. And it was so nice and friendly! Everybody was so familiar and intimate.

"If you want anyone to speak to you, leave all the junk here," Sophy told Leah, who had put on the greater part of her jewelry for the occasion.

The Goldsteins rented an apartment on Tenth Street, but this time the old people furnished it. They bought good soft chairs, the kind they had had before, and a multicolored carpet for the floor of the front room, and a red settee which did not look severe and stylish, but inviting. It was just one step ahead in point of comfort and luxury from the one they had had before the adventure on the Drive. It was home again.

The Drive apartment was sublet, all furnished. Maurice came back to Sophy, Joseph to Leah, and every time one of the family bought clothes or jewelry great care was taken not to overdo—not to scare away old friends, not to soar too high with the first wind. Every time some expensive dress was suggested by some friends they exclaimed in chorus.

"We can't afford it. Times are hard."

But they were happy again.

How I contemplated the world from the Detroit House of Correction and began my life all over again

JOYCE CAROL OATES

NOTES FOR AN ESSAY for an English class at Baldwin Country Day School; poking around in debris; disgust and curiosity; a revelation of the meaning of life; a happy ending . . .

I. EVENTS

1. The girl (myself) is walking through Branden's, that excellent store. Suburb of a large famous city that is a symbol for large famous American cities. The event sneaks up on the girl, who believes she is herding it along with a small fixed smile, a girl of fifteen, innocently experienced. She dawdles in a certain style by a counter of costume jewelry. Rings, earrings, necklaces. Prices from $5 to $50, all within reach. All ugly. She eases over to the glove counter, where everything is ugly too. In her close-fitted coat with its black fur collar she contemplates the luxury of Branden's, which she has known for many years: its many mild pale lights, easy on the eye and the soul, its elaborate tinkly decorations, its women shoppers with their excellent shoes and coats and hairdos, all dawdling gracefully, in no hurry.

Who was ever in a hurry here?

2. The girl seated at home. A small library, paneled walls of oak. Someone is talking to me. An earnest husky female voice drives itself against my ears, nervous, frightened, groping around my heart, saying, "If you wanted gloves why didn't you say so? Why didn't you ask for them?" That store, Branden's, is owned by Raymond Forrest who lives on Du-Maurier Drive. We live on Sioux Drive. Raymond Forrest. A handsome man? An ugly man? A man of fifty or sixty, with gray hair, or a man of forty with earnest courteous eyes, a good golf game, who is Raymond Forrest,

this man who is my salvation? Father has been talking to him. Father is not his physician; Dr. Berg is his physician. Father and Dr. Berg refer patients to each other. There is a connection. Mother plays bridge with . . . On Mondays and Wednesdays our maid Billie works at . . . The strings draw together in a cat's cradle, making a net to save you when you fall . . .

3. *Harriet Arnold's.* A small shop, better than Branden's. Mother in her black coat, I in my close-fitted blue coat. Shopping. Now look at this, isn't this cute, do you want this, why don't you want this, try this on, take this with you to the fitting room, take this also, what's wrong with you, what can I do for you, why are you so strange . . . ? "I wanted to steal but not to buy," I don't tell her. The girl droops along in her coat and gloves and leather boots, her eyes scan the horizon which is pastel pink and decorated like Branden's, tasteful walls and modern ceilings with graceful glimmering lights.

4. Weeks later, the girl at a bus stop. Two o'clock in the afternoon, a Tuesday, obviously she has walked out of school.

5. The girl stepping down from a bus. Afternoon, weather changing to colder. Detroit. Pavement and closed-up stores; grillwork over the windows of a pawnshop. What is a pawnshop, exactly?

II. CHARACTERS

1. The girl stands five feet five inches tall. An ordinary height. Baldwin Country Day School draws them up to that height. She dreams along the corridors and presses her face against the Thermoplex glass. No frost or steam can ever form on that glass. A smudge of grease from her forehead . . . could she be boiled down to grease? She wears her hair loose and long and straight in suburban teen-age style, 1968. Eyes smudged with pencil, dark brown. Brown hair. Vague green eyes. A pretty girl? An ugly girl? She sings to herself under her breath, idling in the corridor, thinking of her many secrets (the thirty dollars she once took from the purse of a friend's mother, just for fun, the basement window she smashed in her own house just for fun) and thinking of her brother who is at Susquehanna Boys'

Academy, an excellent preparatory school in Maine, remembering him unclearly . . . he has long manic hair and a squeaking voice and he looks like one of the popular teen-age singers of 1968, one of those in a group, The Certain Forces, The Way Out, The Maniacs Responsible. The girl in her turn looks like one of those fieldsful of girls who listen to the boys' singing, dreaming and mooning restlessly, breaking into high sullen laughter, innocently experienced.

2. The mother. A midwestern woman of Detroit and suburbs. Belongs to the Detroit Athletic Club. Also the Detroit Golf Club. Also the Bloomfield Hills Country Club. The Village Women's Club at which lectures are given each winter on Genet and Sartre and James Baldwin, by the director of the adult education program at Wayne State University . . . The Bloomfield Art Association. Also the Founders Society of the Detroit Institute of Arts. Also . . . Oh, she is in perpetual motion, this lady, hair like blown-up gold and finer than gold, hair and fingers and body of inestimable grace. Heavy weighs the gold on the back of her hairbrush and hand mirror. Heavy heavy the candlesticks in the dining room. Very heavy is the big car, a Lincoln, long and black, that on one cool autumn day split a squirrel's body in two unequal parts.

3. The father. Dr. ———. He belongs to the same clubs as #2. A player of squash and golf; he has a golfer's umbrella of stripes. Candy stripes. In his mouth nothing turns to sugar, however, saliva works no miracles here. His doctoring is of the slightly sick. The sick are sent elsewhere (to Dr. Berg?), the deathly sick are sent back for more tests and their bills are sent to their homes, the unsick are sent to Dr. Coronet (Isabel, a lady), an excellent psychiatrist for unsick people who angrily believe they are sick and want to do something about it. If they demand a male psychiatrist, the unsick are sent by Dr. ——— (my father) to Dr. Lowenstein, a male psychiatrist, excellent and expensive, with a limited practice.

4. Clarita. She is twenty, twenty-five, she is thirty or more? Pretty, ugly, what? She is a woman lounging by the side of a road, in jeans and a sweater, hitchhiking, or she is slouched on a stool at a counter in some roadside diner. A hard line of jaw. Curious eyes. Amused eyes. Behind her eyes processions move, funeral pageants, cartoons. She says, "I never can figure

out why girls like you bum around down here. What are you looking for anyway?" An odor of tobacco about her. Unwashed underclothes, or no underclothes, unwashed skin, gritty toes, hair long and falling into strands, not recently washed.

5. Simon. In this city the weather changes abruptly, so Simon's weather changes abruptly. He sleeps through the afternoon. He sleeps through the morning. Rising, he gropes around for something to get him going, for a cigarette or a pill to drive him out to the street, where the temperature is hovering around 35°. Why doesn't it drop? Why, why doesn't the cold clean air come down from Canada, will he have to go up into Canada to get it, will he have to leave the Country of his Birth and sink into Canada's frosty fields . . . ? Will the FBI (which he dreams about constantly) chase him over the Canadian border on foot, hounded out in a blizzard of broken glass and horns . . . ?

"Once I was Huckleberry Finn," Simon says, "but now I am Roderick Usher." Beset by frenzies and fears, this man who makes my spine go cold, he takes green pills, yellow pills, pills of white and capsules of dark blue and green . . . he takes other things I may not mention, for what if Simon seeks me out and climbs into my girl's bedroom here in Bloomfield Hills and strangles me, what then . . . ? (As I write this I begin to shiver. Why do I shiver? I am now sixteen and sixteen is not an age for shivering.) It comes from Simon, who is always cold.

III. WORLD EVENTS

Nothing.

IV. PEOPLE & CIRCUMSTANCES CONTRIBUTING TO THIS
    DELINQUENCY

Nothing.

V. SIOUX DRIVE

George, Clyde G. 240 Sioux. A manufacturer's representative; children, a dog; a wife. Georgian with the usual columns. You think of the White House, then of Thomas Jefferson, then your mind goes blank on the white pillars and you think of nothing. Norris, Ralph W. 246 Sioux. Public relations. Colonial. Bay window, brick, stone, concrete, wood, green shutters, sidewalk, lantern, grass, trees, blacktop drive, two children, one of them my classmate Esther (Esther Norris) at Baldwin. Wife, cars. Ramsey, Michael D. 250 Sioux. Colonial. Big living room, thirty by twenty-five, fireplaces in living room library recreation room, paneled walls wet bar five bathrooms five bedrooms two lavatories central air conditioning automatic sprinkler automatic garage door three children one wife two cars a breakfast room a patio a large fenced lot fourteen trees a front door with a brass knocker never knocked. Next is our house. Classic contemporary. Traditional modern. Attached garage, attached Florida room, attached patio, attached pool and cabana, attached roof. A front door mail slot through which pour *Time* magazine, *Fortune, Life, Business Week, The Wall Street Journal,* the *New York Times, New Yorker, Saturday Review, M.D., Modern Medicine, Disease of the Month* . . . and also . . . And in addition to all this a quiet sealed letter from Baldwin saying: *Your daughter is not doing work compatible with her performance on the Stanford-Binet* . . . And your son is not doing well, not well at all, very sad. Where is your son anyway? Once he stole trick-and-treat candy from some six-year-old kids, he himself being a robust ten. The beginning. Now your daughter steals. In the Village Pharmacy she made off with, yes she did, don't deny it, she made off with a copy of *Pageant* magazine for no reason, she swiped a roll of Life Savers in a green wrapper and was in no need of saving her life or even in need of sucking candy, when she was no more than eight years old she stole, don't blush, she stole a package of Tums only because it was out on the counter and available, and the nice lady behind the counter (now dead) said nothing . . . Sioux Drive. Maples, oaks, elms. Diseased elms cut down. Sioux Drive runs into Roosevelt Drive. Slow turning lanes, not streets, all drives and lanes and ways and passes. A private police force. Quiet private police, in unmarked cars. Cruising on Saturday evenings with paternal smiles for the residents who are streaming in and out of houses, going to and from par-

104

ties, a thousand parties, slightly staggering, the women in their furs alighting from automobiles bought of Ford and General Motors and Chrysler, very heavy automobiles. No foreign cars. Detroit. In 275 Sioux, down the block, in that magnificent French Normandy mansion, lives ———— ———— himself, who has the C—— account itself, imagine that! Look at where he lives and look at the enormous trees and chimneys, imagine his many fireplaces, imagine his wife and children, imagine his wife's hair, imagine her fingernails, imagine her bathtub of smooth clean glowing pink, imagine their embraces, his trouser pockets filled with odd coins and keys and dust and peanuts, imagine their ecstasy on Sioux Drive, imagine their income tax returns, imagine their little boy's pride in his experimental car, a scaled-down C——, as he roars around the neighborhood on the sidewalks frightening dogs and Negro maids, oh imagine all these things, imagine everything, let your mind roar out all over Sioux Drive and Du Maurier Drive and Roosevelt Drive and Ticonderoga Pass and Burning Bush Way and Lincolnshire Pass and Lois Lane.

When spring comes its winds blow nothing to Sioux Drive, no odors of hollyhocks or forsythia, nothing Sioux Drive doesn't already possess, everything is planted and performing. The weather vanes, had they weather vanes, don't have to turn with the wind, don't have to content with the weather. There is no weather.

VI. DETROIT

There is always weather in Detroit. Detroit's temperature is always 32°. Fast falling temperatures. Slow rising temperatures. Wind from the north northeast four to forty miles an hour, small craft warnings, partly cloudy today and Wednesday changing to partly sunny through Thursday . . . small warnings of frost, soot warnings, traffic warnings, hazardous lake conditions for small craft and swimmers, restless Negro gangs, restless cloud formations, restless temperatures aching to fall out the very bottom of the thermometer or shoot up over the top and boil everything over in red mercury.

Detroit's temperature is 32°. Fast falling temperatures. Slow rising temperatures. Wind from the north northeast four to forty miles an hour . . .

VII. EVENTS

1. The girl's heart is pounding. In her pocket is a pair of gloves! In a plastic bag! Airproof breathproof plastic bag, gloves selling for twenty-five dollars on Branden's counter! In her pocket! Shoplifted! . . . In her purse is a blue comb, not very clean. In her purse is a leather billfold (a birthday present from her grandmother in Philadelphia) with snapshots of the family in clean plastic windows, in the billfold are bills, she doesn't know how many bills . . . In her purse is an ominous note from her friend Tykie *What's this about Joe H. and the kids hanging around at Louise's Sat. night? You heard anything?* . . . passed in French class. In her purse is a lot of dirty yellow Kleenex, her mother's heart would break to see such very dirty Kleenex, and at the bottom of her purse are brown hairpins and safety pins and a broken pencil and a ballpoint pen (blue) stolen from somewhere forgotten and a purse-size compact of Cover Girl Make-up, Ivory Rose . . . Her lipstick is Broken Heart, a corrupt pink; her fingers are trembling like crazy; her teeth are beginning to chatter; her insides are alive; her eyes glow in her head; she is saying to her mother's astonished face *I want to steal but not to buy.*

2. At Clarita's. Day or night? What room is this? A bed, a regular bed, and a mattress on the floor nearby. Wallpaper hanging in strips. Clarita says she tore it like that with her teeth. She was fighting a barbaric tribe that night, high from some pills she was battling for her life with men wearing helmets of heavy iron and their faces no more than Christian crosses to breathe through, every one of those bastards looking like her lover Simon, who seems to breathe with great difficulty through the slits of mouth and nostrils in his face. Clarita has never heard of Sioux Drive. Raymond Forrest cuts no ice with her, not does the C—account and its millions; Harvard Business School could be at the corner of Vernor and 12th Street for all she cares, and Vietnam might have sunk by now into the Dead Sea under its tons of debris, for all the amazement she could show . . . her face is overworked, overwrought, at the age of twenty (thirty?) it is already exhausted but fanciful and ready for a laugh. Clarita says mournfully to me *Honey somebody is going to turn you out let me give you warning.* In a movie shown on late television Clarita is not a mess like this but a nurse,

106

with short neat hair and a dedicated look, in love with her doctor and her doctor's patients and their diseases, enamored of needles and sponges and rubbing alcohol . . . Or no: she is a private secretary. Robert Cummings is her boss. She helps him with fantastic plots, the canned audience laughs, no, the audience doesn't laugh because nothing is funny, instead her boss is Robert Taylor and they are not boss and secretary but husband and wife, she is threatened by a young starlet, she is grim, handsome, wifely, a good companion for a good man . . . She is Claudette Colbert. Her sister too is Claudette Colbert. They are twins, identical. Her husband Charles Boyer is a very rich handsome man and her sister, Claudette Colbert, is plotting her death in order to take her place as the rich man's wife, no one will know because they are *twins* . . . All these marvelous lives Clarita might have lived, but she fell out the bottom at the age of thirteen. At the age when I was packaging my overnight case for a slumber party at Toni Deshield's she was tearing filthy sheets off a bed and scratching up a rash on her arms . . . Thirteen is uncommonly young for a white girl in Detroit, Miss Brook of the Detroit House of Correction said in a sad newspaper interview for the *Detroit News;* fifteen and sixteen are more likely. Eleven, twelve, thirteen are not surprising in colored . . . they are more precocious. What can we do? Taxes are rising and the tax base is falling. The temperature rises slowly but falls rapidly. Everything is falling out the bottom. Woodward Avenue is filthy, Livernois Avenue is filthy! Scraps of paper flutter in the air like pigeons, dirt flies up and hits you right in the eye, oh Detroit is breaking up into dangerous bits of newspaper and dirt, watch out . . .

Clarita's apartment is over a restaurant. Simon her lover emerges from the cracks at dark. Mrs. Olesko, a neighbor of Clarita's, an aged white wisp of a woman, doesn't complain but sniffs with contentment at Clarita's noisy life and doesn't tell the cops, hating cops, when the cops arrive. I should give more fake names, more blanks, instead of telling all these secrets. I myself am a secret; I am a minor.

3. My father reads a paper at a medical convention in Los Angeles. There he is, on the edge of the North American continent, when the unmarked detective put his hand so gently on my arm in the aisle of Branden's and said, "Miss, would you like to step over here for a minute?"

And where was he when Clarita put her hand on my arm, that wintry dark sulphurous aching day in Detroit, in the company of closed-down barbershops, closed-down diners, closed-down movie houses, homes, windows, basements, faces . . . she put her hand on my arm and said, "Honey, are you looking for somebody down here?"

And was he home worrying about me, gone for two weeks solid, when they carried me off . . . ? It took three of them to get me in the police cruiser, so they said, and they put more than their hands on my arm.

4. I work on this lesson. My English teacher is Mr. Forest, who is from Michigan State. Not handsome, Mr. Forest, and his name is plain unlike Raymond Forrest's, but he is sweet and rodentlike, he has conferred with the principal and my parents, and everything is fixed . . . treat her as if nothing has happened, a new start, begin again, only sixteen years old, what a shame, how did it happen?—nothing happened, nothing could have happened, a slight physiological modification known only to a gynecologist or to Dr. Coronet. I work on my lesson. I sit in my pink room. I look around the room with my sad pink eyes. I sigh, I dawdle. I pause, I eat up time. I am limp and happy to be home, I am sixteen years old suddenly, my head hangs heavy as a pumpkin on my shoulders, and my hair has just been cut by Mr. Faye at the Crystal Salon and is said to be very becoming.

(Simon too put his hand on my arm and said, "Honey, you have got to come with me," and in his six-by-six room we got to know each other. Would I go back to Simon again? Would I lie down with him in all that filth and craziness? Over and over again

a Clarita is being betrayed as in front of a Cunningham Drugstore she is nervously eyeing a colored man who may or may not have money, or a nervous white boy of twenty with sideburns and an Appalachian look, who may or may not have a knife hidden in his jacket pocket, or a husky red-faced man of friendly countenance who may or may not be a member of the Vice Squad out for an early twilight walk.)

I work on my lesson for Mr. Forest. I have filled up eleven pages. Words pour out of me and won't stop. I want to tell everything . . . what was the song Simon was always humming, and who was Simon's friend in a very new trench coat with an old high school graduation ring on his finger . . . ? Simon's bearded friend? When I was down too low for him Simon kicked me out and gave me to him for three days, I think, on Fourteenth Street in Detroit, an airy room of cold cruel drafts with newspapers on the floor . . . Do I really remember that or am I piecing it together from what

108

they told me? Did they tell the truth? Did they know how much of the truth?

VIII. CHARACTERS

1. Wednesdays after school, at four; Saturday mornings at ten. Mother drives me to Dr. Coronet. Ferns in the office, plastic or real, they look the same. Dr. Coronet is queenly, an elegant nicotine-stained lady who would have studied with Freud had circumstances not prevented it, a bit of a Catholic, ready to offer you some mystery if your teeth will ache too much without it. Highly recommended by Father! Forty dollars an hour, Father's forty dollars! Progress! Looking up! Looking better! That new haircut is so becoming, says Dr. Coronet herself, showing how normal she is for a woman with an I.Q. of 180 and many advanced degrees.

2. Mother. A lady in a brown suede coat. Boots of shiny black material, black gloves, a black fur hat. She would be humiliated could she know that of all the people in the world it is my ex-lover Simon who walks most like her . . . self-conscious and unreal, listening to distant music, a little bowlegged with craftiness . . .

3. Father. Tying a necktie. In a hurry. On my first evening home he put his hand on my arm and said, "Honey, we're going to forget all about this."

4. Simon. Outside a plane is crossing the sky, in here we're in a hurry. Morning. It must be morning. The girl is half out of her mind, whimpering and vague, Simon her dear friend is wretched this morning . . . he is wretched with morning itself . . . he forces her to give him an injection, with that needle she knows is filthy, she has a dread of needles and surgical instruments and the odor of things that are to be sent into the blood, thinking somehow of her father. . . . This is a bad morning, Simon says that his mind is being twisted out of shape, and so he submits to the needle which he usually scorns and bites his lip with his yellowish teeth, his face going very pale. *Ah baby!* he says in his soft mocking voice, which with all women is a mockery of love, *do it like this—Slowly—*And the girl, terrified, almost

drops the precious needle but manages to turn it up to the light from the window . . . it is an extension of herself, then? She can give him this gift, then? *I wish you wouldn't do this to me*, she says, wise in her terror, because it seems to her that Simon's danger—in a few minutes he might be dead—is a way of pressing her against him that is more powerful than any other embrace. She has to work over his arm, the knotted corded veins of his arm, her forehead wet with perspiration as she pushes and releases the needle, staring at that mixture of liquid now stained with Simon's bright blood . . . When the drug hits him she can feel it herself, she feels that magic that is more than any woman can give him, striking the back of his head and making his face stretch as if with the impact of a terrible sun . . . She tries to embrace him but he pushes her aside and stumbles to his feet. *Jesus Christ*, he says . . .

5. Princess, a Negro girl of eighteen. What is her charge? She is close-mouthed about it, shrewd and silent, you know that no one had to wrestle her to the sidewalk to get her in here; she came with dignity. In the recreation room she sits reading *Nancy Drew and the Jewel Box Mystery*, which inspires in her face tiny wrinkles of alarm and interest: what a face! Light brown skin, heavy shaded eyes, heavy eyelashes, a serious sinister dark brow, graceful fingers, graceful wristbones, graceful legs, tongue, a sugarsweet voice, a leggy stride more masculine than Simon's and my mother's, decked out in a dirty white blouse and dirty white slacks; vaguely nautical is Princess's style . . . At breakfast she is in charge of clearing the table and leans over me, saying, *Honey you sure you ate enough?*

6. The girl lies sleepless, wondering. Why here, why not there? Why Bloomfield Hills and not jail? Why jail and not her pink room? Why downtown Detroit and not Sioux Drive? What is the difference? Is Simon all the difference? The girl's head is a parade of wonders. She is nearly sixteen, her breath is marvelous with wonders, not long ago she was coloring with crayons and now she is smearing the landscape with paints that won't come off and won't come off her fingers either. She says to the matron *I am not talking about anything*, not because everyone has warned her not to talk but because, because she will not talk, because she won't say anything about Simon who is her secret. And she says to the matron *I won't go home* up until that night in the lavatory when everything was changed . . . "No, I won't go home I want to stay here," she says, listening to her own words

110

with amazement thinking that weeds might climb everywhere over the marvelous $86,000 house and dinosaurs might return to muddy the beige carpeting, but never never will she reconcile four o'clock in the morning in Detroit with eight o'clock breakfasts in Bloomfield Hills . . . oh, she aches still for Simon's hands and his caressing breath, though he gave her little pleasure, he took everything from her (five-dollar bills, ten-dollar bills, passed into her numb hands by men and taken out of her hands by Simon) until she herself was passed into the hands of other men, police, when Simon evidently got tired of her and her hysteria . . . *No, I won't go home, I don't want to be bailed out,* the girl thinks as a *Stubborn and Wayward Child* (one of the several charges lodged against her) and the matron understands her crazy white-rimmed eyes that are seeking out some new violence that will keep her in jail, should someone threaten to let her out. Such children try to strangle the matrons, the attendants, or one another . . . they want the locks locked forever, the doors nailed shut . . . and this girl is no different up until that night her mind is changed for her . . .

IX. THAT NIGHT

Princess and Dolly, a little white girl of maybe fifteen, hardy however as a sergeant and in the house of correction for armed robbery, corner her in the lavatory at the farthest sink and the other girls look away and file out to bed, leaving her. God how she is beaten up! Why is she beaten up? Why do they pound her, why such hatred? Princess vents all the hatred of a thousand silent Detroit winters on her body, this girl whose body belongs to me, fiercely she rides across the midwestern plains on this girl's tender bruised body . . . revenge on the oppressed minorities of America! revenge on the slaughtered Indians! revenge on the female sex, on the male sex, revenge on Bloomfield Hills, revenge revenge . . .

X. DETROIT

In Detroit weather weighs heavily upon everyone. The sky looms large. The horizon shimmers in smoke. Downtown the buildings are imprecise in the haze. Perpetual haze. Perpetual motion inside the haze. Across the choppy river is the city of Windsor, in Canada. Part of the continent has bunched up here and is bulging outward, at the tip of Detroit, a cold hard rain is forever falling on the expressways . . . shoppers shop grimly, their cars are not parked in safe places, their windshields may be smashed and graceful ebony hands may drag them out through their shatterproof smashed windshields crying *Revenge for the Indians!* Ah, they all fear leaving Hudson's and being dragged to the very tip of the city and thrown off the parking roof of Cobo Hall, that expensive tomb, into the river . . .

XI. CHARACTERS WE ARE FOREVER ENTWINED WITH

1. Simon drew me into his tender rotting arms and breathed gravity into me. Then I came to earth, weighted down. He said *You are such a little girl*, and he weighted me down with his delight. In the palms of his hands were teeth marks from his previous life experiences. He was thirty-five, they said. Imagine Simon in this room, in my pink room: he is about six feet tall and stoops slightly, in a feline cautious way, always thinking, always on guard, with his scuffed light suede shoes and his clothes which are anyone's clothes, slightly rumpled ordinary clothes that ordinary men might wear to not-bad jobs. Simon has fair, long hair, curly hair, spent languid curls that are like . . . exactly like the curls of wood shavings to the touch, I am trying to be exact . . . and he smells of unheated mornings and coffee and too many pills coating his tongue with a faint green-white scum . . . Dear Simon, who would be panicked in this room and in this house (right now Billie is vacuuming next door in my parents' room: a vacuum cleaner's roar is a sign of all good things), Simon who is said to have come from a home not much different from this, years ago, fleeing all the carpeting and the polished banisters . . . Simon has a deathly face, only desperate people fall in love with it. His face is bony and cautious, the bones of his cheeks prominent as if the rigidity of his ceaseless thinking, plotting, for he has to make money out of girls to whom money means nothing, they're so far gone they can hardly count it, and in a sense money means nothing to him either except as a way of keeping on with his life. *Each Day's Proud Struggle*, the title of a novel we could read at jail . . . Each day he needs a certain amount of money. He devours it. It wasn't love he uncoiled in me with his

112

hollowed-out eyes and his courteous smile, that remnant of a prosperous past, but a dark terror that needed to press itself flat against him, or against another man . . . but he was the first, he came over to me and took my arm, a claim. We struggled on the stairs and I said, "Let me loose, you're hurting my neck, my face," it was such a surprise that my skin hurt where he rubbed it, and afterward we lay face to face and he breathed everything into me. In the end I think he turned me in.

2. Raymond Forrest. I just read this morning that Raymond Forrest's father, the chairman of the board at ———, died of a heart attack on a plane bound for London. I would like to write Raymond Forrest a note of sympathy. I would like to thank him for not pressing charges against me one hundred years ago, saving me, being so generous . . . well, men like Raymond Forrest are generous men, not like Simon. I would like to write him a letter telling of my love, or of some other emotion that is positive and healthy. Not like Simon and his poetry, which he scrawled down when he was high and never changed a word . . . but when I try to think of something to say it is Simon's language that comes back to me, caught in my head like a bad song, it is always Simon's language:

There is no reality only dreams
Your neck may get snapped when you wake
My love is drawn to some violent end
She keeps wanting to get away
My love is heading downward
And I am heading upward
She is going to crash on the sidewalk
And I am going to dissolve into the clouds

XII. EVENTS

1. Out of the hospital, bruised and saddened and converted, with Princess's grunts still tangled in my hair . . . and Father in his overcoat looking like a prince himself, come to carry me off. Up the expressway and out north to home. Jesus Christ but the air is thinner and cleaner here. Monumental houses. Heartbreaking sidewalks, so clean.

2. Weeping in the living room. The ceiling is two stories high and two chandeliers hang from it. Weeping, weeping, though Billie the maid is *probably listening*. I will never leave home again. Never. Never leave home. Never leave this home again, never.

3. Sugar doughnuts for breakfast. The toaster is very shiny and my face is distorted in it. Is that my face?

4. The car is turning in the driveway. Father brings me home. Mother embraces me. Sunlight breaks in movieland patches on the roof of our traditional contemporary home, which was designed for the famous automotive stylist whose identity, if I told you the name of the famous car he designed, you would all know, so I can't tell you because my teeth chatter at the thought of being sued . . . or having someone climb into my bedroom window with a rope to strangle me . . . The car turns up the blacktop drive. The house opens to me like a doll's house, so lovely in the sunlight, the big living room beckons to me with its walls falling away in a delirium of joy at my return, Billie the maid is *no doubt* listening from the kitchen as I burst into tears and the hysteria Simon got so sick of. Convulsed in Father's arms I say I will never leave again, never, why did I leave, where did I go, what happened, my mind is gone wrong, my body is one big bruise, my backbone was sucked dry, it wasn't the men who hurt me and Simon never hurt me but only those girls . . . my God how they hurt me . . . I will never leave home again . . . The car is perpetually turning up the drive and I am perpetually breaking down in the living room and we are perpetually taking the right exit from the expressway (Lahser Road) and the wall of the rest room is perpetually banging against my head and perpetually are Simon's hands moving across my body and adding everything up and so too are Father's hands on my shaking bruised back, far from the surface of my skin on the surface of my good blue cashmere coat (dry-cleaned for my release) . . . I weep for all the money here, for God in gold and beige carpeting, for the beauty of chandeliers and the miracle of a clean polished gleaming toaster and faucets that run both hot and cold water, and I tell them *I will never leave home, this is my home, I love everything here, I am in love with everything here* . . .

D. C.

KARL SHAPIRO

The bad breed of the natives with their hates
That border on a Georgian night,
The short vocabularly, the southern look
That writes a volume on your past, the men
Freeholders of the city-state, the women
Polite for murder—these happen to be;
The rest arrive and never quite remain.

The rest live with an easy homelessness
And common tastelessness, their souls
Weakly lit up blazing screens and tales
Told by a newspaper. Holidays the vast
Basilicas of the railroad swallow up
Hundreds of thousands, struggling in the tide
For home, the one identity and past.

The noble riches keep themselves, the miles
Of marble breast the empty wind,
The halls of books and pictures manufacture
Their deep patinas, the fountains coldly splash
To the lone sailor, the boulevards stretch out
Farther than Arlington, where all night long
One living soldier marches for the dead.

Only the very foreign, the very proud,
The richest and the very poor
Hid in their creepy purlieus white or black

City People

Adore this whole Augustan spectacle,
And chancelleries perceive the porch of might
Surmounted by the dome in which there lies
No Bonaparte, no Lenin, but a floor.

Yet those who govern live in quaintness, close
In the Georgian ghetto of the best;
What was the simplest of the old becomes
The exquisite palate of the new. Their names
Are admirals and paternalists, their ways
The ways of Lee who, having lost the slaves,
Died farther south, a general in the wrong.

Paul's Case

A Study in Temperament

WILLA CATHER

It was Paul's afternoon to appear before the faculty of the Pittsburgh High School to account for his various misdemeanors. He had been suspended a week ago, and his father had called at the Principal's office and confessed his perplexity about his son. Paul entered the faculty room suave and smiling. His clothes were a trifle outgrown, and the tan velvet on the collar of his open overcoat was frayed and worn; but for all that there was something of the dandy about him, and he wore an opal pin in his neatly knotted black four-in-hand, and a red carnation in his buttonhole. This latter adornment the faculty somehow felt was not properly significant of the contrite spirit befitting a boy under the ban of suspension.

Paul was tall for his age and very thin, with high, cramped shoulders and a narrow chest. His eyes were remarkable for a certain hysterical brilliancy, and he continually used them in a conscious, theatrical sort of way, peculiarly offensive in a boy. The pupils were abnormally large, as though he were addicted to belladonna, but there was a glassy glitter about them which that drug does not produce.

When questioned by the Principal as to why he was there Paul stated, politely enough, that he wanted to come back to school. This was a lie, but Paul was quite accustomed to lying; found it, indeed, indispensable for overcoming friction. His teachers were asked to state their respective charges against him, which they did with such a rancor and aggrievedness as evinced that this was not a usual case. Disorder and impertinence were among the offenses named, yet each of his instructors felt that it was scarcely possible to put into words the real cause of the trouble, which lay in a sort of hysterically defiant manner of the boy's; in the contempt which they all knew he felt for them, and which he seemingly made not the least effort to conceal. Once, when he had been making a synopsis of a paragraph at the blackboard, his English teacher had stepped to his side and attempted to guide his hand. Paul had started back with a shudder and thrust

117

his hands violently behind him. The astonished woman could scarcely have been more hurt and embarrassed had he struck at her. The insult was so involuntary and definitely personal as to be unforgettable. In one way and another he had made all his teachers, men and women alike, conscious of the same feeling of physical aversion. In one class he habitually sat with his hand shading his eyes; in another he always looked out of the window during the recitation; in another he made a running commentary on the lecture, with humorous intention.

His teachers felt this afternoon that his whole attitude was symbolized by his shrug and his flippantly red carnation flower, and they fell upon him without mercy, his English teacher leading the pack. He stood through it smiling, his pale lips parted over his white teeth. (His lips were continually twitching, and he had a habit of raising his eyebrows that was contemptuous and irritating to the last degree.) Older boys than Paul had broken down and shed tears under that baptism of fire, but his set smile did not once desert him, and his only sign of discomfort was the nervous trembling of the fingers that toyed with the buttons of his overcoat, and an occasional jerking of the other hand that held his hat. Paul was always smiling, always glancing about him, seeming to feel that people might be watching him and trying to detect something. This conscious expression, since it was as far as possible from boyish mirthfulness, was usually attributed to insolence or "smartness."

As the inquisition proceeded one of his instructors repeated an impertinent remark of the boy's, and the Principal asked him whether he thought that a courteous speech to have made a woman. Paul shrugged his shoulders slightly and his eyebrows twitched.

"I don't know," he replied. "I didn't mean to be polite or impolite, either. I guess it's a sort of way I have of saying things regardless."

The Principal, who was a sympathetic man, asked him whether he didn't think that a way it would be well to get rid of. Paul grinned and said he guessed so. When he was told that he could go he bowed gracefully and went out. His bow was but a repetition of the scandalous red carnation.

His teachers were in despair, and his drawing master voiced the feeling of them all when he declared there was something about the boy which none of them understood. He added: "I don't really believe that smile of his comes altogether from insolence; there's something sort of haunted about it. The boy is not strong, for one thing. I happen to know that he was born in

Colorado, only a few months before his mother died out there of a long illness. There is something wrong about the fellow."

The drawing master had come to realize that, in looking at Paul, one saw only his white teeth and the forced animation of his eyes. One warm afternoon the boy had gone to sleep at his drawing board, and his master had noted with amazement what a white, blue-veined face it was; drawn and wrinkled like an old man's about the eyes, the lips twitching even in his sleep, and stiff with a nervous tension that drew them back from his teeth.

His teachers left the building dissatisfied and unhappy; humiliated to have felt so vindictive toward a mere boy, to have uttered this feeling in cutting terms, and to have set each other on, as it were, in the gruesome game of intemperate reproach. Some of them remembered having seen a miserable street cat set at bay by a ring of tormentors.

As for Paul, he ran down the hill whistling the "Soldiers' Chorus" from *Faust,* looking wildly behind him now and then to see whether some of his teachers were not there to writhe under his lightheartedness. As it was now late in the afternoon and Paul was on duty that evening as usher at Carnegie Hall, he decided that he would not go home to supper. When he reached the concert hall the doors were not yet open and, as it was chilly outside, he decided to go up into the picture gallery—always deserted at this hour— where there were some of Raffelli's gay studies of Paris streets and an airy blue Venetian scene or two that always exhilarated him. He was delighted to find no one in the gallery but the old guard, who sat in one corner, a newspaper on his knee, a black patch over one eye and the other closed. Paul possessed himself of the place and walked confidently up and down, whistling under his breath. After a while he sat down before a blue Rico and lost himself. When he bethought him to look at his watch, it was after seven o'clock, and he rose with a start and ran downstairs, making a face at Augustus, peering out from the cast room, and an evil gesture at the Venus de Milo as he passed her on the stairway.

When Paul reached the ushers' dressing room half a dozen boys were there already, and he began excitedly to tumble into his uniform. It was one of the few that at all approached fitting, and Paul thought it very becoming—though he knew that the tight, straight coat accentuated his narrow chest, about which he was exceedingly sensitive. He was always considerably excited while he dressed, twanging all over to the tuning of the strings and the preliminary flourishes of the horns in the music room; but

119

tonight he seemed quite beside himself, and he teased and plagued the boys until, telling him tht he was crazy, they put him down on the floor and sat on him.

Somewhat calmed by his suppression, Paul dashed out to the front of the house to seat the early comers. He was a model usher; gracious and smiling he ran up and down the aisles; nothing was too much trouble for him; he carried messages and brought programs as though it were his greatest pleasure in life, and all the people in his section thought him a charming boy, feeling that he remembered and admired them. As the house filled, he grew more and more vivacious and animated, and the color came to his cheeks and lips. It was very much as though this were a great reception and Paul were the host. Just as the musicians came out to take their places, his English teacher arrived with checks for the seats which a prominent manufacturer had taken for the season. She betrayed some embarrassment when she handed Paul the tickets, and a hauteur which subsequently made her feel very foolish. Paul was startled for a moment, and had the feeling of wanting to put her out; what business had she here among all these fine people and gay colors? He looked her over and decided that she was not appropriately dressed and must be a fool to sit downstairs in such togs. The tickets had probably been sent her out of kindness, he reflected as he put down a seat for her, and she had about as much right to sit there as he had.

When the symphony began Paul sank into one of the rear seats with a long sigh of relief, and lost himself as he had done before the Rico. It was not that symphonies, as such, meant anything in particular to Paul, but the first sigh of the instruments seemed to free some hilarious and potent spirit within him; something that struggled there like the genie in the bottle found by the Arab fisherman. He felt a sudden zest of life; the lights danced before his eyes and the concert hall blazed into unimaginable splendor. When the soprano soloist came on Paul forgot even the nastiness of his teacher's being there and gave himself up to the peculiar stimulus such personages always had for him. The soloist chanced to be a German woman, by no means in her first youth, and the mother of many children; but she wore an elaborate gown and a tiara, and above all she had that indefinable air of achievement, that world-shine upon her, which, in Paul's eyes, made her a veritable queen of Romance.

After a concert was over Paul was always irritable and wretched until he got to sleep, and tonight he was even more than usually restless. He had

120

the feeling of not being able to let down, of its being impossible to give up this delicious excitement which was the only thing that could be called living at all. During the last number he withdrew and, after hastily changing his clothes in the dressing room, slipped out to the side door where the soprano's carriage stood. Here he began pacing rapidly up and down the walk, waiting to see her come out.

Over yonder, the Schenley, in its vacant stretch, loomed big and square through the fine rain, the windows of its twelve stories glowing like those of a lighted cardboard house under a Christmas tree. All the actors and singers of the better class stayed there when they were in the city, and a number of the big manufacturers of the place lived there in the winter. Paul had often hung about the hotel, watching the people go in and out, longing to enter and leave schoomasters and dull care behind him forever.

At last the singer came out, accompanied by the conductor, who helped her into her carriage and closed the door with a cordial *auf wiedersehen* which set Paul to wondering whether she were not an old sweetheart of his. Paul followed the carriage over to the hotel, walking so rapidly as not to be far from the entrance when the singer alighted, and disappeared behind the swinging glass doors that were opened by a Negro in a tall hat and a long coat. In the moment that the door was ajar it seemed to Paul that he, too, entered. He seemed to feel himself go after her up the steps, into the warm, lighted building, into an exotic, tropical world of shiny, glistening surfaces and basking ease. He reflected upon the mysterious dishes that were brought into the dining room, the green bottles in buckets of ice, as he had seen them in the supper party pictures of the *Sunday World* supplement. A quick gust of wind brought the rain down with sudden vehemence, and Paul was startled to find that he was still outside in the slush of the gravel driveway; that his boots were letting in the water and his scanty overcoat was clinging wet about him; that the lights in front of the concert hall were out and that the rain was driving in sheets between him and the orange glow of the windows above him. There it was, what he wanted—tangibly before him, like the fairy world of a Christmas pantomime—but mocking spirits stood guard at the doors, and, as the rain beat in his face, Paul wondered whether he were destined always to shiver in the black night outside, looking up at it.

He turned and walked reluctantly toward the car tracks. The end had to come sometime; his father in his night-clothes at the top of the stairs, expla-

121

nations that did not explain, hastily improvised fictions that were forever tripping him up, his upstairs room and its horrible yellow wallpaper, the creaking bureau with the greasy plush collarbox, and over his painted wooden bed the pictures of George Washington and John Calvin, and the framed motto, "Feed my Lambs," which had been worked in red worsted by his mother.

Half an hour later Paul alighted from his car and went slowly down one of the side streets off the main thoroughfare. It was a highly respectable street, where all the houses were exactly alike, and where businessmen of moderate means begot and reared large families of children, all of whom went to Sabbath school and learned the shorter catechism, and were interested in arithmetic; all of whom were as exactly alike as their homes, and of a piece with the monotony in which they lived. Paul never went up Cordelia Street without a shudder of loathing. His home was next to the house of the Cumberland minister. He approached it tonight with the nerveless sense of defeat, the hopeless feeling of sinking back forever into ugliness and commonness that he had always had when he came home. The moment he turned into Cordelia Street he felt the waters close above his head. After each of these orgies of living he experienced all the physical depression which follows a debauch; the loathing of respectable beds, of common food, of a house penetrated by kitchen odors; a shuddering repulsion for the flavorless, colorless mass of everyday existence; a morbid desire for cool things and soft lights and fresh flowers.

The nearer he approached the house, the more absolutely unequal Paul felt to the sight of it all: his ugly sleeping chamber; the cold bathroom with the grimy zinc tub, the cracked mirror, the dripping spiggots; his father, at the top of the stairs, his hairy legs sticking out from his nightshirt, his feet thrust into carpet slippers. He was so much later than usual that there would certainly be inquiries and reproaches; Paul stopped short before the door. He felt that he could not be accosted by his father tonight; that he could not toss again on that miserable bed. He would not go in. He would tell his father that he had no carfare and it was raining so hard he had gone home with one of the boys and stayed all night.

Meanwhile, he was wet and cold. He went around to the back of the house and tried one of the basement windows, found it open, raised it cautiously, and scrambled down the cellar wall to the floor. There he stood, holding his breath, terrified by the noise he had made, but the floor above him was silent, and there was no creak on the stairs. He found a soapbox, and carried it over to the soft ring of light that streamed from the furnace door, and sat down. He was horribly afraid of rats, so he did not try to sleep, but sat looking distrustfully at the dark, still terrified lest he might have awakened his father. In such reactions, after one of the experiences which made days and nights out of the dreary blanks of the calendar, when his senses were deadened, Paul's head was always singularly clear. Suppose his father had heard him getting in at the window and had come down and shot him for a burglar? Then, again, suppose his father had come down, pistol in hand, and he had cried out in time to save himself, and his father had been horrified to think how nearly he had killed him? Then, again, suppose a day should come when his father would remember that night, and wish there had been no warning cry to stay his hand? With this last supposition Paul entertained himself until daybreak.

The following Sunday was fine; the sodden November chill was broken by the last flash of autumnal summer. In the morning Paul had to go to church and Sabbath school, as always. On seasonable Sunday afternoons the burghers of Cordelia Street always sat out on their front stoops and talked to their neighbors on the next stoop, or called to those across the street in neighborly fashion. The men usually sat on gay cushions placed upon the steps that led down to the sidewalk, while the women, in their Sunday "waists," sat in rockers on the cramped porches, pretending to be greatly at their ease. The children played in the streets; there were so many of them that the place resembled the recreation grounds of a kindergarten. The men on the steps—all in their shirt sleeves, their vests unbuttoned—sat with their legs well apart, their stomachs comfortably protruding, and talked of the prices of things, or told anecdotes of the sagacity of their various chiefs and overlords. They occasionally looked over the multitude of squabbling children, listened affectionately to their high pitched, nasal voices, smiling to see their own proclivities reproduced in their offspring, and interspersed their legends of the iron kings with remarks about their sons' progress at school, their grades in arithmetic, and the amounts they had saved in their toy banks.

On this last Sunday of November Paul sat all the afternoon on the lowest step of his stoop, staring into the street, while his sisters, in their rockers, were talking to the minister's daughters next door about how many shirtwaists they had made in the last week, and how many waffles someone had

eaten at the last church supper. When the weather was warm, and his father was in a particularly jovial frame of mind, the girls made lemonade,
which was always brought out in a red-glass pitcher, ornamented with
forget-me-nots in blue enamel. This the girls thought very fine, and the
neighbors always joked about the suspicious colour of the pitcher.

Today Paul's father sat on the top step, talking to a young man who
shifted a restless baby from knee to knee. He happened to be the young
man who was daily held up to Paul as a model, and after whom it was his father's dearest hope that he would pattern. This young man was of a ruddy
complexion, with a compressed, red mouth, and faded nearsighted eyes,
over which he wore thick spectacles, with gold bows that curved about his
ears. He was clerk to one of the magnates of a great steel corporation, and
was looked upon in Cordelia Street as a young man with a future. There was
a story that, some five years ago—he was now barely twenty-six—he had
been a trifle dissipated, but in order to curb his appetites and save the loss
of time and strength that a sowing of wild oats might have entailed, he had
taken his chief's advice, oft reiterated to his employees, and at twenty-one
had married the first woman whom he could persuade to share his fortunes. She happened to be an angular schoolmistress, much older than he,
who also wore thick glasses, and who had now borne him four children, all
nearsighted, like herself.

The young man was relating how his chief, now cruising in the Mediterranean, kept in touch with all the details of the business, arranging his office
hours on his yacht just as though he were at home, and "knocking off work
enough to keep two stenographers busy." His father told, in turn, the plan
his corporation was considering, of putting in an electric railway plant at
Cairo. Paul snapped his teeth; he had an awful apprehension that they
might spoil it all before he got there. Yet he rather liked to hear these
legends of the iron kings that were told and retold on Sundays and holidays;
these stories of palaces in Venice, yachts on the Mediterranean, and high
play at Monte Carlo appealed to his fancy, and he was interested in the
triumphs of these cash boys who had become famous, though he had no
mind for the cash-boy stage.

After supper was over and he had helped to dry the dishes, Paul nervously asked his father whether he could go to George's to get some help in
his geometry, and still more nervously asked for carfare. This latter request
he had to repeat, as his father, on principle, did not like to hear requests for

money, whether much or little. He asked Paul whether he could not go to some boy who lived nearer, and told him that he ought not leave his school-work until Sunday; but he gave him the dime. He was not a poor man, but he had a worthy ambition to come up in the world. His only reason for allowing Paul to usher was that he thought a boy ought to be earning a little.

Paul bounded upstairs, scrubbed the greasy odor of the dishwater from his hands with the ill-smelling soap he hated, and then shook over his fingers a few drops of violet water from the bottle he kept hidden in his drawer. He left the house with his geometry conspicuously under his arm, and the moment he got out of Cordelia Street and boarded a downtown car, he shook off the lethargy of two deadening days and began to live again.

The leading juvenile of the permanent stock company which played at one of the downtown theaters was an acquaintance of Paul's, and the boy had been invited to drop in at the Sunday-night rehearsals whenever he could. For more than a year Paul had spent every available moment loitering about Charley Edwards's dressing room. He had won a place among Edwards's following not only because the young actor, who could not afford to employ a dresser, often found him useful, but because he recognized in Paul something akin to what churchmen term "vocation."

It was at the theater and at Carnegie Hall that Paul really lived; the rest was but a sleep and a forgetting. This was Paul's fairy tale, and it had for him all the allurement of a secret love. The moment he inhaled the gassy, painty, dusty odor behind the scenes, he breathed like a prisoner set free, and felt within him the possibility of doing or saying splendid, brilliant, poetic things. The moment the cracked orchestra beat out the overture from *Martha*, or jerked at the serenade from *Rigoletto*, all stupid and ugly things slid from him, and his senses were deliciously, yet delicately fired.

Perhaps it was because, in Paul's world, the natural nearly always wore the guise of ugliness, that a certain element of artificiality seemed to him necessary in beauty. Perhaps it was because his experience of life elsewhere was so full of Sabbath-school picnics, petty economies, wholesome advice as to how to succeed in life, and the inescapable odors of cooking, that he found this existence so alluring, these smartly clad men and women so attractive, that he was so moved by these starry apple orchards that bloomed perennially under the limelight.

It would be difficult to put it strongly enough how convincingly the stage entrance of that theater was for Paul the actual portal of Romance. Certainly none of the company ever suspected it, least of all Charley Edwards. It was very like the old stories that used to float about London of fabulously rich Jews, who had subterranean halls there, with palms, and fountains, and soft lamps and richly appareled women who never saw the disenchanting light of London day. So, in the midst of that smoke-palled city, enamored of figures and grimy toil, Paul had his secret temple, his wishing carpet, his bit of blue-and-white Mediterranean shore bathed in perpetual sunshine.

Several of Paul's teachers had a theory that his imagination had been perverted by garish fiction, but the truth was that he scarcely ever read at all. The books at home were not such as would either tempt or corrupt a youthful mind, and as for reading the novels that some of his friends urged upon him—well, he got what he wanted much more quickly from music; any sort of music, from an orchestra to a barrel organ. He needed only the spark, the indescribable thrill that made his imagination master of his senses, and he could make plots and pictures enough of his own. It was equally true that he was not stage-struck—not, at any rate, in the usual acceptation of that expression. He had no desire to become an actor, any more than he had to become a musician. He felt no necessity to do any of these things; what he wanted was to see, to be in the atmosphere, float on the wave of it, to be carried out, blue league after blue league, away from everything.

After a night behind the scenes Paul found the schoolroom more than ever repulsive; the bare floors and naked walls; the prosy men who never wore frock coats, or violets in their buttonholes; the women with their dull gowns, shrill voices, and pitiful seriousness about prepositions that govern the dative. He could not bear to have the other pupils think, for a moment, that he took these people seriously; he must convey to them that he considered it all trivial, and was there only by way of a jest, anyway. He had autographed pictures of all the members of the stock company which he showed his classmates, telling them the most incredible stories of his familiarity with these people, of his acquaintance with the soloists who came to Carnegie Hall, his suppers with them and the flowers he sent them. When these stories lost their effect, and his audience grew listless, he became desperate and would bid all the boys good-by, announcing that he was going to travel for a while; going to Naples, to Venice, to Egypt. Then, next Monday, he would slip back, conscious and nervously smiling; his sister was ill, and he should have to defer his voyage until spring.

Matters went steadily worse with Paul at school. In the itch to let his instructors know how heartily he despised them and their homilies, and how thoroughly he was appreciated elsewhere, he mentioned once or twice that he had no time to fool with theorems; adding—with a twitch of the eyebrows and a touch of that nervous bravado which so perplexed them—that he was helping the people down at the stock company; they were old friends of his.

The upshot of the matter was that the Principal went to Paul's father, and Paul was taken out of school and put to work. The manager at Carnegie Hall was told to get another usher in his stead; the doorkeeper at the theater was warned not to admit him to the house; and Charley Edwards remorsefully promised the boy's father not to see him again.

The members of the stock company were vastly amused when some of Paul's stories reached them—especially the women. They were hard-working women, most of them supporting indigent husbands or brothers, and they laughed rather bitterly at having stirred the boy to such fervid and florid inventions. They agreed with the faculty and with his father that Paul's was a bad case.

The eastbound train was plowing through a January snowstorm; the dull dawn was beginning to show gray when the engine whistled a mile out of Newark. Paul started up from the seat where he had lain curled in uneasy slumber, rubbed the breath-misted window glass with his hand, and peered out. The snow was whirling in curling eddies above the white bottom lands, and the drifts lay already deep in the fields and along the fences, while here and there the long dead grass and dried weed stalks protruded black above it. Lights shone from the scattered houses, and a gang of laborers who stood beside the track waved their lanterns.

Paul had slept very little, and he felt grimy and uncomfortable. He had made the all-night journey in a day coach, partly because he was ashamed, dressed as he was, to go into a Pullman, and partly because he was afraid of being seen there by some Pittsburgh businessman, who might have noticed him in Denny & Carson's office. When the whistle awoke him, he clutched quickly at his breast pocket, glancing about him with an uncertain smile. But the little, clay-bespattered Italians were still sleeping, the slatternly women across the aisle were in open-mouthed oblivion, and even the crumby, crying babies were for the nonce stilled. Paul settled back to struggle with his impatience as best he could.

When he arrived at the Jersey City station he hurried through his breakfast, manifestly ill at ease and keeping a sharp eye about him. After he reached the Twenty-third Street station, he consulted a cabman and had himself driven to a men's furnishings establishment that was just opening for the day. He spent upward of two hours there, buying with endless reconsidering and great care. His new street suit he put on in the fitting room; the frock coat and dress clothes he had bundled into the cab with his linen. Then he drove to a hatter's and a shoe house. His next errand was at Tiffany's, where he selected his silver and a new scarf pin. He would not wait to have his silver marked, he said. Lastly, he stopped at a trunk shop on Broadway and had his purchases packed into various traveling bags.

It was a little after one o'clock when he drove up to the Waldorf, and after settling with the cabman, went into the office. He registered from Washington; said his mother and father had been abroad, and that he had come down to await the arrival of their steamer. He told his story plausibly and had no trouble, since he volunteered to pay for them in advance, in engaging his rooms; a sleeping room, sitting room, and bath.

Not once, but a hundred times, Paul had planned this entry into New York. He had gone over every detail of it with Charley Edwards, and in his scrapbook at home there were pages of description about New York hotels, cut from the Sunday papers. When he was shown to his sitting room on the eighth floor he saw at a glance that everything was as it should be; there was but one detail in his mental picture that the place did not realize, so he rang for the bellboy and sent him down for flowers. He moved about nervously until the boy returned, putting away his new linen and fingering it delightedly as he did so. When the flowers came he put them hastily into water, and then tumbled into a hot bath. Presently he came out of his white bathroom, resplendent in his new silk underwear, and playing with the tassels of his red robe. The snow was whirling so fiercely outside his windows that he could scarcely see across the street, but within the air was deliciously soft and fragrant. He put the violets and jonquils on the taboret beside the couch, and threw himself down, with a long sigh, covering himself with a Roman blanket. He was thoroughly tired; he had been in such haste, he had stood up to such a strain, covered so much ground in the last twenty-four hours, that he wanted to think how it had all come about.

Lulled by the sound of the wind, the warm air, and the cool fragrance of the flowers, he sank into deep, drowsy retrospection.

It had been wonderfully simple; when they had shut him out of the theater and concert hall, when they had taken away his bone, the whole thing was virtually determined. The rest was a mere matter of opportunity. The only thing that at all surprised him was his own courage—for he realized well enough that he had always been tormented by fear, a sort of apprehensive dread that, of late years, as the meshes of the lies he had told closed about him, had been pulling the muscles of his body tighter and tighter. Until now he could not remember the time when he had not been dreading something. Even when he was a little boy it was always there—behind him, or before, or on either side. There had always been the shadowed corner, the dark place into which he dared not look but from which something seemed always to be watching him—and Paul had done things that were not pretty to watch, he knew.

But now he had a curious sense of relief, as though he had at last thrown down the gauntlet to the thing in the corner.

Yet it was but a day since he had been sulking in the traces; but yesterday afternoon that he had been sent to the bank with Denny & Carson's deposit, as usual—but this time he was instructed to leave the book to be balanced. There was above two thousand dollars in checks, and nearly a thousand in the bank notes which he had taken from the book and quietly transferred to his pocket. At the bank he had made out a new deposit slip. His nerves had been steady enough to permit of his returning to the office, where he had finished his work and asked for a full day's holiday tomorrow, Saturday, giving a perfectly reasonable pretext. The bankbook, he knew, would not be returned before Monday or Tuesday, and his father would be out of town for the next week. From the time he slipped the bank notes into his pocket until he boarded the night train for New York, he had not known a moment's hesitation. It was not the first time Paul had steered through treacherous waters.

How astonishingly easy it had all been; here he was, the thing done; and this time there would be no awakening, no figure at the top of the stairs. He watched the snowflakes whirling by his window until he fell asleep.

When he awoke, it was three o'clock in the afternoon. He bounded up with a start; half of one of his precious days gone already! He spent more than an hour in dressing, watching every stage of his toilet carefully in the

129

mirror. Everything was quite perfect; he was exactly the kind of boy he had always wanted to be.

When he went downstairs Paul took a carriage and drove up Fifth Avenue toward the Park. The snow had somewhat abated; carriages and tradesmen's wagons were hurrying soundlessly to and fro in the winter twilight; boys in woolen mufflers were shoveling off the doorsteps; the avenue stages made fine spots of color against the white street. Here and there on the corners were stands, with whole flower gardens blooming under glass cases, against the sides of which the snowflakes stuck and melted; violets, roses, carnations, lilies of the valley—somehow vastly more lovely and alluring that they blossomed thus unnaturally in the snow. The Park itself was a wonderful stage winter-piece.

When he returned, the pause of the twilight had ceased and the tune of the streets had changed. The snow was falling faster, lights streamed from the hotels that reared their dozen stories fearlessly up into the storm, defying the raging Atlantic winds. A long, black stream of carriages poured down the avenue, intersected here and there by other streams, tending horizontally. There were a score of cabs about the entrance of his hotel, and his driver had to wait. Boys in livery were running in and out of the awning stretched across the sidewalk, up and down the red velvet carpet laid from the door to the street. Above, about, within it all was the rumble and roar, the hurry and toss of thousands of human beings as hot for pleasure as himself, and on every side of him towered the glaring affirmation of the omnipotence of wealth.

The boy set his teeth and drew his shoulders together in a spasm of realization; the plot of all dramas, the text of all romances, the nerve-stuff of all sensations was whirling about him like the snowflakes. He burnt like a faggot in a tempest.

When Paul went down to dinner the music of the orchestra came floating up the elevator shaft to greet him. His head whirled as he stepped into the thronged corridor, and he sank back into one of the chairs against the wall to get his breath. The lights, the chatter, the perfumes, the bewildering medley of color—he had, for a moment, the feeling of not being able to stand it. But only for a moment; these were his own people, he told himself. He went slowly about the corridors, through the writing rooms, smoking rooms, reception rooms, as though he were exploring the chambers of an enchanted palace, built and peopled for him alone.

130

When he reached the dining room he sat down at a table near a window. The flowers, the white linen, the many-colored wineglasses, the gay toilettes of the women, the low popping of corks, the undulating repetitions of the *Blue Danube* from the orchestra, all flooded Paul's dream with bewildering radiance. When the roseate tinge of his champagne was added—that cold, precious, bubbling stuff that creamed and foamed in his glass—Paul wondered that there were honest men in the world at all. This was what all the world was fighting for, he reflected; this was what all the struggle was about. He doubted the reality of his past. Had he ever known a place called Cordelia Street, a place where fagged-looking businessmen got on the early car; mere rivets in a machine they seemed to Paul,—sickening men, with combings of children's hair always hanging to their coats, and the smell of cooking in their clothes. Cordelia Street—Ah, that belonged to another time and country; had he not always been thus, had he not sat here night after night, from as far back as he could remember, looking pensively over just such shimmering textures and slowly twirling the stem of a glass like this one between his thumb and middle finger? He rather thought he had.

He was not in the least abashed or lonely. He had no especial desire to meet or to know any of these people; all he demanded was the right to look on and conjecture, to watch the pageant. The mere stage properties were all he contended for. Nor was he lonely later in the evening, in his lodge at the Metropolitan. He was now entirely rid of his nervous misgivings, of his forced aggressiveness, of the imperative desire to show himself different from his surroundings. He felt now that his surroundings explained him. Nobody questioned the purple; he had only to wear it passively. He had only to glance down at his attire to reassure himself that here it would be impossible for anyone to humiliate him.

He found it hard to leave his beautiful sitting-room to go to bed that night, and sat long watching the raging storm from his turret window. When he went to sleep it was with the lights turned on in his bedroom; partly because of his old timidity, and partly so that, if he should wake in the night, there would be no wretched moment of doubt, no horrible suspicion of yellow wallpaper, or of Washington and Calvin above his bed.

Sunday morning the city was practically snowbound. Paul breakfasted late, and in the afternoon he fell in with a wild San Francisco boy, a freshman at Yale, who said he had run down for a "little flyer" over Sunday. The young man offered to show Paul the night side of the town, and the two boys went out together after dinner, not returning to the hotel until seven o'clock the next morning. They had started out in the confiding warmth of a champagne friendship, but their parting in the elevator was singularly cool. The freshman pulled himself together to make his train, and Paul went to bed. He awoke at two o'clock in the afternoon, very thirsty and dizzy, and rang for ice-water, coffee, and the Pittsburgh papers.

On the part of the hotel management, Paul excited no suspicion. There was this to be said for him, that he wore his spoils with dignity and in no way made himself conspicuous. Even under the glow of his wine he was never boisterous, though he found the stuff like a magician's wand for wonder-building. His chief greediness lay in his ears and eyes, and his excesses were not offensive ones. His dearest pleasures were the gray winter twilights in his sitting room; his quiet enjoyment of his flowers, his clothes, his wide divan, his cigarette, and his sense of power. He could not remember a time when he had felt so at peace with himself. The mere release from the necessity of petty lying, lying every day and every day, restored his self-respect. He had never lied for pleasure, even at school; but to be noticed and admired, to assert his difference from other Cordelia Street boys; and he felt a good deal more manly, more honest, even, now that he had no need for boastful pretensions, now that he could, as his actor friends used to say, "dress the part." It was characteristic that remorse did not occur to him. His golden days went by without a shadow, and he made each as perfect as he could.

On the eighth day after his arrival in New York he found the whole affair exploited in the Pittsburgh papers, exploited with a wealth of detail which indicated that local news of a sensational nature was at a low ebb. The firm of Denny & Carson announced that the boy's father had refunded the full amount of the theft and that they had no intention of prosecuting. The Cumberland minister had been interviewed, and expressed his hope of yet reclaiming the motherless lad, and his Sabbath-school teacher declared that she would spare no effort to that end. The rumor had reached Pittsburgh that the boy had been seen in a New York hotel, and his father had gone East to find him and bring him home.

Paul had just come in to dress for dinner; he sank into a chair, weak to the knees, and clasped his head in his hands. It was to be worse than jail, even; the tepid waters of Cordelia Street were to close over him finally and forever. The gray monotony stretched before him in hopeless unrelieved years; Sabbath school, Young People's Meeting, the yellow-papered room, the damp dishtowels; it all rushed back upon him with a sickening vividness. He had the old feeling that the orchestra had suddenly stopped; the sinking sensation that the play was over. The sweat broke out on his face, and he sprang to his feet, looked about him with his white, conscious smile, and winked at himself in the mirror. With something of the old childish belief in miracles with which he had so often gone to class, all his lessons unlearned, Paul dressed and dashed whistling down the corridor to the elevator.

He had no sooner entered the dining room and caught the measure of the music than his remembrance was lightened by his old elastic power of claiming the moment, mounting with it, and finding it all sufficient. The glare and glitter about him, the mere scenic accessories had again, and for the last time, their old potency. He would show himself that he was game, he would finish the thing splendidly. He doubted, more than ever, the existence of Cordelia Street, and for the first time he drank his wine recklessly. Was he not, after all, one of those fortunate beings born to the purple, was he not still himself and in his own place? He drummed a nervous accompaniment to the Pagliacci music and looked about him, telling himself over and over that it had paid.

He reflected drowsily, to the swell of the music and the chill sweetness of his wine, that he might have done it more wisely. He might have caught an outbound steamer and been well out of their clutches before now. But the other side of the world had seemed too far away and too uncertain then; he could not have waited for it; his need had been too sharp. If he had to choose over again, he would do the same thing tomorrow. He looked affectionately about the dining room, now gilded with a soft mist. Ah, it had paid indeed!

Paul was awakened next morning by a painful throbbing in his head and feet. He had thrown himself across the bed without undressing, and had slept with his shoes on. His limbs and hands were lead heavy, and his tongue and throat were parched and burnt. There came upon him one of those fateful attacks of clearheadedness that never occurred except when he was physically exhausted and his nerves hung loose. He lay still, closed his eyes, and let the tide of things wash over him.

His father was in New York; "stopping at some joint or other," he told himself. The memory of successive summers on the front stoop fell upon him like a weight of black water. He had not a hundred dollars left; and he knew now, more than ever, that money was everything, the wall that stood between all he loathed and all he wanted. The thing was winding itself up; he had thought of that on his first glorious day in New York, and had even provided a way to snap the thread. It lay on his dressing table now: he had got it out last night when he came blindly up from dinner, but the shiny metal hurt his eyes, and he disliked the looks of it.

He rose and moved about with a painful effort, succumbing now and again to attacks of nausea. It was the old depression exaggerated; all the world had become Cordelia street. Yet somehow he was not afraid of anything, was absolutely calm; perhaps because he had looked into the dark corner at last and knew. It was bad enough, what he saw there, but somehow not so bad as his long fear of it had been. He saw everything clearly now. He had a feeling that he had made the best of it, that he had lived the sort of life he was meant to live, and for half an hour he sat staring at the revolver. But he told himself that was not the way, so he went downstairs and took a cab to the ferry.

When Paul arrived at Newark he got off the train and took another cab, directing the driver to follow the Pennsylvania tracks out of the town. The snow lay heavy on the roadways and had drifted deep in the open fields. Only here and there the dead grass or dried weed stalks projected, singularly black, above it. Once well into the country, Paul dismissed the carriage and walked, floundering along the tracks, his mind a medley of irrelevant things. He seemed to hold in his brain an actual picture of everything he had seen that morning. He remembered every feature of both his drivers, of the toothless old woman from whom he had bought the red flowers in his coat, the agent from whom he had got his ticket, and all of his fellow passengers on the ferry. His mind, unable to cope with vital matters near at hand, worked feverishly and deftly at sorting and grouping these images. They made for him a part of the ugliness of the world, of the ache in his head, and the bitter burning on his tongue. He stooped and put a handful of snow into his mouth as he walked, but that, too, seemed hot. When he reached a little hillside, where the track ran through a cut some twenty feet below him, he stopped and sat down.

The carnations in his coat were drooping with the cold, he noticed, their red glory all over. It occurred to him that all the flowers he had seen in the glass cases that first night must have gone the same way, long before this. It

134

was only one splendid breath they had, in spite of their brave mockery at the winter outside the glass; and it was a losing game in the end, it seemed, this revolt against the homilies by which the world is run. Paul took one of the blossoms carefully from his coat and scooped a little hole in the snow, where he covered it up. Then he dozed a while, from his weak condition, seemingly insensible to the cold.

The sound of an approaching train awoke him, and he started to his feet, remembering only his resolution, and afraid lest he should be too late. He stood watching the approaching locomotive, his teeth chattering, his lips drawn away from them in a frightened smile; once or twice he glanced nervously sidewise, as though he were being watched. When the right moment came, he jumped. As he fell, the folly of his haste occurred to him with merciless clearness, the vastness of what he had left undone. There flashed through his brain, clearer than ever before, the blue of Adriatic water, the yellow of Algerian sands.

He felt something strike his chest, and that his body was being thrown swiftly through the air, on and on, immeasurably far and fast, while his limbs were gently relaxed. Then, because the picture-making mechanism was crushed, the disturbing visions flashed into black, and Paul dropped back into the immense design of things.

Back Bay Conservatory

MARK HELPRIN

Boston is a city of libraries and darkness, winter darkness, when lights shine through a cold mist or the clear air. If the wind has come from New Hampshire it is possible to see every star from every street and in the day the blue of the sky is absolute. But if the wind is off the sea the entire city is dark and close, the sparkling crystals not faraway stars but luminous white ice and snow. You can see the snow fall even in the dark, and though there is complete silence each descending particle has its own sound. Libraries shelter students and give the impression that strong fires burn in adjoining rooms. Of course there are no fires but the impression remains as one takes off coat and scarf. At night the windows of reading rooms are black and astonishingly cold.

Victoria had not been named after the Queen but rather her mother's sister who was not, as Victoria said, drowned on the *Lusitania* but killed as a child in a great fire which took most of the town and left the rest in despair. It happened one January night in Vermont before the First World War, and the father of the first Victoria had gone over the border into Canada to find laborers to build him a new house. It made no difference; she had been his hope, the little girl who when burned to death had been clothed in flannel the color of flame.

Victoria played the piano and was taught by a man named Andreyev. He kept his studio in a building devoted to music on Massachusetts Avenue near Symphony Hall, near enough anyway so that when Victoria caught a glimpse of it on her way to the lesson she thought how she always thought of playing to a mythical audience of professors and music critics. There were thousands of music critics. They came from every publication ever published, even Turkish technical journals and African joke magazines. And there were friends, all the friends she had ever known, especially the ones who had slighted her, the ones who had somehow gained on her in competition at remote and remembered times, and the front row was reserved for those she had loved who were no longer in her life.

Leaning over the piano, Andreyev looked out his window and saw a golden dome on a hill of brick houses, and a white dome on buildings grayer than Westminster. He knew that Victoria often took a long tour around the hill before her lesson. A magnificent pianist, she was his best pupil. She did not always practice as much as she might have, and was not as disciplined as many others, but she had so much love for what she played that she could not help but play it well. She knew she was good and her career in the literal sense was fast and musical, forward without hesitation; she enjoyed even the strain.

They always talked while her hands warmed. Sometimes when it was very cold it took fifteen or twenty minutes for the frost to pass so that she was dexterous. He wanted to warm her hands in his hands. He might have done it. She wanted him to, but instead they talked about his silver medals. They were won in his twenties and they impressed her greatly. He thought she knew she was going to win gold medals, but she knew neither that nor that at thirty-five he believed himself to be not good any more as a pianist, only passable as a teacher, and too old for girls of their early twenties—girls like Victoria, whose diversionary walks around Beacon Hill were so that her face might be red and the cold would cling to her coat and refresh the room.

Ascending the staircase she progressed faster and faster, gliding up like a rising angel to the sound of strings from the many rooms all about her. She felt like heat itself rising and when she entered to find serious Andreyev there came to her a sudden reddening which reminded him of all the Provençal and early Italian poetry he had been forced to read, which in Victoria suddenly seemed quite real.

She walked to the window and looked at the vanishing light, at the gold-rimmed snow on buildings, at the flat white basin of the Charles River—not a river because it does not flow—and her heart danced. The sun glinted off her glasses, and her black hair came near the thick white edge of the lens. She had bad eyes but they were large and brown. Her hair was as black as if she had been Chinese, and her face was long and fine. She knew that when she left her lesson it would be dark and she would ride the green-sided trolley back to Cambridge.

After his five o'clock lesson with Victoria, Andreyev usually walked to his small house in Brookline, a house with white rooms and two pianos, a house where there were never any women. In summer when Boston was hot, and Victoria went back to Vermont to swim in the Baker River's rapids, when he was most lonely, when the city seemed quiet and green as if a dream of the Middle East, in summer he thought of departed students and played better than winter ever heard because there was no one to listen.

Andreyev found that his convictions backed him into corners. At first it had been welcome, since he was sure he would eventually triumph. He was all right until his confidence began to erode, after many meetings with other great pianists who in truth were failures. He was at a time in his life when he could not accept failure and yet did not have success. Enough strength remained in him to keep away the comfort of being only a man, blessed with a trade but completely mortal. He was still bent upon being a great pianist—but so feebly and passively that it became just a thought to have on the trolley as he sped across a landscape of gray rain and wet trees. The less he thought of breaking into public life like a long overdue baby bird cracking its shell, the more he delighted in things he had not noticed in years and years since the beginnings of his ambition, and the less he wanted to be alone. He began to be proud of his fierce black eyes, his height, and his Russianness—things which for so many years he had considered only for their effect on concert audiences. He bought himself a suit and new glasses, for the old ones were heavy and contradicted his face. He found that when he abandoned his ambition he regained strength enough to become again ambitious. Meanwhile Boston passed him on all sides and above, and he lamented that his students were like clouds going to sea as he remained rooted firmly on the barest place of land. There had been a time when he might have given up his dreams, but he had kept them and it soon was too late ever to release them. He felt the twenty years. He was already old enough to dream of abandoning his dreams. He imagined that his girl students were loved by his boy students and that they danced together. Victoria was the kindest of them all, and unfortunately the most beautiful.

With the sun making her gold glasses shine she turned to him and smiled. Her hands were warm, she said, they could begin. She was to play a piece he had adapted from guitar music by Gianocelli. The timing was difficult but he had arranged it well and she had practiced for many hours the day it snowed. She played while he counted time, coming down doubly hard on the stresses he had indicated in red pencil. They went through it three times. Then she played at smooth pace without him. There were mis-

Boston

takes and she once hesitated. She became as red as when she had come in from the cold. Again, he said. She played with no mistakes.

While doing it once more, simply because she liked it, she told him at intervals in the long rests that . . . she was going to stay . . . in Boston for the summer . . . she was glad . . . and she planned mainly to practice. She wondered if he too were going to be in Boston and if he would have time to continue the lessons.

He walked to the brown marble mantel where his medals were framed on black felt, silver medals all. She was playing with great speed and energy.

"I am going to be in Boston this summer," he said, turning down the frames one by one, "and although I myself must practice I will have time for you. As you know, or perhaps you don't, I haven't performed in eight or nine years. If the summer goes well I plan to give a concert in the fall."

She stopped playing and turned to look at him. "Keep playing," he said, and she returned to play faster and almost as if in anger. "I know it's difficult to play when someone is talking, but people always talk. Gianocelli is especially beautiful. No one knows him and he wrote little but I think he is among the best." There was a silence. "Most of my students are absent in the summer." He looked at her, at her black dress and gold chain necklace. "If you want you can practice here. The windows are open in the summer and the light is better."

She stopped playing and looked out at the blackness of the night which had descended. She was confused, and although she saw like silver on jeweler's felt a thousand white lights of cars moving on the long bridge from Cambridge, she was frightened and could only say, as if she were older than he, Andreyev, Andreyev, Andreyev. But she did not feel older. She couldn't have.

Ballad of the Landlord

LANGSTON HUGHES

Landlord, landlord,
My roof has sprung a leak.
Don't you 'member I told you about it
Way last week?

Landlord, landlord,
These steps is broken down.
When you come up yourself
It's a wonder you don't fall down.

Ten Bucks you say I owe you?
Ten Bucks you say is due?
Well, that's Ten Bucks more'n I'll pay you
Till you fix this house up new.

What? You gonna get eviction orders?
You gonna cut off my heat?
You gonna take my furniture and
Throw it in the street?

Um-huh! You talking high and mighty.
Talk on—till you get through.
You ain't gonna be able to say a word
If I land my fist on you.

City People

Police! Police!
Come and get this man!
He's trying to ruin the government
And overturn the land!

Copper's whistle!
Patrol bell!
Arrest.

Precinct Station.
Iron cell.
Headlines in press:

MAN THREATENS LANDLORD

TENANT HELD NO BAIL

JUDGE GIVES NEGRO 90 DAYS IN COUNTY JAIL

Only the Dead Know Brooklyn

THOMAS WOLFE

Dere's no guy livin' dat knows Brooklyn t'roo an' t'roo, because it'd take a guy a lifetime just to find his way aroun' duh f——town.

So like I say, I'm waitin' for my train t' come when I sees dis big guy standin' deh—dis is duh foist I eveh see of him. Well, he's lookin' wild, y'know, an' I can see dat he's had plenty, but still he's holdin' it; he talks good an' is walkin' straight enough. So den, dis big guy steps up to a little guy dat's standin' deh, an' says, "How d'yuh get t' Eighteent' Avenoo an' Sixty-sevent' Street?" he says.

"Jesus! Yuh got me, chief," duh little guy says to him. "I ain't been heah long myself. Where is duh place?" he says. "Out in duh Flatbush section somewhere?"

"Nah," duh big guy says. "It's out in Bensonhoist. But I was neveh deh befoeh. How d'yuh get deh?"

"Jesus," duh little guy says, scratchin' his head, y'know—yuh could see duh little guy didn't know his way about—"yuh got me, chief. I neveh hoid of it. Do any of youse guys know where it is?" he says to me.

"Sure," I says. "It's out in Bensonhoist. Yuh take duh Fourt' Avenoo express, get off at Fifty-nint' Street, change to a Sea Beach local deh, get off at Eighteent' Avenoo an' Sixty-toid, an' den walk down foeh blocks. Dat's all yuh got to do," I says.

"G'wan!" some wise guy dat I neveh seen befoeh pipes up. "Whatcha talkin' about?" he says—oh, he was wise, y'know. "Duh guy is crazy I tell yuh what yuh do," he says to duh big guy. "Yuh change to duh West End line at Toity-sixt'," he tells him. "Get off at Noo Utrecht an' Sixteent' Avenoo," he says. "Walk two blocks oveh, foeh blocks up," he says, "an' you'll be right deh." Oh, a *wise* guy, y'know.

"Oh, yeah?" I says. "Who told *you* so much?" He got me sore because he was so wise about it. "How long you been livin' heah?" I says.

143

"All my life," he says. "I was bawn in Williamsboig," he says. "An' I can tell you t'ings about dis town you neveh hoid of," he says.

"Yeah?" I says.

"Yeah," he says.

"Well, den, you can tell me t'ings about dis town dat nobody else has eveh hoid of either. Maybe you make it all up yoehself at night," I says, "befoeh you go to sleep—like cuttin' out papeh dolls, or somp'n."

"Oh, yeah?" he says. "You're pretty wise, ain't yuh?"

"Oh, I dont know," I says. "Duh boids ain't usin' my head for Lincoln's statue yet," I says. "But I'm wise enough to know a phony when I see one."

"Yeah?" he says. "A wise guy, huh? Well, you're so wise dat someone's goin' t'bust yuh one right on duh snoot some day," he says. "Dat's how wise *you* are."

Well, my train was comin', or I'da smacked him den and dere, but when I seen duh train was comin,' all I said was, "All right, mugg! I'm sorry I can't stay to take keh of you, but I'll be seein' yuh sometime, I hope, out in duh cemetery." So den I says to duh big guy, who'd been standin' deh all duh time, "You come wit me," I says. So when we gets onto duh train I says to him, "Where yuh goin' out in Bensonhoist?" I says. "What numbeh are yuh lookin' for?" I says. *You* know—I t'ought if he told me duh address I might be able to help him out.

'Oh," he says. "I'm not lookin' for no one. I don't know no one out deh."

"Then whatcha goin' out deh for?" I says.

"Oh," duh guy says, "I'm just goin' out to see duh place," he says. "I like duh sound of duh name—Bensonhoist, y'know—so I t'ought I'd go out an' have a look at it."

"Whatcha tryin t'hand me?" I says. "Whatcha tryin t'do—kid me?" *You* know, I t'ought duh guy was bein' wise wit me.

"No," he says, "I'm tellin' yuh duh troot. I like to go out an' take a look at places wit nice names like dat. I like to go out an' look at all kinds of places," he says.

"How'd yuh know deh was such a place," I says, "if yuh neveh been deh befoeh?"

"Oh," he says, "I got a map."

"A *map?*" I says.

"Sure," he says, "I got a map dat tells me about all dese places. I take it wit me every time I come out heah," he says.

And Jesus! Wit dat, he pulls it out of his pocket, an' so help me, but he's *got* it—he's tellin' duh troot—a big map of duh whole f——— place with all duh different pahts mahked out. You know—Canarsie an' East Noo Yawk an' Flatbush, Bensonhoist, Sout' Brooklyn, duh Heights, Bay Ride, Green-pernt—duh whole goddam layout, he's got it right deh on duh map.

"You been to any of dose places?" I says.

"Sure," he says, "I been to most of 'em. I was down in Red Hook just last night," he says.

"Jesus! Red Hook!" I says. "Whatcha do down deh?"

"Oh," he says, "nuttin' much. I just walked aroun'. I went into a coupla places an' had a drink," he says, "but most of the time I just walked aroun'."

"Just walked aroun'?" I says.

"Sure," he says, "just lookin' at t'ings, y'know."

"Where'd yuh go?" I asts him.

"Oh," he says, "I don't know duh name of duh place, but I could find it on my map," he says. "One time I was walkin' across some big fields where deh ain't no houses," he says, "but I could see ships oveh deh all lighted up. Dey was loadin'. So I walks across duh fields," he says, "to where duh ships are."

"Sure," I says, "I know where you was. You was down to duh Erie Basin."

"Yeah," he says, "I gues dat was it. Dey had some of dose big elevators an' cranes an' dey was loadin' ships, an' I could see some ships in drydock all lighted up, so I walks across duh fields to where dey are," he says.

"Den what did yuh do?" I says.

"Oh," he says, "nuttin' much. I came on back across duh fields after a while an' went into a coupla places an' had a drink."

"Didn't nuttin' happen while yuh was in dere?" I says.

"No," he says. "Nuttin' much. A couple guys was drunk in one of duh places an' started a fight, but dey bounced 'em out," he says, "an' den one of duh guys stahted to come back again, but duh bartender gets his baseball bat out from under duh counteh, so duh guy goes on."

"Jesus!" I said. "Red Hook!"

"Sure," he says. "Dat's where it was, all right."

"Well, you keep outa deh," I says. "You stay away from deh."

"Why?" he says. "What's wrong wit it?"

"Oh," I says, "It's a good place to stay away from, dat's all. It's a good place to keep out of."

"Why?" he says. "Why is it?"

Jesus! Whatcha gonna do wit a guy as dumb as dat? I saw it wasn't no use to try to tell him nuttin', he wouldn't know what I was talkin' about, so I just says to him, "Oh, nuttin'. Yuh might get lost down deh, dat's all."

"Lost?" he says. "No, I wouldn't get lost. I got a map," he says.

A map! Red Hook! Jesus.

So den duh guy begins to ast me all kinds of nutty questions: how big was Brooklyn an' could I find my way aroun' in it, an' how long would it take a guy to know duh place.

"Listen!" I says. "You get dat idea outa yoeh head right now," I says. "You ain't neveh gonna get to know Brooklyn," I says. "Not in a hundred yeahs. I been livin' heah all my life," I says, "an' I don't even know all deh is to know about it, so how do you expect to know duh town," I says, "when you don't even live heah?"

"Yes," he says, "but I got a map to help me find my way about."

"Map or no map," I says, "yuh ain't gonna get to know Brooklyn wit no map," I says.

"Can you swim?" he says, just like dat. Jesus! By dat time, y'know, I begun to see dat duh guy was some kind of nut. He'd had plenty to drink of course, but he had dat crazy look in his eye I didn't like. "Can you swim?" he says.

"Sure," I says. "Can't you?"

"No, he says. "Not more'n a stroke or two. I neveh loined good."

"Well, it's easy," I says. "All yuh need is a little confidence. Duh way I loined, me older bruddeh pitched me off duh dock one day when I was eight yeahs old, cloes an' all. 'You'll swim,' he says. "You'll swim all right— or drown.' An' believe me, I *swam!* When yuh know yuh got to, you'll do it. Duh only t'ing yuh need is confidence. An' once you've loined," I says, "you've got nuttin' else to worry about. You'll neveh forget it. It's somp'n dat stays wit yuh as long as yuh live."

"Can yuh swim good?" he says.

"Like a fish," I tells him. "I'm a regulah fish in duh wateh," I says. "I loined to swim right off duh docks wit all duh oddeh kids," I says.

"What would you do if yuh saw a man drownin'?" duh guy says.

"Do? Why, I'd jump in an' pull him out," I says. "Dat's what I'd do."

"Did yuh eveh see a man drown?" he says.

"Sure," I says. "I see two guys—bot' times at Coney Island. Dey got out

146

too far, an' neider one could swim. Dey drowned befoeh anyone could get to 'em."

"What becomes of people after dey've drowned out heah?" he says.

"Drowned out where?" I says.

"Out heah in Brooklyn."

"I don't know whatcha mean," I says. "Neveh hoid of no one drownin' heah in Brooklyn, unless you mean a swimmin' pool. Yuh can't drown in Brooklyn," I says. "Yuh gotta drown somewhere else—in duh ocean, where dere's wateh."

"Drownin'," duh guy says, lookin' at his map. "Drownin'." Jesus! I could see by den he was some kind of nut, he had dat crazy expression in his eyes when he looked at you, an' I didn't know what he might do. So we was comin' to a station, an' it wasn't my stop, but I got off anyway, an' waited for duh next train.

"Well, so long, chief," I says. "Take it easy, now."

"Drownin'," duh guy says, lookin' at his map. "Drownin'."

Jesus! I've t'ought about dat guy a t'ousand times since den an' wondered what eveh happened to 'm goin' out to look at Bensonhoist because he liked duh name! Walkin' aroun' t'roo Red Hook by himself at night an' lookin' at his map! How many people did I see get drowned out heah in Brooklyn! How long would it take a guy wit a good map to know all deh was to know about Brooklyn!

Jesus! What a nut *he* was! I wondeh what eveh happened to 'im, anyway! I wondeh if someone knocked him on duh head, or if he's still wanderin' aroun' in duh subway in duh middle of duh night wit his little map! Duh poor guy! Say, I've got to laugh, at dat, when I t'ink about him! Maybe he's found out by now dat he'll neveh live long enough to know duh whole of Brooklyn. It'd take a guy a lifetime to know Brooklyn t'roo an' t'roo. An' even den, yuh wouldn't know it all.

View of St. Louis, ca. 1939, Joe Jones

City Scenes

In 1948 E. B. White spent the summer in New York—living alone, wandering through the city streets, recording his impressions with the journalist's eye and the humorist's wit that have endeared him to so many readers. The result was his essay "Here Is New York," a delightful sketch which has since become a classic. James Baldwin's essay "Fifth Avenue, Uptown" is a brilliant and impassioned portrait of modern-day Harlem, in all its sadness, frustration, and decay. The Washington, D.C. which Arthur Hoppe satirizes in his essay is a scene of hyperbole and impermanence, of inflated symbols and curious anthropological rites—a purposeful city with an amusing self-awareness.

Poet William Carlos Williams writes of city winters; Melville Cane sketches a city park; Witter Bynner, Donald Hall, and John Updike give us their impressions of Pittsburgh, Detroit, Harlem, and San Francisco. Borden Deal's short story "Antaeus" points out the contrasts between country life and city life. In all of these selections it is the artist's expressive gift that takes hold of the ordinary, the commonplace, and transforms it into another kind of experience altogether.

Here Is New York

E. B. WHITE

On any person who desires such queer prizes, New York will bestow the gift of loneliness and the gift of privacy. It is this largess that accounts for the presence within the city's walls of a considerable section of the population; for the residents of Manhattan are to a large extent strangers who have pulled up stakes somewhere and come to town, seeking sanctuary or fulfillment or some greater or lesser grail. The capacity to make such dubious gifts is a mysterious quality of New York. It can destroy an individual, or it can fulfill him, depending a good deal on luck. No one should come to New York to live unless he is willing to be lucky.

New York is the concentrate of art and commerce and sport and religion and entertainment and finance, bringing to a single compact arena the gladiator, the evangelist, the promoter, the actor, the trader and the merchant. It carries on its lapel the unexpungeable odor of the long past, so that no matter where you sit in New York you feel the vibrations of great times and tall deeds, of queer people and events and undertakings. I am sitting at the moment in a stifling hotel room in 90-degree heat, halfway down an air shaft, in midtown. No air moves in or out of the room, yet I am curiously affected by emanations from the immediate surroundings. I am twenty-two blocks from where Rudolph Valentino lay in state, eight blocks from where Nathan Hale was executed, five blocks from the publisher's office where Ernest Hemingway hit Max Eastman on the nose, four miles from where Walt Whitman sat sweating out editorials for the Brooklyn Eagle, thirty-four blocks from the street Willa Cather lived in when she came to New York to write books about Nebraska, one block from where Marceline used to clown on the boards of the Hippodrome, thirty-six blocks from the spot where the historian Joe Gould kicked a radio to pieces in full view of the public, thirteen blocks from where Harry Thaw shot Stanford White, five blocks from where I used to usher at the Metropolitan Opera and only a hundred and twelve blocks from the spot where Clarence Day the Elder was washed of

World Trade Center, New York

his sins in the Church of the Epiphany (I could continue this list indefinitely); and for that matter I am probably occupying the very room that any
number of exalted and somewise memorable characters sat in, some of them
on hot, breathless afternoons, lonely and private and full of their own sense
of emanations from without. . . .

New York blends the gift of privacy with the excitement of participation;
and better than most dense communities it succeeds in insulating the individual (if he wants it, and almost everybody wants or needs it) against all
enormous and violent and wonderful events that are taking place every minute. Since I have been sitting in this miasmic air shaft, a good many rather
splashy events have occurred in town. A man shot and killed his wife in a fit
of jealousy. It caused no stir outside his block and got only small mention in
the papers. I did not attend. Since my arrival, the greatest air show ever
staged in all the world took place in town. I didn't attend and neither did
most of the eight million other inhabitants, although they say there was
quite a crowd. I didn't even hear any planes except a couple of westbound
commercial airliners that habitually use this air shaft to fly over. The biggest
ocean-going ships on the North Atlantic arrived and departed. I didn't notice them and neither did most other New Yorkers. I am told this is the
greatest seaport in the world, with six hundred and fifty miles of water
front, and ships calling here from many exotic lands, but the only boat I've
happened to notice since my arrival was a small sloop tacking out of the East
River night before last on the ebb tide when I was walking across the
Brooklyn Bridge. I heard the *Queen Mary* blow one midnight, though, and
the sound carried the whole history of departure and longing and loss. The
Lions have been in convention. I've seen not one Lion. A friend of mine
saw one and told me about him. (He was lame, and was wearing a bolero.)
At the ballgrounds and horse parks the greatest sporting spectacles have
been enacted. I saw no ballplayer, no race horse. The governor came to
town. I heard the siren scream, but that was all there was to that—an
eighteen-inch margin again. A man was killed by a falling cornice. I was not
a party to the tragedy, and again the inches counted heavily.

I mention these merely to show that New York is peculiarly constructed
to absorb almost anything that comes along (whether a thousand-foot liner
out of the East or a twenty-thousand-man convention out of the West)
without inflicting the event on its inhabitants; so that every event is, in a
sense, optional, and the inhabitant is in the happy position of being able to

choose his spectacle and so conserve his soul. In most metropolises, small and large, the choice is often not with the individual at all. He is thrown to the Lions. The Lions are overwhelming; the event is unavoidable. A cornice falls, and it hits every citizen on the head, every last man in town. I sometimes think that the only event that hits every New Yorker on the head is the annual St. Patrick's Day parade, which is fairly penetrating—the Irish are a hard race to tune out, there are 500,000 of them in residence, and they have the police force right in the family.

The quality in New York that insulates its inhabitants from life may simply weaken them as individuals. Perhaps it is healthier to live in a community where, when a cornice falls, you feel the blow; where, when the governor passes, you see at any rate his hat.

I am not defending New York in this regard. Many of its settlers are probably here merely to escape, not face, reality. But whatever it means, it is a rather rare gift, and I believe it has a positive effect on the creative capacities of New Yorkers—for creation is in part merely the business of forgoing the great and small distractions.

Although New York often imparts a feeling of great forlornness or forsakenness, it seldom seems dead or unresourceful; and you always feel that either by shifting your location ten blocks or by reducing your fortune by five dollars you can experience rejuvenation. Many people who have no real independence of spirit depend on the city's tremendous variety and sources of excitement for spiritual sustenance and maintenance of morale. In the country there are a few chances of sudden rejuvenation—a shift in weather, perhaps, or something arriving in the mail. But in New York the chances are endless. I think that although many persons are here from some excess of spirit (which caused them to break away from their small town), some, too, are here from a deficiency of spirit, who find in New York a protection, or an easy substitution. . . .

A poem compresses much in a small space and adds music, thus heightening its meaning. The city is like poetry: it compresses all life, all races and breeds, into a small island and adds music and the accompaniment of internal engines. The island of Manhattan is without any doubt the greatest human concentrate on earth, the poem whose magic is comprehensible to millions of permanent residents but whose full meaning will always remain illusive. At the feet of the tallest and plushiest offices lie the crummiest slums. The genteel mysteries housed in the Riverside Church are only a few

154

Skating in Central Park, 1894

blocks from the voodoo charms of Harlem. The merchant princes, riding to Wall Street in their limousines down the East River Drive, pass within a few hundred yards of the gypsy kings; but the princes do not know they are passing kings, and the kings are not up yet anyway—they live a more leisurely life than the princes and get drunk more consistently.

New York is nothing like Paris; it is nothing like London; and it is not Spokane multiplied by sixty, or Detroit multiplied by four. It is by all odds the loftiest of cities. It even managed to reach the highest point in the sky at the lowest moment of the depression. The Empire State Building shot twelve hundred and fifty feet into the air when it was madness to put out as much as six inches of new growth. (The building has a mooring mast that no dirigible has ever tied to; it employs a man to flush toilets in slack times; it has been hit by an airplane in a fog, struck countless times by lightning, and been jumped off of by so many unhappy people that pedestrians instinctively quicken step when passing Fifth Avenue and 34th Street.)

Manhattan has been compelled to expand skyward because of the absence of any other direction in which to grow. This, more than any other thing, is responsible for its physical majesty. It is to the nation what the white church spire is to the village—the visible symbol of aspiration and faith, the white plume saying that the way is up. The summer traveler swings in over Hell Gate Bridge and from the window of his sleeping car as it glides above the pigeon lofts and back yards of Queens looks southwest to where the morning light first strikes the steel peaks of midtown, and he sees its upward thrust unmistakable: the great walls and towers rising, the smoke rising, the heat not yet rising, the hopes and ferments of so many awakening millions rising—this vigorous spear that presses heaven hard.

It is a miracle that New York works at all. The whole thing is implausible. Every time the residents brush their teeth, millions of gallons of water must be drawn from the Catskills and the hills of Westchester. When a young man in Manhattan writes a letter to his girl in Brooklyn, the love message gets blown to her through a pneumatic tube—*pfft*—just like that. The subterranean system of telephone cables, power lines, steam pipes, gas mains and sewer pipes is reason enough to abandon the island to the gods and the weevils. Every time an incision is made in the pavement, the noisy surgeons expose ganglia that are tangled beyond belief. By rights New York should have destroyed itself long ago, from panic or fire or rioting or failure of some vital supply line in its circulatory system or from some deep labyrinthine short circuit. Long ago the city should have experienced an insoluble traffic snarl at some impossible bottleneck. It should have perished of hunger when food lines failed for a few days. It should have been wiped out by a plague starting in its slums or carried in by ships' rats. It should have been overwhelmed by the sea that licks at it on every side. The workers in its myriad cells should have succumbed to nerves, from the fearful pall of smoke-fog that drifts over every few days from Jersey, blotting out all light at noon and leaving the high offices suspended, men groping and depressed, and the sense of world's end. It should have been touched in the head by the August heat and gone off its rocker.

Mass hysteria is a terrible force, yet New Yorkers seem always to escape it by some tiny margin: they sit in stalled subways without claustrophobia, they extricate themselves from panic situations by some lucky wisecrack, they meet confusion and congestion with patience and grit—a sort of perpetual muddling through. Every facility is inadequate—the hospitals and schools and playgrounds are overcrowded, the express highways are feverish, the unimproved highways and bridges are bottlenecks; there is not enough air and not enough light, and there is usually either too much heat or too little. But the city makes up for its hazards and its deficiencies by supplying its citizens with massive doses of a supplementary vitamin—the sense of belonging to something unique, cosmopolitan, mighty and unparalleled. . . .

157

Harlem Sounds: Hallelujah Corner

WILLIAM BROWNE

Cymbals clash,
and in this scene
of annulled jazz,
gay-stepping stompers
roll in
shouting 'Hallelujah'
at a deposed 'Spirit'
until,
like a mimic-child,
it rages,
stumbles,
and lies exhausted,
strung like Jesus.

The honky-tonk
riffs,
runs,
and breaks,
are superimposed
on the sounds
of
weeping
amens.

The mandrill sounds
of tuba snorts,
coned by applauding tambourines;
laugh
at the banjo-dance
of amen-women
shouting
at the
boogie-woogie
voice
of God.

Fifth Avenue, Uptown:
A Letter from Harlem*

JAMES BALDWIN

There is a Housing Project standing now where the house in which we grew up once stood, and one of those stunted city trees is snarling where our doorway used to be. This is on the rehabilitated side of the avenue. The other side of the avenue—for progress takes time—has not been rehabilitated yet and it looks exactly as it looked in the days when we sat with our noses pressed against the windowpane, longing to be allowed to go "across the street." The grocery store which gave us credit is still there, and there can be no doubt that it is still giving credit. The people in the project certainly need it—far more, indeed, than they ever needed the project. The last time I passed by, the Jewish proprietor was still standing among his shelves, looking sadder and heavier but scarcely any older. Farther down the block stands the shoe-repair store in which our shoes were repaired until reparation became impossible and in which, then, we bought all our "new" ones. The Negro proprietor is still in the window, head down, working at the leather.

These two, I imagine, could tell a long tale if they would (perhaps they would be glad to if they could), having watched so many, for so long, struggling in the fishhooks, the barbed wire, of this avenue.

The avenue is elsewhere the renowned and elegant Fifth. The area I am describing, which, in today's gang parlance, would be called "the turf," is bounded by Lenox Avenue on the west, the Harlem River on the east, 135th Street on the north, and 130th Street on the south. We never lived beyond these boundaries; this is where we grew up. Walking along 145th Street—for example—familiar as it is, and similar, does not have the same impact because I do not know any of the people on the block. But when I turn east on 131st Street and Lenox Avenue, there is first a soda-pop joint, then a shoeshine "parlor," then a grocery store, then a dry cleaners', then

*Selection from *Nobody Knows My Name*.

160

the houses. All along the street there are people who watched me grow up, people who grew up with me, people I watched grow up along with my brothers and sisters; and, sometimes in my arms, sometimes underfoot, sometimes at my shoulder—or on it—their children, a riot, a forest of children, who include my nieces and nephews.

When we reach the end of this long block, we find ourselves on wide, filthy, hostile Fifth Avenue, facing that project which hangs over the avenue like a monument to the folly, and the cowardice, of good intentions. All along the block, for anyone who knows it, are immense human gaps, like craters. These gaps are not created merely by those who have moved away, inevitably into some other ghetto; or by those who have risen, almost always into a greater capacity for self-loathing and self-delusion; or yet by those who, by whatever means—War II, the Korean war, a policeman's gun or billy, a gang war, a brawl, madness, an overdose of heroin, or, simply, un-natural exhaustion—are dead. I am talking about those who are left, and I am talking principally about the young. What are they doing? Well, some, a minority, are fanatical churchgoers, members of the more extreme of the Holy Roller sects. Many, many more are "moslems," by affiliation or sympathy, that is to say that they are united by nothing more—and nothing less—than a hatred of the white world and all its works. They are present, for example, at every Buy Black street-corner meeting—meetings in which the speaker urges his hearers to cease trading with white men and establish a separate economy. Neither the speaker nor his hearers can possibly do this, of course, since Negroes do not own General Motors or RCA or the A & P, nor, indeed, do they own more than a wholly insufficient fraction of anything else in Harlem (those who *do* own anything are more interested in their profits than in their fellows). But these meetings nevertheless keep alive in the participators a certain pride of bitterness without which, however futile this bitterness may be, they could scarcely remain alive at all. Many have given up. They stay home and watch the TV screen, living on the earnings of their parents, cousins, brothers, or uncles, and only leave the house to go to the movies or to the nearest bar. "How're you making it?" one may ask, running into them along the block, or in the bar. "Oh, I'm TV-ing it"; with the saddest, sweetest, most shamefaced of smiles, and from a great distance. This distance one is compelled to respect; anyone who has traveled so far will not easily be dragged again into the world. There are further retreats, of course, than the TV screen or the bar. There are those who

161

are simply sitting on their stoops, "stoned," animated for a moment only, and hideously, by the approach of someone who may lend them the money for a "fix." Or by the approach of someone from whom they can purchase it, one of the shrewd ones, on the way to prison or just coming out.

And the others, who have avoided all of these deaths, get up in the morning and go downtown to meet "the man." They work in the white man's world all day and come home in the evening to this fetid block. They struggle to instill in their children some private sense of honor or dignity which will help the child to survive. This means, of course, that they must struggle, stolidly, incessantly, to keep this sense alive in themselves, in spite of the insults, the indifference, and the cruelty they are certain to encounter in their working day. They patiently browbeat the landlord into fixing the heat, the plaster, the plumbing; this demands prodigious patience; nor is patience usually enough. In trying to make their hovels habitable, they are perpetually throwing good money after bad. Such frustration, so long endured, is driving many strong, admirable men and women whose only crime is color to the very gates of paranoia.

One remembers them from another time—playing handball in the playground, going to church, wondering if they were going to be promoted at school. One remembers them going off to war—gladly, to escape this block. One remembers their return. Perhaps one remembers their wedding day. And one sees where the girl is now—vainly looking for salvation from some other embittered, trussed, and struggling boy—and sees the all-but-abandoned children in the streets.

Now I am perfectly aware that there are other slums in which white men are fighting for their lives, and mainly losing. I know that blood is also flowing through those streets and that the human damage there is incalculable. People are continually pointing out to me the wretchedness of white people in order to console me for the wretchedness of blacks. But an itemized account of the American failure does not console me and it should not console anyone else. That hundreds of thousands of white people are living, in effect, no better than the "niggers" is not a fact to be regarded with complacency. The social and moral bankruptcy suggested by this fact is of the bitterest, most terrifying kind.

The people, however, who believe that this democratic anguish has some consoling value are always pointing out that So-and-So, white, and So-and-So, black, rose from the slums into the big time. The existence—the public existence—of, say, Frank Sinatra and Sammy Davis, Jr. proves to them that America is still the land of opportunity and that inequalities vanish before the determined will. It proves nothing of the sort. The determined will is rare—at the moment, in this country, it is unspeakably rare—and the inequalities suffered by the many are in no way justified by the rise of a few. A few have always risen—in every country, every era, and in the teeth of regimes which can by no stretch of the imagination be thought of as free. Not all of these people, it is worth remembering, left the world better than they found it. The determined will is rare, but it is not invariably benevolent. Furthermore, the American equation of success with the big times reveals an awful disrespect for human life and human achievement. This equation has placed our cities among the most dangerous in the world and has placed our youth among the most empty and most bewildered. The situation of our youth is not mysterious. Children have never been very good at listening to their elders, but they have never failed to imitate them. They must, they have no other models. That is exactly what our children are doing. They are imitating our immorality, our disrespect for the pain of others.

All other slum dwellers, when the bank account permits it, can move out of the slum and vanish altogether from the eye of persecution. No Negro in this country has ever made that much money and it will be a long time before any Negro does. The Negroes in Harlem, who have no money, spend what they have on such gimcracks as they are sold. These include "wider" TV screens, more "faithful" hi-fi sets, more "powerful" cars, all of which, of course, are obsolete long before they are paid for. Anyone who has ever struggled with poverty knows how extremely expensive it is to be poor; and if one is a member of a captive population, economically speaking, one's feet have simply been placed on the treadmill forever. One is victimized, economically, in a thousand ways—rent, for example, or car insurance. Go shopping one day in Harlem—for anything—and compare Harlem prices and quality with those downtown.

The people who have managed to get off this block have only got as far as a more respectable ghetto. This respectable ghetto does not even have the advantages of the disreputable one—friends, neighbors, a familiar church, and friendly tradesmen; and it is not, moreover, in the nature of any ghetto to remain respectable long. Every Sunday, people who have left the block take the lonely ride back, dragging their increasingly discontented

163

children with them. They spend the day talking, not always with words, about the trouble they've seen and the trouble—one must watch their eyes as they watch their children—they are only too likely to see. For children do not like ghettos. It takes them nearly no time to discover exactly why they are there.

The projects in Harlem are hated. They are hated almost as much as policemen, and this is saying a great deal. And they are hated for the same reason: both reveal, unbearably, the real attitude of the white world, no matter how many liberal speeches are made, no matter how many lofty editorials are written, no matter how many civil-rights commissions are set up.

The projects are hideous, of course, there being a law, apparently respected throughout the world, that popular housing shall be as cheerless as a prison. They are lumped all over Harlem, colorless, bleak, high, and revolting. The wide windows look out on Harlem's invincible and indescribable squalor: the Park Avenue railroad tracks, around which, about forty years ago, the present dark community began; the unrehabilitated houses, bowed down, it would seem, under the great weight of frustration and bitterness they contain; the dark, the ominous schoolhouses from which the child may emerge maimed, blinded, hooked, or enraged for life; and the churches, churches, block upon block of churches, niched in the walls like cannon in the walls of a fortress. Even if the administration of the projects were not so insanely humiliating (for example: one must report raises in salary to the management, which will then eat up the profit by raising one's rent; the management has the right to know who is staying in your apartment; the management can ask you to leave, at their discretion), the projects would still be hated because they are an insult to the meanest intelligence.

Harlem got its first private project, Riverton *—which is now, naturally,

* The inhabitants of Riverton were much embittered by this description; they have, apparently, forgotten how their project came into being; and have repeatedly informed me that I cannot possibly be referring to Riverton, but to another housing project which is directly across the street. It is quite clear, I think, that I have no interest in accusing any individuals or families of the depredations herein described: but neither can I deny the evidence of my own eyes. Nor do I blame anyone in Harlem for making the best of a dreadful bargain. But anyone who lives in Harlem and imagines that he has *not* struck this bargain, or that what he takes to be his status (in whose eyes?) protects him against the common pain, demoralization, and danger, is simply self deluded.

a slum—about twelve years ago because at that time Negroes were not allowed to live in Stuyvesant Town. Harlem watched Riverton go up, therefore, in the most violent bitterness of spirit, and hated it long before the builders arrived. They began hating it at about the time people began moving out of their condemned houses to make room for this additional proof of how thoroughly the white world despised them. And they had scarcely moved in, naturally, before they began smashing windows, defacing walls, urinating in the elevators, and fornicating in the playgrounds. Liberals, both white and black, were appalled at the spectacle. I was appalled by the liberal innocence—or cynicism, which comes out in practice as much the same thing. Other people were delighted to be able to point to proof positive that nothing could be done to better the lot of the colored people. They were, and are, right in one respect: that nothing can be done as long as they are treated like colored people. The people in Harlem know they are living there because white people do not think they are good enough to live anywhere else. No amount of "improvement" can sweeten this fact. Whatever money is now being earmarked to improve this, or any other ghetto, might as well be burnt. A ghetto can be improved in one way only: out of existence.

Similarly, the only way to police a ghetto is to be oppressive. None of the Police Commissioner's men, even with the best will in the world, have any way of understanding the lives led by the people they swagger about in twos and threes controlling. Their very presence is an insult, and it would be, even if they spent their entire day feeding gumdrops to children. They represent the force of the white world, and that world's real intentions are, simply, for that world's criminal profit and ease, to keep the black man corraled up here, in his place. The badge, the gun in the holster, and the swinging club make vivid what will happen should his rebellion become overt. Rare, indeed, is the Harlem citizen, from the most circumspect church member to the most shiftless adolescent, who does not have a long tale to tell of police incompetence, injustice, or brutality. I myself have witnessed and endured it more than once. The businessmen and racketeers also have a story. And so do the prostitutes. (And this is not, perhaps, the place to discuss Harlem's very complex attitude toward black policemen, nor the reasons, according to Harlem, that they are nearly all downtown.)

It is hard, on the other hand, to blame the policeman, blank, good-natured, thoughtless, and insuperably innocent, for being such a perfect representative of the people he serves. He, too, believes in good intentions and is astounded and offended when they are not taken for the deed. He has never, himself, done anything for which to be hated—which of us has?—and yet he is facing, daily and nightly, people who would gladly see him dead, and he knows it. There is no way for him not to know it: there are few things under heaven more unnerving than the silent, accumulating contempt and hatred of a people. He moves through Harlem, therefore, like an occupying soldier in a bitterly hostile country; which is precisely what, and where, he is, and is the reason he walks in twos and threes. And he is not the only one who knows why he is always in company: the people who are watching him know why, too. Any street meeting, sacred or secular, which he and his colleagues uneasily cover has as its explicit or implicit burden the cruelty and injustice of the white domination. And these days, of course, in terms increasingly vivid and jubilant, it speaks of the end of that domination. The white policeman standing on a Harlem street corner finds himself at the very center of the revolution now occurring in the world. He is not prepared for it—naturally, nobody is—and, what is possibly much more to the point, he is exposed, as few white people are, to the anguish of the black people around him. Even if he is gifted with the merest mustard grain of imagination, something must seep in. He cannot avoid observing that some of the children, in spite of their color, remind him of children he has known and loved, perhaps even of his own children. He knows that he certainly does not want *his* children living this way. He can retreat from his uneasiness in only one direction: into a callousness which very shortly becomes second nature. He becomes more callous, the population becomes more hostile, the situation grows more tense, and the police force is increased. One day, to everyone's astonishment, someone drops a match in the powder keg and everything blows up. Before the dust has settled or the blood congealed, editorials, speeches, and civil-rights commissions are loud in the land, demanding to know what happened. What happened is that Negroes want to be treated like men.

Negroes want to be treated like men: a perfectly straightforward statement, containing only seven words. People who have mastered Kant, Hegel, Shakespeare, Marx, Freud, and the Bible find this statement utterly impenetrable. The idea seems to threaten profound, barely conscious assumptions. A kind of panic paralyzes their features, as though they found themselves trapped on the edge of a steep place. I once tried to describe to

166

a very well-known American intellectual the conditions among Negroes in the South. My recital disturbed him and made him indignant; and he asked me in perfect innocence, "Why don't all the Negroes in the South move North?" I tried to explain what *has* happened, unfailingly, whenever a significant body of Negroes move North. They do not escape Jim Crow: they merely encounter another, not-less-deadly variety. They do not move to Chicago, they move to the South Side; they do not move to New York, they move to Harlem. The pressure within the ghetto causes the ghetto walls to expand, and this expansion is always violent. White people hold the line as long as they can, and in as many ways as they can, from verbal intimidation to physical violence. But inevitably the border which has divided the ghetto from the rest of the world falls into the hands of the ghetto. The white people fall back bitterly before the black horde; the landlords make a tidy profit by raising the rent, chopping up the rooms, and all but dispensing with the upkeep; and what has once been a neighborhood turns into a "turf." This is precisely what happened when the Puerto Ricans arrived in their thousands—and the bitterness thus caused is, as I write, being fought out all up and down those streets.

Northerners indulge in an extremely dangerous luxury. They seem to feel that because they fought on the right side during the Civil War, and won, they have earned the right merely to deplore what is going on in the South, without taking any responsibility for it; and that they can ignore what is happening in Northern cities because what is happening in Little Rock or Birmingham is worse. Well, in the first place, it is not possible for anyone who has not endured both to know which is "worse." I know Negroes who prefer the South and white Southerners, because "At least there, you haven't got to play any guessing games!" The guessing games referred to have driven more than one Negro into the narcotics ward, the madhouse, or the river. I know another Negro, a man very dear to me, who says, with conviction and with truth, "The spirit of the South is the spirit of America." He was born in the North and did his military training in the South. He did not, as far as I can gather, find the South "worse"; he found it, if anything, all too familiar. In the second place, though, even if Birmingham *is* worse, no doubt Johannesburg, South Africa, beats it by several miles, and Buchenwald was one of the worst things that ever happened in the entire history of the world. The world has never lacked for horrifying examples; but I do not believe that these examples are meant to be used as justification for our own crimes. This perpetual justification empties the heart of all human feeling. The emptier our hearts become, the greater will be our crimes. Thirdly, the South is not merely an embarrassingly backward region, but a part of this country, and what happens there concerns every one of us.

As far as the color problem is concerned, there is but one great difference between the Southern white and the Northerner: the Southerner remembers, historically and in his own psyche, a kind of Eden in which he loved black people and they loved him. Historically, the flaming sword laid across this Eden is the Civil War. Personally, it is the Southerner's sexual coming of age, when, without any warning, unbreakable taboos are set up between himself and his past. Everything, thereafter, is permitted him except the love he remembers and has never ceased to need. The resulting, indescribable torment affects every Southern mind and is the basis of the Southern hysteria.

None of this is true for the Northerner. Negroes represent nothing to him personally, except, perhaps, the dangers of carnality. He never sees Negroes. Southerners see them all the time. Northerners never think about them whereas Southerners are never really thinking of anything else. Negroes are, therefore, ignored in the North and are under surveillance in the South, and suffer hideously in both places. Neither the Southerner nor the Northerner is able to look on the Negro simply as a man. It seems to be indispensable to the national self-esteem that the Negro be considered either as a kind of ward (in which case we are told how many Negroes, comparatively, bought Cadillacs last year and how few, comparatively, were lynched), or as a victim (in which case we are promised that he will never vote in our assemblies or go to school with our kids). They are two sides of the same coin and the South will not change—*cannot* change—until the North changes. The country will not change until it re-examines itself and discovers what it really means by freedom. In the meantime, generations keep being born, bitterness is increased by incompetence, pride, and folly, and the world shrinks around us.

It is a terrible, an inexorable, law that one cannot deny the humanity of another without diminishing one's own: in the face of one's victim, one sees oneself. Walk through the streets of Harlem and see what we, this nation, have become.

Pittsburgh

WITTER BYNNER

Coming upon it unawares,
A town of men and millionaires,
A town of coal-dust and of churches,
I thought of moons, I thought of birches,
Goals forgotten in the faces
Of the swift who run the races,
Whip-poor-wills and misty meadows,
Musk-rats in the river-shadows,
Robins whistling five o'clock,
Mornings naked on a rock.

Approach to a City

WILLIAM CARLOS WILLIAMS

Getting through with the world—
I never tire of the mystery
of these streets: the three baskets
of dried flowers in the high

bar-room window, the gulls wheeling
above the factory, the dirty
snow—the humility of the snow that
silvers everything and is

trampled and lined with use—yet
falls again, the silent birds
on the still wires of the sky, the blur
of wings as they take off

together. The flags in the heavy
air move against a leaden
ground—the snow
pencilled with the stubble of old

weeds: I never tire of these sights
but refresh myself there
always for there is small holiness
to be found in braver things.

Interesting Native Customs in Washington and Other Savage Lands

ARTHUR HOPPE

When visiting a strange country like Washington, it's incumbent on us responsible ace newsmen to file what we call "a backgrounder." You know, a lengthy review of annual rainfall and grazing conditions with a few paragraphs about quaint native courting customs thrown in to sex things up a little.

Well, Washington is several miles square and about as tall, say, as the Washington Monument, give or take a little. It is surrounded on all four sides by reality. The winters aren't too hot. Neither is the rest of the climate. The natives, in general, are sullen.

While the outside world refers to it as "Washington," the natives call it "the District," short for "District of Columbia." And the natives, of course, do not think of themselves as "natives." They think of themselves as "experts." The population, at the moment, consists of 998,762 experts and two tourists from Camden, Ohio, who, on being interviewed, said they hadn't the foggiest notion of what was wrong with U.S. foreign policy.

The main industries are eating, drinking, and talking. The major import and export—indeed, the staple of the economy—is money. As with many other countries these days, Washington imports more from us than it exports. This creates what we economists call "an unfavorable trade balance." Which, in this case, it certainly is.

The local unit of currency is "the Million Dollar." Usually written "$1 million." Many of these, however, are required to purchase anything. So they are generally referred to in the plural, such as "thus and so many Million Dollars." In recent years, a new denomination, "the Billion Dollar" (written "$1 billion") has come into wide use. And lately one even hears "the Trillion Dollar" mentioned on occasion. But only in referring to the national debt.

It is exceedingly difficult to calculate a rate of exchange between Washington money and our money because the essential characteristic of Washington money is that it's not real. No native, to my knowledge, has even seen "a Million Dollar," much less "a Billion Dollar," although they remain the chief topic of conversation.

Lesser denominations, such as "the Thousand Dollar" or "the Hundred Dollar" have, like the old French centime, virtually disappeared from circulation. And the only place the natives use real money, such as the dollar, is after office hours. Indeed, any mention of real money tends for some unexplained reason to make the natives restless. Take, for example, the case of the underground garage.

The Solons, a local tribe living on Capitol Hill, recently decided to build an underground garage so their cars wouldn't get sunburned. This would cost only four "Million Dollars," and everybody was quite content. But then someone, presumably an anthropologist from the real world, announced, after much calculation, that this figure came to somewhere around $25,000 per car. Which sounded like real money. And it was suggested that the Solons might economize by merely buying cheap cars and throwing them away each day on arriving at their meeting place. This talk about real money made the Solons terribly nervous. Not nervous enough, of course, to cancel their plans for the four "Million Dollar" garage. But terribly nervous.

Despite the obvious need for a drastic currency reform, however, the local economy is booming. Everywhere the visitor looks, new buildings are going up. And when you realize that the natives neither manufacture nor produce anything of salable value, this expansion is all the more fantastic.

The new buildings are, of course, all being constructed in the Foursquare Monolithic Style of modern native architecture. The natives, it is believed, pour a solid cube of concrete, hollow out the inside, and stick a flagpole on top. The result, it is generally agreed, is much more permanent than the thatched huts of the Wambeesi. If not as pleasing to the eye.

But it is certainly clear to even the most casual observer that all this activity indicates the natives, due to our help, have at last reached "the economic takeoff point." And while my heart goes out to them in their struggle to better themselves, I feel it is now our grim duty to cut back drastically on our financial-aid program so that they may learn to stand on their own two feet. I feel strongly that we should take this step before April 15 at the latest.

Let us now turn to the social structure of the country. As in many of the new African nations, the natives of Washington belong not to one, but to numerous separate and distinct tribes, each spiritedly warlike and fiercely jealous of its prerogatives. The best known of the local tribes are, of course, the Solons, occupying the strategic heights of Capitol Hill, and the Presidents, who live on the flats perhaps a mile away. . . . Lesser known are the numerous other interesting tribes of the flats, such as "State," "Commerce," "Interior," "NRA" (now extinct), and so forth. While nominally joined by treaty with the Presidents, these lesser tribes devote most of their energies to battling each other. . . .

The young warriors of each tribe are prepared for leadership in these devious wars by a rite known as Shafting—a test similar to the trial-by-fire dance for young Ugulaps in North Borneo. Unlike the fire dance, which is a one-time fling for the young Ugulap, Shafting remains the prime occupation of the Washingtonian from his entry into the tribe until his death or retirement.

The goal in the rites of Shafting is telephone buttons. A telephone without buttons is a symbol of shame, and the native who has one invariably keeps it turned away from his visitors. A phone with two buttons is the symbol of having arrived at manhood, and so forth on up. Status is carefully equated. A six-button native, for instance, would never telephone a four-button native. Except through his secretary. The current scepter of chiefhood in all tribes is a conference phone, a light green model with chromium hooks and no fewer than eighteen plastic buttons, two of them red. With this goes a corner office, a conference table, two flags in standards, and four in-and-out baskets.

Most of the inordinately complex rituals of Shafting are fathomable only by anthropologists. Three of the simpler forms will be discussed here: Leaking, Copy-to-ing and Jack Hornering.

Leaking is practiced only at the highest levels in each tribe. Usually by subchieftans. When a mistake is made, Subchief X announces quickly that no mistake was made. Then he Leaks the inside information to the Columnists (a tribe of local historians of tremendous unimportance) that in reality it was a horrendous mistake. And that Subchief Y made it. When three or more Columnists print the leak, it becomes known as a *fact*. And Subchief Y is stripped of one secretary, his leather couch, and four buttons from his telephone. . . .

Copy-to-ing is practiced on the lower levels. Should Al Z, a young native working under Chief Y, make a minor slip, he will immediately receive fourteen interoffice memos from his fellow tribesmen. Such as: "Al, I was very sorry to see us get in that awful bind. But I did warn you at Staff beforehand. How about talking it over? Perhaps something can still be saved from the wreckage."

At the bottom of each memo is typed: COPY TO CHIEF Y. While no chief could possibly read all the scores of copies of memos he receives each day, the psychological damage on Al Z of those words, COPY TO CHIEF Y, can well be imagined.

I stumbled on Jack Hornering by making friends with a young native barely of the Executive Dining Room level. I found him busily initialing each page of an eight-page report to his chief.

"It cuts the chance of being Jack Hornered," he said.

Jack Hornered? "Sure," he said. "This report's loaded with good ideas. And it's got to pass through a lot of hands on its way to the top. Each hand's got a thumb. Remember? 'So he stuck in his thumb and pulled out a plum and said, "What a good boy am I." ' Sometimes an eight-page report gets to the top saying nothing but: 'Dear Chief: Yrs Truly.' I figure if I initial every page it will be a psychological burglar lock. To tell you the truth, though," he added gloomily, "it never works."

In my forthcoming book, *Interesting Native Customs in Washington and Other Savage Lands*, I've decided to prepare the gentler readers for the bloody accounts of Washington tribal shafting by building up to them gradually. For example, the early chapters will deal with less gruesome customs of more civilized tribes. Like: "Disembowelment Techniques Among the Mau Mau."

With all this intertribal and intratribal warfare, the natives, understandably enough, have little interest in the outside world, except as its events affect their internecine quarrels. Indeed, many modern anthropologists feel that if the natives could ever be knit into one homogeneous unit, their skill and deviousness in the arts of warfare would inevitably mean that Washington would soon come to rule the world.

As of now, however, this danger appears extremely remote.

Detroit

DONALD HALL

There is a cool river
which flows among the red and yellow
pennants of the gas stations,
and through the black brick
of the car factories.
Smoke does not dirty it.
Children splash through it
on their Lambrettas.
It does not disturb the drought
which burns the evergreens
on the square lawns of foremen.
Yet willows grow
from the moss on the bank.
Under the mist of the branches
sit William Blake,
Thomas Jefferson,
Huckleberry Finn,
and Henry James.
They are thinking about fish.
They are watching the river: it flows
through the city of America
without fish.

Park Pigeons

MELVILLE CANE

Still blue stones,
Dull gray rocks,
Sunk in grass.
A child flings a peanut.
Stones flutter,
Rocks circle in the sun.

Antaeus

BORDEN DEAL

This was during the wartime, when lots of people were coming North for jobs in factories and war industries, when people moved around a lot more than they do now and sometimes kids were thrown into new groups and new lives that were completely different from anything they had ever known before. I remember this one kid; T. J. his name was, from somewhere down South, whose family moved into our building during that time. They'd come North with everything they owned piled into the back seat of an old-model sedan that you wouldn't expect could make the trip, with T. J. and his three younger sisters riding shakily atop the load of junk.

Our building was just like all the others there, with families crowded into a few rooms, and I guess there were twenty-five or thirty kids about my age in that one building. Of course, there were a few of us who formed a gang and ran together all the time after school, and I was the one who brought T. J. in and started the whole thing.

The building right next door to us was a factory where they made walking dolls. It was a low building with a flat, tarred roof that had a parapet all around it about head-high and we'd found out a long time before that no one, not even the watchman, paid any attention to the roof because it was higher than any of the other buildings around. So my gang used the roof as a headquarters. We could get up there by crossing over to the fire escape from our own roof on a plank and then going on up. It was a secret place for us, where nobody else could go without our permission.

I remember the day I first took T. J. up there to meet the gang. He was a stocky, robust kid with a shock of white hair, nothing sissy about him except his voice—he talked different from any of us and you noticed it right away. But I liked him anyway, so I told him to come on up.

We climbed up over the parapet and dropped down on the roof. The rest of the gang were already there.

178

"Hi," I said. I jerked my thumb at T. J. "He just moved into the building yesterday."

He just stood there, not scared or anything, just looking, like the first time you see somebody you're not sure you're going to like.

"Hi," Blackie said. "Where you from?"

"Marion County," T. J. said.

We laughed. "Marion County?" I said. "Where's that?"

He looked at me like I was a stranger, too. "It's in Alabama," he said, like I ought to know where it was.

"What's your name?" Charley said.

"T. J.," he said, looking back at him. He had pale blue eyes that looked washed-out but he looked directly at Charley, waiting for his reaction. He'll be all right, I thought. No sissy in him . . . except that voice. Who ever talked like that?

"T. J.," Blackie said. "That's just initials. What's your real name? Nobody in the world has just initials."

"I do," he said. "And they're T. J. That's all the name I got."

His voice was resolute with the knowledge of his rightness and for a moment no one had anything to say. T. J. looked around at the rooftop and down at the black tar under his feet. "Down yonder where I come from," he said, "we played out in the woods. Don't you-all have no woods around here?"

"Naw," Blackie said. "There's the park a few blocks over, but it's full of kids and cops and old women. You can't do a thing."

T. J. kept looking at the tar under his feet. "You mean you ain't got no fields to raise nothing in? No watermelons or nothing?"

"Naw," I said scornfully. "What do you want to grow something for? The folks can buy everything they need at the store."

He looked at me again with that strange, unknowing look. "In Marion County," he said, "I had my own acre of cotton and my own acre of corn. It was mine to plant ever' year."

He sounded like it was something to be proud of, and in some obscure way it made the rest of us angry. "Heck!" Blackie said. "Who'd want to have their own acre of cotton and corn? That's just work. What can you do with an acre of cotton and corn?"

T. J. looked at him. "Well, you get part of the bale offen your acre," he said seriously. "And I fed my acre of corn to my calf."

We didn't really know what he was talking about, so we were more puzzled than angry; otherwise, I guess, we'd have chased him off the roof and wouldn't let him be part of our gang. But he was strange and different and we were all attracted by his stolid sense of rightness and belonging, maybe by the strange softness of his voice contrasting our own tones of speech into harshness.

He moved his foot against the black tar. "We could make our own field right here," he said softly, thoughtfully. "Come spring we could raise us what we want to . . . watermelons and garden truck and no telling what all."

"You'd have to be a good farmer to make these tar roofs grow any watermelons," I said. We all laughed.

But T. J. looked serious. "We could haul us some dirt up here," he said. "And spread it out even and water it and before you know it we'd have us a crop in here." He looked at us intently. "Wouldn't that be fun?"

"They wouldn't let us," Blackie said quickly.

"I thought you said this was you-all's roof," T. J. said to me. "That you-all could do anything you wanted up here."

"They've never bothered us," I said. I felt the idea beginning to catch fire in me. It was a big idea and it took a while for it to sink in but the more I thought about it the better I liked it. "Say," I said to the gang, "he might have something there. Just make us a regular roof garden, with flowers and grass and trees and everything. And all ours, too," I said. "We wouldn't let anybody up here except the ones we wanted to."

"It'd take a while to grow trees," T. J. said quickly, but we weren't paying any attention to him. They were all talking about it suddenly, all excited with the idea after I'd put it in a way they could catch hold of it. Only rich people had roof gardens, we knew, and the idea of our own private domain excited them.

"We could bring it up in sacks and boxes," Blackie said. "We'd have to do it while the folks weren't paying any attention to us. We'd have to come up to the roof of our building and then cross over with it."

"Where could we get the dirt?" somebody said worriedly.

"Out of those vacant lots over close to school," Blackie said. "Nobody'd notice if we scraped it up."

I slapped T. J. on the shoulder. "Man, you had a wonderful idea," I

180

said, and everybody grinned at him, remembering he had started it. "Our own private roof garden."

He grinned back. "It'll be ourn," he said. "All ourn." Then he looked thoughtful again. "Maybe I can lay my hands on some cotton seed, too. You think we could raise us some cotton?"

We'd started big projects before at one time or another, like any gang of kids, but they'd always petered out for lack of organization and direction. But this one didn't . . . somehow or other T. J. kept it going all through the winter months. He kept talking about the watermelons and the cotton we'd raise, come spring, and when even that wouldn't work he'd switch around to my idea of flowers and grass and trees though he was always honest enough to add that it'd take a while to get any trees started. He always had it on his mind and he'd mention it in school, getting them lined up to carry dirt that afternoon, saying in a casual way that he reckoned a few more weeks ought to see the job through.

Our little area of private earth grew slowly. T. J. was smart enough to start in one corner of the building, heaping up the carried earth two or three feet thick, so that we had an immediate result to look at, to contemplate with awe. Some of the evenings T. J. alone was carrying earth up to the building, the rest of the gang distracted by other enterprises or interests, but T. J. kept plugging along on his own and eventually we'd all come back to him again and then our own little acre would grow more rapidly.

He was careful about the kind of dirt he'd let us carry up there and more than once he dumped a sandy load over the parapet in the areaway below because it wasn't good enough. He found out the kinds of earth in all the vacant lots for blocks around. He'd pick it up and fell it and smell it, frozen though it was sometimes, and then he'd say it was good growing soil or it wasn't worth anything and we'd have to go on somewhere else.

Thinking about it now I don't see how he kept us at it. It was hard work, lugging paper sacks and boxes of dirt all the way up the stairs of our own building, keeping out of the way of the grownups so they wouldn't catch on to what we were doing. They probably wouldn't have cared, for they didn't pay much attention to us, but we wanted to keep it secret anyway. Then we had to go through the trap door to our roof, teeter over a plank to the fire escape, then climb two or three stories to the parapet and drop down onto the roof. All that for a small pile of earth that sometimes didn't seem worth the effort. But T. J. kept the vision bright within us, his words shrewd and calculated toward the fulfillment of his dream; and he worked harder than any of us. He seemed driven toward a goal that we couldn't see, a particular point in time that would be definitely marked by signs and wonders that only he could see.

The laborious earth just lay there during the cold months, inert and lifeless, the clods lumpy and cold under our feet when we walked over it. But one day it rained and afterward there was a softness in the air and the earth was alive and giving again with moisture and warmth. That evening T. J. smelled the air, his nostrils dilating with the odor of the earth under his feet.

"It's spring," he said, and there was a gladness rising in his voice that filled us all with the same feeling. "It's mighty late for it, but it's spring. I'd just about decided it wasn't never gonna get here at all."

We were all sniffing at the air, too, trying to smell it the way that T. J. did, and I can still remember the sweet odor of the earth under our feet. It was the first time in my life that spring and spring earth had meant anything to me. I looked at T. J. then, knowing in a faint way the hunger within him through the toilsome winter months, knowing the dream that lay behind his plan. He was a new Antaeus, preparing his own bed of strength.

"Planting time," he said. "We'll have to find us some seed."

"What do we do?" Blackie said. "How do we do it?"

"First we'll have to break up the clods," T. J. said. "That won't be hard to do. Then we plant the seed and after a while they come up. Then you got you a crop." He frowned. "But you ain't got it raised yet. You got to tend it and hoe it and take care of it and all the time it's growing and growing while you're awake and while you're asleep. Then you lay it by when it's growed and let it ripen and then you got you a crop."

"There's those wholesale seed houses over on Sixth," I said. "We could probably swipe some grass seed over there."

T. J. looked at the earth. "You-all seem mighty set on raising some grass," he said. "I ain't never put no effort into that. I spent all my life trying not to raise grass."

"But it's pretty," Blackie said. "We could play on it and take sunbaths on it. Like having our own lawn. Lots of people got lawns."

"Well," T. J. said. He looked at the rest of us, hesitant for the first time.

182

He kept on looking at us for a moment. "I did have it in mind to raise some corn and vegetables. But we'll plant grass."

He was smart. He knew where to give in. And I don't suppose it made any difference to him really. He just wanted to grow something, even if it was grass.

"Of course," he said, "I do think we ought to plant a row of watermelons. They'd be mighty nice to eat while we was a-laying on that grass."

We all laughed. "All right," I said. "We'll plant us a row of watermelons."

Things went very quickly then. Perhaps half the roof was covered with the earth, the half that wasn't broken by ventilators, and we swiped pocketfuls of grass seed from the open bins in the wholesale seed house, mingling among the buyers on Saturdays and during the school lunch hour. T. J. showed us how to prepare the earth, breaking up the clods and smoothing it and sowing the grass seed. It looked rich and black now with moisture, receiving of the seed, and it seemed that the grass sprang up overnight, pale green in the early spring.

We couldn't keep from looking at it, unable to believe that we had created this delicate growth. We looked at T. J. with understanding now, knowing the fulfillment of the plan he had carried alone within his mind. We had worked without full understanding of the task but he had known all the time.

We found that we couldn't walk or play on the delicate blades, as we had expected to, but we didn't mind. It was enough just to look at it, to realize that it was the work of our own hands, and each evening the whole gang was there, trying to measure the growth that had been achieved that day.

One time a foot was placed on the plot of ground . . . one time only Blackie stepping onto it with sudden bravado. Then he looked at the crushed blades and there was shame in his face. He did not do it again. This was his grass, too, and not to be desecrated. No one said anything, for it was not necessary.

T. J. had reserved a small section for watermelons and he was still trying to find some seed for it. The wholesale house didn't have any watermelon seed and we didn't know where we could lay our hands on them. T. J. shaped the earth into mounds, ready to receive them, three mounds lying in a straight line along the edge of the grass plot.

We had just about decided that we'd have to buy the seed if we were to get them. It was a violation of our principles but we were anxious to get the watermelons started. Somewhere or other, T. J. got his hands on a seed catalogue and brought it one evening to our roof garden.

"We can order them now," he said, showing us the catalogue. "Look!"

We all crowded around, looking at the fat, green watermelons pictured in full color on the pages. Some of them were split open, showing the red, tempting meat, making our mouths water.

"Now we got to scrape up some seed money," T. J. said, looking at us. "I got a quarter. How much you-all got?"

We made up a couple of dollars between us and T. J. nodded his head. "That'll be more than enough. Now we got to decide what kind to get. I think them Kleckley Sweets. What do you-all think?"

He was going into esoteric matters beyond our reach. We hadn't even known there were different kinds of melons. So we just nodded our heads and agreed that yes, we thought the Kleckley Sweets, too.

"I'll order them tonight," T. J. said. "We ought to have them in a few days."

Then an adult voice said behind us: "What are you boys doing up here?"

It startled us for no one had ever come up here before, in all the time we had been using the roof of the factory. We jerked around and saw three men standing near the trap door at the other end of the roof. They weren't policemen, or night watchmen, but three men in plump business suits, looking at us. They walked toward us.

"What are you boys doing up here?" the one in the middle said again.

We stood still, guilt heavy among us, levied by the tone of voice, and looked at the three strangers.

The men stared at the grass flourishing behind us. "What's this?" the man said. "How did this get up here?"

"Sure is growing good, ain't it?" T. J. said conversationally. "We planted it."

The men kept looking at the grass as if they didn't believe it. It was a thick carpet over the earth now, a patch of deep greenness startling in the sterile industrial surroundings.

"Yes, sir," T. J. said proudly. "We toted that earth up here and planted that grass." He fluttered the seed catalogue. "And we're just fixing to plant us some watermelon."

The man looked at him then, his eyes strange and faraway. "What do

184

you mean, putting this on the roof of my building?" he said. "Do you want to go to jail?"

T. J. looked shaken. The rest of us were silent, frightened by the authority of his voice. We had grown up aware of adult authority, of policemen and night watchmen and teachers, and this man sounded like all the others. But it was a new thing to T. J.

"Well, you wan't using the roof," T. J. said. He paused a moment and added shrewdly, "So we just thought to pretty it up a little bit."

"And sag it so I'd have to rebuild it," the man said sharply. He turned away, saying to a man beside him, "See that all that junk is shoveled off by tomorrow."

"Yes, sir," the man said.

T. J. started forward. "You can't do that," he said. "We toted it up here and it's our earth. We planted it and raised it and toted it up here."

The man stared at him coldly. "But it's my building," he said. "It's to be shoveled off tomorrow."

"It's our earth," T. J. said desperately. "You ain't got no right!"

The men walked on without listening and descended clumsily through the trap door. T. J. stood looking after them, his body tense with anger, until they had disappeared. They wouldn't even argue with him, wouldn't let him defend his earth-rights.

He turned to us. "We won't let 'em do it," he said fiercely. "We'll stay up here all day tomorrow and the day after that and we won't let 'em do it."

We just looked at him. We knew that there was no stopping it. He saw it in our faces and his face wavered for a moment before he gripped it into determination.

"They ain't got no right," he said. "It's our earth. It's our land. Can't nobody touch a man's own land."

We kept on looking at him, listening to the words but knowing that it was no use. The adult world had descended on us even in our richest dream and we knew there was no calculating the adult world, no fighting it, no winning against it.

We started moving slowly toward the parapet and the fire escape, avoiding a last look at the green beauty of the earth that T. J. had planted for us . . . had planted deeply in our minds as well as in our experience. We liked slowly over the edge and down the steps to the plank, T. J. coming last, and all of us could feel the weight of his grief behind us.

"Wait a minute," he said suddenly, his voice harsh with the effort of calling. We stopped and turned, held by the tone of his voice, and looked up at him standing above us on the fire escape.

"We can't stop them?" he said, looking down at us, his face strange in the dusky light. "There ain't no way to stop 'em?"

"No," Blackie said with finality. "They own the building."

We stood still for a moment, looking up at T. J., caught into inaction by the decision working in his face. He stared back at us and his face was pale and mean in the poor light, with a bald nakedness in his skin like cripples have sometimes.

"They ain't gonna touch my earth," he said fiercely. "They ain't gonna lay a hand on it! Come on."

He turned around and started up the fire escape again, almost running against the effort of climbing. We followed more slowly, not knowing what he intended. By the time we reached him, he had seized a board and thrust it into the soil, scooping it up and flinging it over the parapet into the areaway below. He straightened and looked us squarely in the face.

"They can't touch it," he said. "I won't let 'em lay a dirty hand on it!"

We saw it then. He stooped to his labor again and we followed, the gusts of his anger moving in frenzied labor among us as we scattered along the edge of earth, scooping it and throwing it over the parapet, destroying with anger the growth we had nurtured with such tender care. The soil carried so laboriously upward to the light and the sun cascaded swiftly into the dark areaway, the green blades of grass crumpled and twisted in the falling.

It took less time than you would think . . . the task of destruction is infinitely easier than that of creation. We stopped at the end, leaving only a scattering of loose soil, and when it was finally over a stillness stood among the group and over the dreary building. We looked down at the bare sterility of black tar, felt the harsh texture of it under the soles of our shoes, and the anger had gone out of us, leaving only a sore aching in our minds like over-stretched muscles.

T. J. stooped for a moment, his breathing slowing from anger and effort, caught into the same contemplation of destruction as all of us. He stooped slowly, finally, and picked up a lonely blade of grass left trampled under our feet and put it between his teeth tasting it, sucking the greenness out of it into his mouth. Then he started walking toward the fire escape, moving before any of us were ready to move, and disappared over the edge while we stared after him.

186

We followed him but he was already halfway down to the ground, going on past the board where we crossed over, climbing down into the areaway. We saw the last section swing down with his weight and then he stood on the concrete below us, looking at the small pile of anonymous earth scattered by our throwing. Then he walked across the place where we could see him and disappeared toward the street without glancing back, without looking up to see us watching him.

They did not find him for two weeks. Then the Nashville police caught him just outside the Nashville freight yards. He was walking along the railroad track; still heading south, still heading home.

As for us, who had no remembered home to call us . . . none of us ever again climbed the escape-way to the roof.

Scenic

JOHN UPDIKE

O when in San Francisco do
As natives do: they sit and stare
And smile and stare again. The view
Is visible from anywhere.

Here hills are white with houses whence,
Across a multitude of sills,
The owners, lucky residents,
See other houses, other hills.

The meanest San Franciscan knows,
No matter what his past has been,
There are a thousand patios
Whose view he is included in.

The Golden Gate, the cable cars,
Twin Peaks, the Spreckles habitat,
The local ocean, sun, and stars—
When fog falls, one admires *that*.

Here homes are stacked in such a way
That every picture window has
An unmarred prospect of the Bay
And, in its center, Alcatraz.

City Reminiscences

I remember, I remember. The writer looks back into the past, into the mind, and out of this backward glance comes a host of memories and impressions, brought forth and transformed by the literary imagination into something very different from the raw material that helped inspire it. For the writers whose selections follow, the city is catalyst: an extraordinary trigger for the mind.

H. L. Mencken looks back to a young Baltimore: a panorama of waterfronts and crab fisherman, canneries and fertilizer factories, of summer cleaning sprees and noisy, vigorous street living—an energetic and optimistic pastoral life quickly becoming urban. Ralph Ellison reaches back into his memory for the people with whom he lived in the black section of Oklahoma City: the bootleggers, jazz musicians, the fire-and-brimstone preachers, the old who had endured, survived, and conquered slavery. John Dos Passos reminisces about San Francisco and gives us vivid pictures of its striking urban topography.

Gerald Green and Mark Helprin look back with mixed feelings. The Brooklyn of Green's youth has disappeared into thin air; the present that has replaced it is an alien, unfamiliar stretch of time and space. The Bronx that was part of Helprin's adolescence exists only in the imagination—along with thoughtful speculation about how that adolescence might have been different.

What emerges here in these selections is the dislocating effect of time—the uneasy, even obscure connection between past and present, the delicate line between memory and nostalgia, perception and fantasy. William Saroyan, however, looking back, finds both present and future. His turbulent memories of boyhood in early twentieth-century San Francisco are a brilliant affirmation of the relationship between time and imagination.

FROM *Happy Days*

H. L. MENCKEN

The city into which I was born in 1880 had a reputation all over for what the English, in their real-estate advertising, are fond of calling the amenities. So far as I have been able to discover by a labored search of contemporary travel-books, no literary tourist, however waspish he may have been about Washington, Niagara Falls, the prairies of the West, or even Boston and New York, ever gave Baltimore a bad notice. They all agreed, often with lubricious gloats and gurgles, (*a*) that its indigenous victualry was unsurpassed in the Republic, (*b*) that its native Caucasian females of all ages up to thirty-five were of incomparable pulchritude, and as amiable as they were lovely, and (*c*) that its home-life was spacious, charming, full of creature comforts, and highly conducive to the facile and orderly propagation of the species.

There was some truth in all these articles, but not, I regret to have to add, too much. Perhaps the one that came closest to meeting scientific tests was the first. Baltimore lay very near the immense protein factory of Chesapeake Bay, and out of the bay it ate divinely. I well recall the time when prime hard crabs of the channel species, blue in color, at least eight inches in length along the shell, and with snow-white meat almost as firm as soap, were hawked in Hollins street of Summer mornings at ten cents a dozen. The supply seemed to be almost unlimited, even in the polluted waters of the Patapsco river, which stretched up fourteen miles from the bay to engulf the slops of the Baltimore canneries and fertilizer factories. Any poor man could go down to the banks of the river, armed with no more than a length of stout cord, a home-made net on a pole, and a chunk of cat's meat, and come home in a couple of hours with enough crabs to feed his family for two days. Soft crabs, of course, were scarcer and harder to snare, and hence higher in price, but not much. More than once, hiding behind my mother's apron, I helped her to buy them at the door for two-and-a-twelfth cents a piece. And there blazes in my memory like a comet the day when she came

193

home from Hollins market complaining with strange and bitter indignation that the fishmongers there—including old Harris, her favorite—had begun to *sell* shad roe. Hitherto, stretching back to the first settlement of Baltimore Town, they had always thrown it in with the fish. Worse, she reported that they had now entered upon an illegal combination to lift the price of the standard shad of twenty inches—enough for the average family, and to spare—from forty cents to half a dollar. When my father came home for lunch and heard this incredible news, he predicted formally that the Republic would never survive the Nineteenth Century.

Terrapin was not common eating in those days, any more than it is in these, but that was mainly because few women liked it, just as few like it today. It was then assumed that their distaste was due to the fact that its consumption involved a considerable lavage with fortified wines, but they still show no honest enthusiasm for it, though Prohibition converted many of them into very adept and eager boozers. It was not, in my infancy, within the reach of the proletariat, but it was certainly not beyond the bourgeoisie. My mother, until well past the turn of the century, used to buy pint jars of the picked meat in Hollins market, with plenty of rich, golden eggs scattered through it, for a dollar a jar. For the same price it was possible to obtain *two* wild ducks of respectable if not royal species—and the open season ran gloriously from the instant the first birds wandered in from Labrador to the time the last stragglers set sail for Brazil. So far as I can remember, my mother never bought any of these ducks, but that was only because the guns, dogs and eagle eye of my uncle Henry, who lived next door, kept us oversupplied all Winter.

Garden-truck was correspondingly cheap, and so was fruit in season. Out of season we seldom saw it at all. Oranges, which cost sixty cents a dozen, came in at Christmas, and not before. We had to wait until May for strawberries, asparagus, fresh peas, carrots, and even radishes. But when the huge, fragrant strawberries of Anne Arundel county (pronounced Ann'ran'l) appeared at last they went for only five cents a box. All Spring the streets swarmed with hucksters selling such things: they called themselves, not hucksters, but Arabs (with the first *a* as in *day*), and announced their wares with loud, raucous, unintelligible cries, much worn down by phonetic decay. In Winter the principal howling was done by colored men selling shucked oysters out of huge cans. In the dark backward and abysm of time their cry must have been simply "Oysters!", but generations of Aframerican

194

larynxes had debased it to "Awneeeeeee!", with the final *e*'s prolonged until
the vendor got out of breath. He always wore a blue-and-white checked
apron, and that apron was also the uniform of the colored butlers of the Baltimore gentry when engaged upon their morning work—sweeping the sidewalk, scouring the white marble front steps, polishing up the handle of the
big front door, and bragging about their white folks to their colleagues to
port and starboard.

Oysters were not too much esteemed in the Baltimore of my youth, nor
are they in the Baltimore of today. They were eaten, of course, but not
often, for serving them raw at the table was beyond the usual domestic
technic of the time, and it was difficult to cook them in any fashion that
made them consonant with contemporary ideas of elegance. Fried, they
were fit only to be devoured at church oyster-suppers, or gobbled in oyster-
bays by drunks wandering home from scenes of revelry. The more cele-
brated oyster-houses of Baltimore—for example, Kelly's in Eutaw street—
were patronized largely by such lamentable characters. It was their playful
custom to challenge foolishlooking strangers to wash down a dozen raw
Chincoteagues with half a tumbler of Maryland rye: the town belief was that
this combination was so deleterious as to be equal to the kick of a mule. If
the stranger survived, they tried to inveigle him into eating another dozen
with sugar sprinkled on them: this dose was supposed to be almost certainly
fatal. I grew up believing that the only man in history who had ever actually
swallowed it and lived was John L. Sullivan.

There is a saying in Baltimore that crabs may be prepared in fifty ways
and that all of them are good. The range of oyster dishes is much narrower,
and they are much less attractive. Fried oysters I have just mentioned.
Stewed, they are undoubtedly edible, but only in the sorry sense that oat-
meal or boiled rice is edible. Certainly no Baltimorean not insane would
argue that an oyster stew has any of the noble qualities of the two great crab
soups—shore style (with vegetables) and bisque (with cream). Both of these
masterpieces were on tap in the old Rennert Hotel when I lunched there
daily (years after the term of the present narrative) and both were magnificent. The Rennert also offered an oyster pot-pie that had its points, but the
late Jeff Davis, manager of the hotel (and the last public virtuoso of Maryland cookery), once confessed to me that its flavor was really due to a sly use
of garlic. Such concoctions as panned and scalloped oysters have never been
eaten in my time by connoisseurs, and oyster fritters (always called flitters

195

in Baltimore) are to be had only at free-for-all oyster-roasts and along the wharves. A roasted oyster, if it be hauled off the fire at the exact instant the shell opens, is not to be sniffed at, but getting it down is a troublesome business, for the shell is too hot to be handled without mittens. Despite this inconvenience, there are still oyster-roasts in Baltimore on Winter Sunday afternoons, and since the collapse of Prohibition they have been drawing pretty good houses. When the Elks give one they hire a militia armory, lay in a thousand kegs of beer, engage 200 waiters, and prepare for a mob. But the mob is not attracted by the oysters alone; it comes mainly to eat hot-dogs, barbecued beef and sauerkraut and to wash down these lowly victuals with the beer.

The greatest crab cook of the days I remember was Tom McNulty, origi-nally a whiskey drummer but in the end sheriff of Baltimore, and the most venerated oyster cook was a cop named Fred. Tom's specialty was made by spearing a slice of bacon on a large fork, jamming a soft crab down on it, holding the two over a charcoal brazier until the bacon had melted over the crab, and then slapping both upon a slice of hot toast. This titbit had its points, I assure you, and I never think of it without deploring Tom's too early translation to bliss eternal. Fred devoted himself mainly to oyster flit-ters. The other cops rolled and snuffled in his masterpieces like cats in cat-nip, but I never could see much virtue in them. It was always my impres-sion, perhaps in error, that he fried them in curve grease borrowed from the street railways. He was an old-time Model T flat-foot, not much taller than a fire-plug, but as big around the middle as a load of hay. At the end of a busy afternoon he would be spattered from head to foot with blobs of flit-ter batter and wild grease.

It was the opinion of my father, as I have recorded, that all the Bal-timore beers were poisonous, but he nevertheless kept a supply of them in the house for visiting plumbers, tinners, cellar-inspectors, tax-assessors and so on, and for Class D social callers. I find by his bill file that he paid $1.20 for a case of twenty-four bottles. His own favorite malt liquor was Anheuser-Busch, but he also made occasional experiments with the other brands that were then beginning to find a national market: some of them to survive to this day, but the most perished under Prohibition. His same bill file shows that on December 27, 1883, he paid Courtney, Fairall & Company, then the favorite fancy grocers of Baltimore, $4 for a gallon of Monticello whis-key. It retails now for from $3 to $3.50 a *quart*. In those days it was always

196

straight, for the old-time Baltimoreans regarded blends with great suspicion, though many of the widely-advertised brands of Maryland rye were of that character. They drank straight whiskey straight, disdaining both diluents and chasers. I don't recall ever seeing my father drink a high-ball; the thing must have existed in his day, for he lived on to 1899, but he probably regarded its use as unmanly and ignoble. Before every meal, including breakfast, he ducked into the cupboard in the dining-room and poured out a substantial hooker of rye, and when he emerged he was always sucking in a great whiff of air to cool off his tonsils. He regarded this appetizer as necessary to his well-being. He said that it was the best medicine he had ever found for toning up his stomach.

How the stomachs of Baltimore survived at all in those days is a pathological mystery. The standard evening meal tended to be light, but the other two were terrific. The repertoire for breakfast, beside all the known varieties of pancake and porridge, included such things as ham and eggs, broiled mackerel, fried smelts, beef hash, pork chops, country sausage, and even—God help us all!—what would now be called Welsh rabbit. My father, save when we were in the country, usually came home for lunch, and on Saturdays, with no school, my brother Charlie and I sat in. Our favorite Winter lunch was typical of the time. Its main dishes were a huge platter of Norfolk spots or other pan-fish, and a Himalaya of corncakes. Along with this combination went succotash, buttered beets, baked potatoes, string beans, and other such hearty vegetables. When oranges and bananas were obtainable they followed for dessert—sliced, and with a heavy dressing of grated cocoanut. The calorie content of two or three helpings of such powerful aliments probably ran to 3000. We'd all be somewhat subdued afterward, and my father always stretched out on the dining-room lounge for a nap. In the evening he seldom had much appetite, and would usually complain that cooking was fast going downhill in Baltimore, in accord with the general decay of human society. Worse, he would warn Charlie and me against eating too much, and often he undertook to ration us. We beat this sanitary policing by laying in a sufficiency in the kitchen before sitting down to table. As a reserve against emergencies we kept a supply of ginger snaps, mushroom crackers, all-day suckers, dried apricots and solferino taffy in a cigar-box in our bedroom. In fear that it might spoil, or that mice might sneak up from the cellar to raid it, we devoured this stock at frequent intervals, and it had to be renewed.

197

City Reminiscences

The Baltimoreans of those days were complacent beyond the ordinary, and agreed with their envious visitors that life in their town was swell. I can't recall ever hearing anyone complain of the fact that there was a great epidemic of typhoid fever every Summer, and a wave of malaria every Autumn, and more than a scattering of smallpox, especially among the colored folk in the alleys, every Winter. Spring, indeed, was the only season free from serious pestilence, and in Spring the communal laying off possible, and boys would come from blocks around to measure and admire it. Whenever an insect of unfamiliar species showed up we tried to capture it, and if we succeeded we kept it alive in a pill-box or baking-powder can. Our favorite among pill-boxes was the one that held Wright's Indian Vegetable Pills (which my father swallowed every time he got into a low state), for it was made of thin sheets of wood veneer, and was thus more durable than the druggists' usual cardboard boxes.

Every public place in Baltimore was so furiously beset by bugs of all sorts that communal gatherings were impossible on hot nights. The very cops on the street corners spent a large part of their time slapping mosquitoes and catching flies. Our pony Frank had a fly-net, but it operated only when he was in motion; in his leisure he was as badly used as the cops. When arc-lights began to light the streets, along about 1885, they attracted so many beetles of gigantic size that their glare was actually obscured. These beetles at once acquired the name of electric-light bugs, and it was believed that the arc carbons produced them by a kind of spontaneous generation, and that their bite was as dangerous as that of a tarantula. But no Baltimorean would ever admit categorically that this Congo-like plague of flying things, taking one day with another, was really serious, or indeed a plague at all. Many a time I have seen my mother leap up from the dinner-table to engage the swarming flies with an improvised punkah, and heard her rejoice and give humble thanks simultaneously that Baltimore was not the sinkhole that Washington was.

These flies gave no concern to my brother Charlie and me; they seemed to be innocuous and even friendly compared to the chiggers, bumble-bees and hornets that occasionally beset us. Indeed, they were a source of pleasant recreation to us, for very often, on hot Summer evenings, we would retire to the kitchen, stretch out flat on our backs on the table, and pop away at them with sling-shots as they roosted in dense clumps upon the ceiling. Our favorite projectile was a square of lemon-peel, roasted by the hired girl.

198

Thus prepared, it was tough enough to shoot straight and kill certainly, but when it bounced back it did not hurt us. The hired girl, when she was in an amiable mood, prepared us enough of these missiles for an hour's brisk shooting, and in the morning she had the Red Cross job of sweeping the dead flies off the ceiling. Sometimes there were hundreds of them, lying dead in sticky windrows. When there were horse-flies from the back alley among them, which was not infrequently, they leaked red mammalian blood, which was an extra satisfaction to us. The stables that lined the far side of the alley were vast hatcheries of such flies, some of which reached a gigantic size. When we caught one we pulled off its wings and watched it try idiotically to escape on foot, or removed its legs and listened while it buzzed in a loud and futile manner. The theory taught in those days was that creatures below the warm-blooded level had no feelings whatever, and in fact rather enjoyed being mutilated. Thus it was an innocent and instructive matter to cut a worm into two halves, and watch them wriggle off in opposite directions. Once my brother and I caught a turtle, chopped off its head, and were amazed to see it march away headless. That experience, in truth, was so astonishing as to be alarming, and we never monkeyed with turtles thereafter. But we got a good deal of pleasure, first and last, out of chasing and butchering toads, though we were always careful to avoid taking them in our hands, for the juice of their kidneys was supposed to cause warts.

At the first smell of hot weather there was a tremendous revolution in Hollins street. All the Brussels carpets in the house were jimmied up and replaced by sleazy Chinese matting, all the haircloth furniture was covered with linen covers, and every picture, mirror, gas bracket and Rogers group was draped in fly netting. The carpets were wheelbarrowed out to Steuart's hill by professional carpet beaters of the African race, and there flogged and flayed until the heaviest lick yielded no more dust. Before the mattings could be laid all the floors had to be scrubbed, and every picture and mirror had to be taken down and polished. Also, the lace curtains had to come down, and the ivory-colored Holland shades that hung in Winter had to be changed to blue ones, to filter out the Summer sun. The lace curtains were always laundered before being put away—a formidable operation involving stretching them on huge frameworks set up on trestles in the backyard. All this uproar was repeated in reverse at the ides of September. The mattings came up, the carpets went down, the furniture was stripped of its covers, the pictures, mirrors and gas brackets lost their netting, and the blue Holland shades were displaced by the ivory ones. It always turned out, of course, that the flies of Summer had got through the nettings with ease, and left every picture peppered with their calling cards. The large pier mirror between the two windows of the parlor usually got a double dose, and it took the hired girl half a day to renovate it, climbing up and down a ladder in the clumsy manner of a policeman getting over a fence, and dropping soap, washrags, hairpins and other gear on the floor.

The legend seems to prevail that there were no sewers in Baltimore until after the World War, but that is something of an exaggeration. Our House in Hollins street was connected with a private sewer down the alley in the rear as early as I have any recollection of it, and so were many other houses, especially in the newer parts of the town. But I should add that we also had a powder room in the backyard for the accommodation of laundresses, whitewashers and other visiting members of the domestic faculty, and that there was a shallow sink under it that inspired my brother and me with considerable dread. Every now and then some child in West Baltimore fell into such a sink, and had to be hauled out, besmeared and howling, by the cops. The one in our yard was pumped out and fumigated every Spring by a gang of colored men who arrived on a wagon that was called an O.E.A.—*i.e.*, odorless excavating apparatus. They discharged this social-minded duty with great fervor and dispatch, and achieved non-odoriferousness, in the innocent Aframerican way, by burning buckets of rosin and tar. The whole neighborhood choked on the black, greasy, pungent smoke for hours afterward. It was thought to be an effective preventive of cholera, smallpox and tuberculosis.

All the sewers of Baltimore, whether private or public, emptied into the Back Basin in those days, just as all those of Manhattan empty into the North and East rivers to this day. But I should add that there was a difference, for the North and East rivers have swift tidal currents, whereas the Back Basin, distant 170 miles from the Chesapeake capes, had only the most lethargic. As a result it began to acquire a powerful aroma every Spring, and by August smelled like a billion polecats. This stench radiated all over downtown Baltimore, though in Hollins street we hardly ever detected it. Perhaps that was due to the fact that West Baltimore had rival perfumes of its own—for example, the emanation from the Wilkins hair factory in the

Frederick road, a mile or so from Union Square. When a breeze from the southwest, bouncing its way over the Wilkins factory, reached Hollins street the effect was almost that of poison gas. It happened only seldom, but when it happened it was surely memorable. The householders of the vicinage always swarmed down to the City Hall the next day and raised blue hell, but they never got anything save promises. In fact, it was not until the Wilkinses went into the red and shut down their factory that the abomination abated—and its place was then taken, for an unhappy year or two, by the degenerate cosmic rays projected from a glue factory lying in the same general direction. No one, so far as I know, ever argued that these mephitic blasts were salubrious, but it is a sober fact that town opinion held that the bouquet of the Back Basin was. In proof thereof it was pointed out that the clerks who sweated all Summer in the little coops of offices along the Light street and Pratt street wharves were so remarkably long-lived that many of them appeared to be at least 100 years old, and that the colored stevedores who loaded and unloaded the Bay packets were the strongest, toughest, drunkest and most thieving in the whole port.

The Baltimore of the eighties was a noisy town, for the impact of iron wagon tires on hard cobblestone was almost like that of a hammer on an anvil. To be sure, there was a dirt road down the middle of every street, kept in repair by the accumulated sweepings of the sidewalks, but this cushioned track was patronized only by hay-wagons from the country and like occasional traffic: milk-men, grocery deliverymen and other such regulars kept to the areas where the cobbles were naked, and so made a fearful clatter. In every way, in fact, city life was much noiser then than it is now. Children at play were not incarcerated in playgrounds and policed by hired ma'ms, but roved the open streets, and most of their games involved singing or yelling. At Christmas time they began to blow horns at least a week before the great day, and kept it up until all the horns were disabled, and in Summer they began celebrating the Fourth far back in June and were still exploding fire-crackers at the end of July. Nearly every house had a dog in it, and nearly all the dogs barked more or less continuously from 4 a.m. until after midnight. It was still lawful to keep chickens in backyards, and many householders did so. All within ear range of Hollins street appeared to divide them as to sex in the proportion of a hundred crowing roosters to one clucking hen. My grandfather Mencken once laid in a coop of Guineas, unquestionably the noisiest species of *Aves* known to science. But his wife, my step-grandmother, had got in a colored clergyman to steal them before the neighbors arrived with the police.

In retired by-streets grass grew between the cobblestones to almost incredible heights, and it was not uncommon for colored rag-and-bone men to pasture their undernourished horses on it. On the steep hill making eastward from the Washington Monument, in the very heart of Baltimore, some comedian once sowed wheat, and it kept on coming up for years thereafter. Every Spring the Baltimore newspapers would report on the prospects of the crop, and visitors to the city were taken to see it. Most Baltimoreans of that era, in fact, took a fierce, defiant pride in the bucolic aspects of their city. They would boast that it was the only great seaport on earth in which dandelions grew in the streets in Spring. They believed that all such vegetation was healthful, and kept down chills and fever. I myself once had proof that the excess of litter in the streets was not without its value to mankind. I was riding the pony Frank when a wild thought suddenly seized him, and he bucked me out of the saddle in the best manner of a Buffalo Bill bronco. Unfortunately, my left foot was stuck in the stirrup, and so I was dragged behind him as he galloped off. He had gone at least a block before a couple of colored boys stopped him. If the cobblestones of Stricker street had been bare I'd not be with you today. As it was, I got no worse damage than a series of harsh scourings running from my neck to my heels. The colored boys took me to Reveille's livery-stable, and stopped the bloodshed with large gobs of spider web. It was the hemostatic of choice in Baltimore when I was young. If, perchance, it spread a little tetanus, then the Baltimoreans blamed the mercies of God.

FROM *To Brooklyn with Love*

GERALD GREEN

As Abrams and his children turned the corner and entered Longview Avenue, the street lights went on. The sudden discharge of light seemed to him overdramatic, a display he had staged, a trick prearranged with Consolidated Edison. Abrams had read somewhere that you could pay the City of Paris to light the Eiffel Tower or the Arc de Triomphe. Why not pay the Borough President of Brooklyn to illuminate his boyhood home?

The three of them—a small, neat man in his thirties, a girl of seven, a boy of five—walked cautiously down the cold, darkening street. Abrams appeared uncomfortable. He was fussily dressed in the manner of certain little men, affecting a pinkish overcoat of military cut (it suggested prior servitude as an envious enlisted man), clay-colored trousers and gleaming cordovan shoes.

Around them rose silvery lamp posts, flooding sidewalks and gutter with fluorescent brilliance, a presumed deterrent to muggers, thieves, the wicked poor.

"I knew something was wrong," he said. "Public School 133 is still there, and the old schoolyard, and the synagogue around the corner, but the trees are gone."

"Y'mean you had trees—in this place?" asked his daughter.

"A row on either side. Maples, catalpas, oaks. My father's tree was the biggest. About halfway down. It was a Lombardy poplar—one of the tallest trees in Brownsville. But it's gone."

"It's crummy here," she said.

"Yes, I guess it isn't much to look at now." He longed to tell them about the schoolyard where they had played salugi, punchball, stickball, boxball, Chinese handball, stoopball, association, but he could not. They were suburban children, reared in station wagons.

"My goodness, there's the old house." He tried to sound proud of his discovery. But he was a poor actor. His voice wavered.

"It's little," his son said.

"And dirty," added his daughter. "How come you could live there?"

Explanations would not help. They lived on a woodland hill and played with the sons of market research directors from North Dakota, the daughters of media men from Georgia.

In front of the yellow brick house—two-storied, narrow, crowned with a chipped cornice—a lavender Pontiac was parked. A Negro in a pale blue windbreaker was peering into its opened jaws, groping at its entrails with a wrench. It was parked adjacent to where the tree had stood. When had it been chopped down? A dignified giant, its upper branches heavy with summer leafage had brushed the upstairs window screens. In the spring it bore red-brown catkins. It had offended no one except some City Hall flunky who claimed its roots were strangling a watermain. He remembered a violent argument between his father and the public servant. His father had probably lost the argument. He usually did.

Through layers of filth, he could see the flaking number on the door—1422. On the brick wall were visible four dark holes where the old man's brass sign had been bolted. Privet bushes had long vanished from the tiny front yard; the wrought-iron rails were rusted.

"There's a kid lookin' at us," Abrams' son said apprehensively.

A shade in what had been his father's waiting room lifted. A brown face studied them. It was the window that had displayed the small illuminated sign:

SOLOMON ABRAMS, M.D.

There are broken toys now, he thought, in the rooms where my father listened to thousands of pulses and hearts, read innumerable thermometers, EKG's, X-rays, laboratory reports. No one could read a pulse the way his father did: head lowered, eyes intent, lips slightly parted. His fingers on your wrist had a soft touch. The touch assured you you would recover; you could feel the power of the healer.

In those rooms the old man had counted out the hours of his life in unpaid bills and unfilled hopes. Desks opened and slammed shut in Abrams' mind. He heard distantly the probing buzz of the ancient X-ray, heard again his father's hard tread—odd in a small man, but his father was all muscle— and the muffled voice coming through the closed office door: Not a goddamn thing in the world wrong with you, go home and act like a mensch.

"Now there's a lady," his son said.

A stout Negro woman stood behind the child. Arms folded, she stared at the three interlopers on the sidewalk. Was her gaze unfriendly? Abrams envisioned peeling walls, buckling floors, an incessant television set humming, the woman sipping beer from cans. Once his mother had sat there placidly reading Gissing and Meredith and Hardy, while from an RCA Victrola a strained Caruso sang La Juive.

"We gonna go in to see your room, like you promised?" asked his daughter.

Abrams frowned. "I don't think so. I don't want to bother those people."

There was a July day in 1934. His father surprised him with a new softball, a genuine Spalding "indoor," whiter than an angel's robe, intoxicating with its odor of bleached polished cowhide. . . .

"Lookin' for somebody?" the owner of the lavender car asked.

"Ah, no. I used to know some people here." Abrams cleared his throat. "Fellow named Pennington. You ever know a Lee Roy Pennington?"

"Nope. I new here."

Where was Lee Roy, Lee Roy of the great brown football head and bandy legs? Lee Roy: nemesis, shadow, persecutor.

They walked slowly toward the corner. As they approached the intersection Abrams imagined he saw his father coming toward them: overcoat flapping open even in December, ruined fedora pushed back on his head, carrying the scuffed black satchel and a white bakery box, a peace offering for his wife. Something to atone for the imminent tirade about the lousy deadbeat who just done him out of a two-dollar fee. But of course it was not his father. It was only a Negro workman with a lunchbox.

"Anyway the corner grocery's still in business," he told his unheeding children. But the sign read ALIMENTACION. "I guess Benny sold it. That man had the greatest pot cheese in the world."

Through dark and silent streets they trudged toward the subway. It had been a short visit, much shorter than he had planned.

FROM *Shadow and Act*

RALPH ELLISON

Negro Oklahoma City was starkly lacking in writers. In fact, there was only Roscoe Dungee, the editor of the local Negro newspaper and a very fine editorialist in that valuable tradition of personal journalism which is now rapidly disappearing; a writer who in his emphasis upon the possibilities for justice offered by the Constitution anticipated the anti-segregation struggle by decades. There were also a few reporters who drifted in and out, but these were about all. On the level of *conscious* culture the Negro community was biased in the direction of music.

These were the middle and late twenties, remember, and the state was still a new frontier state. The capital city was one of the great centers for southwestern jazz, along with Dallas and Kansas City. Orchestras which were to become famous within a few years were constantly coming and going. As were the blues singers, Ma Rainey and Ida Cox, and the old bands like that of King Oliver. But best of all, thanks to Mrs. Zelia N. Breaux, there was an active and enthusiastic school music program through which any child who had the interest and the talent could learn to play an instrument and take part in the band, the orchestra, the brass quartet. And there was a yearly operetta and a chorus and a glee club. Harmony was taught for four years and the music appreciation program was imperative. European folk dances were taught throughout the Negro school system, and we were also taught complicated patterns of military drill.

I tell you this to point out that although there were no incentives to write, there was ample opportunity to receive an artistic discipline. Indeed, once one picked up an instrument it was difficult to escape. If you chafed at the many rehearsals of the school band or orchestra and were drawn to the many small jazz groups, you were likely to discover that the jazzmen were apt to rehearse far more than the school band; it was only that they seemed to enjoy themselves better and to possess a freedom of imagination which we were denied at school. And once one learned that the wild, transcendent moments which occurred at dances or "battles of music," moments in which memorable improvisations were ignited, depended upon a dedication to a discipline which was observed even when rehearsals had to take place in the crowded quarters of Halley Richardson's shoeshine parlor. It was not the place which counted, although a large hall with good acoustics was preferred, but what one did to perfect one's performance.

If this talk of musical discipline gives the impression that there were no forces working to nourish one who would one day blunder, after many a twist and turn, into writing, I am misleading you. And here I might give you a longish lecture on the Ironies and Uses of Segregation. When I was a small child there was no library for Negroes in our city, and not until a Negro minister invaded the main library did we get one. For it was discovered that there was no law, only custom, which held that we could not use these public facilities. The results were the quick renting of two large rooms in a Negro office building (the recent site of a pool hall), the hiring of a young Negro librarian, the installation of shelves and a hurried stocking of the walls with any and every book possible. It was, in those first days, something of a literary chaos.

But how fortunate for a boy who loved to read! I started with the fairy tales and quickly went through the junior fiction; then through the Westerns and the detective novels, and very soon I was reading the classics—only I didn't know it. There were also the Haldeman Julius Blue Books, which seem to have floated on the air down from Girard, Kansas; the syndicated columns of O. O. McIntyre, and the copies of *Vanity Fair* and the *Literary Digest* which my mother brought home from work—how could I ever join uncritically in the heavy-handed attacks on the so-called Big Media which have become so common today?

There were also the pulp magazines and, more important, that other library which I visited when I went to help my adopted grandfather, J. D. Randolph (my parents had been living in his big rooming house when I was born), at his work as custodian of the law library of the Oklahoma State Capitol. Mr. Randolph had been one of the first teachers in what became Oklahoma City; and he'd also been one of the leaders of a group who walked from Gallatin, Tennessee, to the Oklahoma Territory. He was a tall man, as brown as smoked leather, who looked like the Indians with whom he'd herded horses in the early days.

And while his status was merely the custodian of the law library, I was to see the white legislators come down on many occasions to question him on points of law, and often I was to hear him answer without recourse to the uniform rows of books on the shelves. This was a thing to marvel at in itself, and the white lawmakers did so, but even more marvellous, ironic, intriguing, haunting—call it what you will—is the fact that the Negro who knew the answers was named after Jefferson Davis. What Tennessee lost, Oklahoma was to gain, and after gaining it (a gift of courage, intelligence, fortitude and grace), used it only in concealment and, one hopes, with embarrassment . . .

In the loosely structured community of that time, knowledge, news of other ways of living, ancient wisdom, the latest literary fads, hate literature—for years I kept a card warning Negroes away from the polls, which had been dropped by the thousands from a plane which circled over the Negro community—information of all kinds, found its level, catch-as-catch can, in the minds of those who were receptive to it. Not that there was no conscious structuring—I read my first Shaw and Maupassant, my first Harvard Classics in the home of a friend whose parents were products of that stream of New England education which had been brought to Negroes by the young and enthusiastic white teachers who staffed the schools set up for the freedmen after the Civil War. These parents were both teachers and there were others like them in our town.

But the places where a rich oral literature was truly functional were the churches, the schoolyards, the barbershops, the cotton-picking camps; places where folklore and gossip thrived. The drug store where I worked was such a place, where on days of bad weather the older men would sit with their pipes and tell tall tales, hunting yarns and homely versions of the classics. It was here that I heard stories of searching for buried treasure and of headless horsemen, which I was told were my own father's versions told long before. There were even recitals of popular verse, "The Shooting of Dan McGrew," and, along with these, stories of Jesse James, of Negro outlaws and black United States marshals, of slaves who became the chiefs of Indian tribes and of the exploits of Negro cowboys. There was both truth and fantasy in this, intermingled in the mysterious fashion of literature.

Writers, in their formative period, absorb into their consciousness much that has no special value until much later, and often much which is of no special value even then—perhaps, beyond the fact that it throbs with affect and mystery and in it "time and pain and royalty in the blood" are suspended in imagery. So, long before I thought of writing, I was claimed by weather, by speech rhythms, by Negro voices and their different idioms, by husky male voices and by the high shrill singing voices of certain Negro women, by music; by tight spaces and by wide spaces in which the eyes could wander; by death, by newly born babies, by manners of various kinds, company manners and street manners; the manners of white society and those of our own high society; and by interracial manners; by street fights, circuses and minstrel shows; by vaudeville and moving pictures, by prize fights and foot races, baseball games and football matches. By spring floods and blizzards, catalpa worms and jack rabbits; honeysuckle and snapdragons (which smelled like old cigar butts); by sunflowers and hollyhocks, raw sugar cane and baked yams; pigs' feet, chili and blue haw ice cream. By parades, public dances and jam sessions, Easter sunrise ceremonies and large funerals. By contests between fire-and-brimstone preachers and by presiding elders who got "laughing-happy" when moved by the spirit of God.

I was impressed by the expert players of the "dozens" and certain notorious bootleggers of corn whiskey. By jazz musicians and fortunetellers and by men who did anything well; by strange sicknesses and by interesting brick or razor scars; by expert cursing vocabularies as well as by exalted praying and terrifying shouting, and by transcendent playing or singing of the blues. I was fascinated by old ladies, those who had seen slavery and those who were defiant of white folk and black alike; by the enticing walks of prostitutes and by the limping walks affected by Negro hustlers, especially those who wore Stetson hats, expensive shoes with well-starched overalls, usually with a diamond stickpin (when not in hock) in their tieless collars as their gambling uniforms.

And there were the blind men who preached on corners, and the blind men who sang the blues to the accompaniment of washboard and guitar, and the white junkmen who sang mountain music and the famous hucksters of fruit and vegetables.

And there was the Indian-Negro confusion. There were Negroes who were part Indian and who lived on reservations, and Indians who had children who lived in towns as Negroes, and Negroes who were Indians and traveled back and forth between the groups with no trouble. And Indians who were as wild as wild Negroes and others who were as solid and steady as bankers. There were the teachers, too, inspiring teachers and villainous teachers who chased after the girl students, and certain female teachers who one wished would chase after young male students. And a handsome old principal of military bearing who had been blemished by his classmates at West Point when they discovered on the eve of graduation that he was a Negro. There were certain Jews, Mexicans, Chinese cooks, a German orchestra conductor and an English grocer who owned a Franklin touring car. And certain Negro mechanics—"Cadillac Slim," "Sticks" Walker, Buddy Bunn and Oscar Pitman—who had so assimilated the automobile that they seemed to be behind a steering wheel even as they walked the streets or danced with girls. And there were the whites who despised us and the others who shared our hardships and our joys.

There is much more, but this is sufficient to indicate some of what was present even in a segregated community to form the background of my work, my sense of life.

Willis Avenue

MARK HELPRIN

If, when I am drunk or sentimental or prodded by a stupid friend, I think back to the women I have really loved, most of them are covered and hidden by wishes and disappointment. But there is one of whom my memory is clear, and it is strange—she was so unimportant.

She was named Johanna, and I knew her for a summer when I worked in a typewriter-ribbon factory in the Bronx. It was very simple. She sat across from me on the production line all day long, and when either of us lifted our eyes we saw one another. Our job was to put the spools of ribbon in boxes—a very boring job—a job which left our hands automatic, and faces and eyes free so that we spent many days looking and talking. She was not such an attractive girl, and she knew it. These days I don't like beautiful girls so much, any more. It makes them less able to cry and be sad, and I won't have a girl who cannot cry and be sad.

Now Johanna had a big wide face, and big heavy limbs, although she was not fat by any means, just big. She was in fact bigger than me but she thought like a very delicate woman, and so she moved as if she were little. Although she was not in the least self-conscious about her body (I often saw her breasts as she leaned over to get more boxes and her open shirt came more open), she thought that perhaps she should be, and I could always tell that she was thinking to herself, I have to be more delicate about myself. But she could not be, and the exposure she suffered made her no less attractive to me.

I confess that at first this was not so. She was big and my image of women had been so ideal; I imagined them as princesses and perfectly clean. I thought that perhaps I might sleep with her, understanding that it would not lead to anything. Then I took pity on her for her clumsiness and the way she was impressed by me. I am externally slick, rather handsome, people say. She thought I was beyond her reach; I did too. I took her to lunch, and she blushed under the fan in the little restaurant. The heat of

Willis Avenue Bridge, Ben Shahn

that summer was so intense that it made us both sweat in the shade. She was taken by me and I was therefore not very interested in her. After all she was not very pretty. And every day we sat for eight hours sweating, our legs sometimes touching, across from one another under the inky breeze of the big fan. She looked down so much not because she needed to see to put the spool into the box, but because she was shy, and think, I had told her everything, wanting to make her a sister. She was very unhappy when I told her of the women I thought about that summer. When I first mentioned Nina she looked so sad that I stopped, but later I went on, and I would speak to her of my girls, and I think she cried in the women's dressing room. The other women avoided her and thought she was strange.

We had lunch together every day. All she did was keep still, and laugh with me, and smile when I spoke without thinking. She went home to her mother each afternoon; she spoke well, but she was just not pretty.

In the South Bronx one feels as though one is in the hotter part of Naples or the dull part of the Great Plains. Dirt falls from the air, and the heat, the heat, makes everything, even the iron, wet. And the heat changes people. The people I don't like complain about the heat. Johanna, whom I saw every hour of every day, sitting next to a half-painted column in the skylight light of a hot dirty workroom, did not complain about the heat, but wiped her forehead with her hand now and then and seemed to me very much like myself. She seemed to be me when I was not worried about things, when I was quiet and watching, when I had fallen and could learn and feel, in the heat, the rising heat of that time. Johanna, whitefaced and green-eyed, darting-eyed, hands full of ink, wiping her brow with her wrist and getting ink on her wide face anyway. Johanna in the South Bronx in a hot summer when I was stronger and when I thought I would succeed, sat across from me each day. And then I left, and she had to sit there in the same place, and when January came around she was there, accepting whoever sat across from her. I don't think I would have her now, but if she could know that I loved her then more than anything, that I would have married her, loved her, if only I had not been so young, if only I had known myself. Johanna. When she wiped her brow with her wrist she got ink on her face anyway, and she was always smiling.

San Francisco Looks West

JOHN DOS PASSOS

If you happen to be endowed with topographical curiosity the hills of San Francisco fill you with an irresistible desire to walk to the top of each one of them. Whoever laid the town out took the conventional checkerboard pattern of streets and without the slightest regard for the laws of gravity planked it down blind on an irregular peninsula that was a confusion of steep slopes and sandhills. The result is exhilarating. Wherever you step out on the street there's a hilltop in one direction or the other. From the top of each hill you get a view and the sight of more hills to the right and left and ahead that offer the prospect of still broader views. The process goes on indefinitely. You can't help making your way painfully to the top of each hill just to see what you can see. I kept thinking of what an old French seaman said to me once, describing with some disgust the behavior of passengers on a steamboat: *"Le passager c'est comme le perroquet, ça grimpe toujours."*

This particular morning was a windy morning, half sun and blue sky and half pearly tatters of fog blowing in from the Pacific. Before day it had been raining. I had started out from a steamy little lunchroom where I had eaten a magnificent breakfast of eighteen tiny wheat cakes flanked by broiled bacon and washed down by fresh-made coffee. They still know how to cook in old San Paco's town. In my hand was a list of telephone numbers to call and of men to go to see in their offices. It was nine o'clock, just the time to get down to work. Instead of turning down in the direction of offices and the business part of town, I found I had turned the other way and was resolutely walking up the nearest hill.

This one is Nob Hill, I know that. I remember it years ago when there were still gardens on it and big broken-paned mansions of brown stone, and even, if I remember right, a few wind-bleached frame houses with turrets and scalelike shingles imitating stone and scrollsaw woodwork

214

round the porches. Now it's all hotels and apartment houses, but their massive banality is made up for by the freakishness of the terrain. At the top, in front of the last of the old General-Grant-style houses, I stop a second to get my breath and to mop the sweat off my eyebrows.

Ahead of me the hill rises higher and breaks into a bit of blue sky. Sun shines on a block of white houses at the top. Shiny as a toy fresh from a Christmas tree, a little cable car is crawling up it. Back of me under an indigo blur of mist are shadowed roofs and streets and tall buildings with wisps of fog about them, and beyond, fading off into the foggy sky, stretches the long horizontal of the Bay Bridge.

Better go back now and start about my business. The trouble is that down the hill to the right I've caught sight of accented green roofs and curved gables painted jade green and vermilion. That must be Chinatown. Of course the thing to do is take a turn through Chinatown on the way down toward the business district. I find myself walking along a narrow street in a jungle of Chinese lettering, interpreted here and there by signs announcing Chop Suey, Noodles, Genuine Chinese Store. There are ranks of curio stores, and I find myself studying windows full of Oriental goods with as much sober care as a small boy studying the window of a candy store. The street tempts you along. Beyond the curio shops there are drug stores, groceries giving out an old drenched smell like tea and camphor and lychee nuts, vegetable stores, shops of herb merchants that contain very much the same stock of goods as those Marco Polo saw with such wonder on his travels. In another window there are modern posters: raspberry-and-spinach-tinted plum-cheeked pin-up girls and stern lithographs of the Generalissimo; a few yellowing enlargements of photographs of eager-looking young broad-faced men in cadets' uniforms. The gilt lettering amuses the eye. The decorative scroll-work of dragons and lotus flowers leads you along. You forget the time wondering how to size up the smooth Chinese faces. At the end of the street I discover that an hour has passed and that I have been walking the wrong way all the time.

I come out into a broad oblique avenue full of streetcars and traffic. Suddenly the Chop Suey signs are gone and now everything is Spaghetti, Pizza, Ravioli, Bella Napoli, Grotta Azzura, blooming in painted signs along the housefronts. There are Italian bakeries and pastry shops breathing out almond paste and anise. In small bars men sit talking noisily as they drink black coffee out of glasses. Restaurants smell of olive oil and spilled wine. I

215

cross the street and at the top of another hill catch a glimpse of a white tower shaped like a lighthouse. That must be Signal Hill.

As I walk up through a shabby light-gray cheerful quarter where all the doorbells have Italian and Spanish names, and where the air out of doorways smells of garlic and floor polish and there begin to be pots of geraniums on the tops of scaly walls that conceal small gardens, or carnations now and then on a window sill, it suddenly feels like the quiet streets back of Montmartre or, so many years ago, Marseilles. I reach the top of Signal Hill just in time to take refuge in the tower from a spat of driving rain.

From the tower I look down into a swirl of mist, shot with lights and shadows like the inside of a shell, that pours in from the ocean. Now and then the hurrying mist tears apart long enough to let me see wharves crowded with masts and derricks or an expanse of bright ruffled water—and once, rank on rank of sullen-looking gray freighters at anchor. Two young men in khaki are standing beside me, squinting to see through the rain-spattered glass.

"Boy, it won't be long now," says one.

"You mean before we are stuck down in the hold of one of those things."

"You said it." They notice that I am listening. They exchange reproachful looks and their mouths shut up tight and they move away.

When I leave the tower the sun is beginning to burn through dazzling whiteness. There is blue in the puddles on the paved parking place on top of the hill. It has become clear that this isn't any day to call up telephone numbers or to pester people in their offices. It is a day to walk round the town. And the first thing to do is to get a look out through the Golden Gate.

I plunged down the hill in the direction of the harbor, lost my bearings in a warehouse section, found myself beside a little stagnant inner harbor packed with small motor fishing boats painted up Italian style; and then took a freshly painted cable car to the top of another hill. I got off and set out along a street of frame houses that seemed to be leading me in the direction of the ocean. The houses were all alike, painted cream color, with jutting bay windows and odd little columns on each side of the front door. I walked on and on through the pleasant mild sunlight, expecting to see the ocean from the top of each rise.

Eventually the sight of a hill steeper than the rest, topped with green shrubbery and tall gray pillars of blooming eucalyptus trees, made me change my course. From up there you must be able to see the ocean and the Golden Gate and everything. I got up to the top, puffing after a stiff climb. The hilltop was a park. All the city and the Bay clear to Oakland and the bridges and the hills opened out in every direction at my feet. But not the Golden Gate, though I could see the high straw-colored hills beyond. And toward the ocean there was only a bright haze.

An old Mexican was raking fallen eucalyptus leaves and scaled-off bark into a bonfire that trailed stinging sharp tonic-flavored smoke across the path. At the very summit of the path, cut off from the wind by a hedge of shiny-leaved privet, four whiskered old men were seated round a green board table playing cribbage. It was quiet and sunny up there. The billowing blue smoke cut them off from the city. There is something very special about the smell of burning eucalyptus leaves. In the light fragrant air of the late morning the old men sat in relaxed attitudes of passionless calm. They held their cards with the detachment of gods on Olympus. They weren't smoking. They weren't talking. No one was in any hurry to get along with the game. Their pleasure wasn't in the sun or the air or immense view. Maybe it was just in being alive, in the gentle ambrosial coursing of the blood through their veins, in the faint pumping of the heart. That may have been what the Greeks meant when they wrote about the shadowless painless pleasures of the spirits in the Elysian Fields.

I had stopped in my tracks to look at the four old men, and they all four looked up at me and craned their necks at the same moment. They showed such startled surprise at seeing me standing in the path that I might have been a spook from another world. Maybe I was. I hurried off down into the city again.

Eventually I had to ask my way to the ocean. Somebody said I ought to take a car to the Cliff House. Somewhere in the back of my memory there was connected with that name a park on a cliff, full of funny beer-garden statuary under pines—and the disappointment as a child of not being able to spot a sea lion among the spuming rocks off the headland. The streetcar, a full-sized normal streetcar, rattled along through a suburban section of low stucco houses and across wide boulevards planted with palms, described an S through pines down a steep slope, and finally came to rest in a decrepit barn beside a lunch counter. I stepped out onto a road that curved down the steep slope to the old square white restaurant, and farther round the headland to the broad gray beach, where slow rollers very far apart broke

217

and growled and slithered inland in a swirl of gray water and were sucked back in spume.

I went out and leaned over the parapet of the observation platform. The blue-gray Pacific was clear far out to where a fog bank smudged the horizon. Coming round from the Golden Gate—which I still couldn't catch sight of—a gray patrol boat showed white teeth as it chewed its way seaward into the long swells. Still no black heads of sea lions bobbing around Seal Rocks. . . . A few gulls circled screaming over the platform.

Beside me three very black G.I.'s stood in a huddle staring out at the ocean. Farther along two sailors had their backs turned to the view and were watching with envious looks a boy and girl in sweaters and slacks who looked like high-school kids, and were giggling and horsing and pushing each other around. A sergeant of Marines, very snappy in his greens, strutted out of the building that houses the slot machines; a girl with a blue handkerchief tied round her yellow head was holding onto his arm with both hands. For a couple of minutes the two of them stared hard out to sea as if their eyes could pierce the fog bank. Then they hurried back indoors to the slot machines.

Leaning on the parapet over the hushed and heaving expanse of misted indigo that marks for most Americans the beginning of the Pacific Ocean, I wondered what these two had been thinking. I suppose there's the same question in all our minds when we look westward over the Pacific. Beyond the immense bulge of the world, is the ocean ours or is it theirs? When we've made it ours, what will we want to do with it? The young men in uniform know they are going to have the answer to that question printed on their hides. No wonder they keep their lips tight pressed when they stare out toward the western horizon.

In the restaurant on the level above, the tables are all full but the eaters are very quiet. There are many family parties. Old people and middleaged people brooding around a young man or woman in uniform.

At the table next to mine there's a white-haired man and woman and a stoutish lady with pixie frames on her glasses who's evidently a doting female relative and seems to be somewhat in the way. They don't take their eyes off a first lieutenant in khaki with a close-cropped black bullet head and ruddy cheeks who looks barely old enough to be in high school. The minute you see them you know that the old people have come to say good-by.

218

Maybe it's their last meal together. They are all trying to be very self-possessed. The father is always starting to tell little jokes and neglecting to finish them. They keep forgetting where the salt cellar is on the table. The mother handles the plate of rolls when she passes it round as if it were immensely breakable. They fork the food slowly into their mouths. None of them knows what he is eating. All their motions are very careful and precise as if they feared the slightest false move would break the fragile bonds that are holding the day together for them. The slightest fumble, and these last few hours will be split and lost.

It's very different at the table between mine and the window. There a slender young Air Force major, with dark curly hair already thinning on either side of a high forehead, is taking out a strikingly pretty dark-haired girl. She might be his sister. There's something slightly similar about the way the two of them are built, about the way the nostrils are set in their noses. Or she might be his girl or his wife or just the right chance acquaintance. They have had cocktails and oysters. The waiter is bringing them a bottle in a bucket of ice. They have ordered abalone steaks. They aren't saying much but their eyes are shining and they keep looking at each other and at the wine glasses and at the food on their plates and at the fog bank creeping toward them across the black ocean as if they'd never seen anything in the least like these things before. They think they are alone in the restaurant. It's not so much that they are smiling at each other as that smiles are bubbling up all around them. Time, you can see, stands still for them.

Better get going. I had begun to feel lonely. The rest of my lunch didn't have much flavor to it. Coming out of the restaurant, the fog pressed clammy against my face. I turned up my coat collar and went shuffling up the hill toward the streetcar line. My coat felt suddenly out at the elbows. Everything about me felt shabby and frayed. Maybe it is that there are many things a civilian in wartime feels out of.

Resurrection of a Life

WILLIAM SAROYAN

Everything begins with inhale and exhale, and never ends, moment after moment, yourself inhaling, and exhaling, seeing, hearing, smelling, touching, tasting, moving, sleeping, waking, day after day and year after year, until it is now, this moment, the moment of *your* being, the last moment, which is saddest and most glorious. It is because we remember, and I remember having lived among dead moments, now deathless because of my remembrance, among people now dead, having been a part of the flux which is now only a remembrance, of myself and this earth, a street I was crossing and the people I saw walking in the opposite direction, automobiles going away from me. Saxons, Dorts, Maxwells, and the streetcars and trains, the horses and wagons, and myself, a small boy, crossing a street, alive somehow, going somewhere.

First he sold newspapers. It was because he wanted to do something, standing in the city, shouting about what was happening in the world. He used to shout so loud, and he used to need to shout so much, that he would forget he was supposed to be selling papers; he would get the idea that he was only supposd to shout, to make people understand what was going on. He used to go through the city like an alley cat, prowling all over the place, into saloons, upstairs into whore houses, into gambling joints, to see: their faces, the faces of those who were alive with him on the earth, and the expressions of their faces, and their forms, the faces of old whores, and the way they talked, and the smell of all the ugly places, and the drabness of all the old and rotting buildings, all of it, of his time and his life, a part of him. He prowled through the city, seeing and smelling, talking, shouting about the big news, inhaling and exhaling, blood moving to the rhythm of the sea, coming and going, to the shore of self and back again to selflessness, inhale and newness, exhale and new death, and the boy in the city, walking through it like an alley cat, shouting headlines.

The city was ugly, but his being there was splendid and not an ugliness.

220

His hands would be black with the filth of the city and his face would be black with it, but it was splendid to be alive and walking, of the events of the earth, from day to day, new headlines every day, new things happening.

In the summer it would be very hot and his body would thirst for the sweet fluids of melons, and he would long for the shade of thick leaves and the coolness of a quiet stream, but always he would be in the city, shouting. It was his place and he was the guy, and he wanted the city to be the way it was, if that was the way. He would figure it out somehow. He used to stare at rich people sitting at tables in hightone restaurants eating dishes of ice cream, electric fans making breezes for them, and he used to watch them ignoring the city, not going out to it and being of it, and it used to make him mad. Pigs, he used to say, having everything you want, having everything. What do you know of this place? What do you know of me, seeing this place with a clean eye, any of you? And he used to go, in the summer, to the Crystal Bar, and there he would study the fat man who slept in a chair all summer, a mountain of somebody, a man with a face and substance that lived, who slept all day every summer day, dreaming what? This fat man, three hundred pounds? What did he dream, sitting in the saloon, in the corner, not playing poker or pinochle like the other men, only sleeping and sometimes brushing the flies from his fat face? What was there for him to dream, anyway, with a body like that, and what was there hidden beneath the fat of that body, what grace or gracelessness? He used to go into the saloon and spit on the floor as the men did and watch the fat man sleeping, trying to figure it out. Him alive, too? he used to ask. That great big sleeping thing alive? Like myself?

In the winter he wouldn't see the fat man. It would be only in the summer. The fat man was like the hot sun, very near everything, of everything, sleeping, flies on his big nose. In the winter it would be cold and there would be much rain. The rain would fall over him and his clothes would be wet, but he would never get out of the rain, and he would go on prowling around in the city, looking for whatever it was that was there and that nobody else was trying to see, and he would go in and out of all the ugly places to see how it was with the faces of the people when it rained, how the rain changed the expressions of their faces. His body would be wet with the rain, but he would go from one place to another, shouting headlines, telling the city about the things that were going on in the world.

I was this boy and he is dead now, but he will be prowling through the

221

city when my body no longer makes a shadow upon the pavement, and if it is not this boy it will be another, myself again, another boy alive on earth, seeking the essential truth of the scene, seeking the static and precise beneath that which is in motion and which is imprecise.

The theatre stood in the city like another universe, and he entered its darkness, seeking there in the falsity of pictures of man in motion the truth of his own city, and of himself, and the truth of all living. He saw their eyes: *While London Sleeps.* He saw the thin emaciated hand of theft twitching toward crime: *Jean Valjean.* And he saw the lecherous eyes of lust violating virginity. In the darkness the false universe unfolded itself before him and he saw the phantoms of man going and coming, making quiet horrifying shadows: *The Cabinet of Doctor Caligari.* He saw the endless sea, smashing against rocks, birds flying, the great prairie and herds of horses, New York and greater mobs of men, monstrous trains, rolling ships, men marching to war, and a line of infantry charging another line of infantry: *The Birth of a Nation.* And sitting in the secrecy of the theatre he entered the houses of the rich, saw them, the male and the female, the high ceilings, the huge marble pillars, the fancy furniture, great bathrooms, tables loaded with food, rich people laughing and eating and drinking, and then secrecy again and a male seeking a female, and himself watching carefully to understand, one pursuing and the other fleeing, and he felt the lust of man mounting in him, desire for the loveliest of them, the universal lady of the firm white shoulders and the thick round thighs, desire for her, he himself, ten years old, in the darkness.

He is dead and deathless, staring at the magnification of the kiss, straining at the mad embrace of male and female, walking alone from the theatre, insane with the passion to live. And at school their shallowness was too much. Don't try to teach me, he said. Teach the idiots. Don't try to tell me anything. I am getting it direct, straight from the pit, the ugliness with the loveliness. Two times two is many millions all over the earth, lonely and shivering, groaning one at a time, trying to figure it out. Don't try to teach me. I'll figure it out for myself.

Daniel Boone? he said. Don't tell me. I knew him. Walking through Kentucky. He killed a bear. Lincoln? A big fellow walking alone, looking at things as if he pitied them, a face like the face of man. The whole countryside full of dead men, men he loved, and he himself alive. Don't ask me to memorize his speech. I know all about it, the way he stood, the way the words came from his being.

He used to get up before daybreak and walk to the San Joaquin Baking Company. It was good, the smell of freshly baked bread, and it was good to see the machine wrapping the loaves in wax paper. *Chicken bread,* he used to say, and the important man in the fine suit of clothes used to smile at him. The important man used to say. What kind of chickens you got at your house, kid? And the man would smile nicely so that there would be no insult, and he would never have to tell the man that he himself and his brother and sisters were eating the chicken bread. He would just stand by the bin, not saying anything, not asking for the best loaves, and the important man would understand, and he would pick out the best of the loaves and drop them into the sack the boy held open. If the man happened to drop a bad loaf into the sack the boy would say nothing, and a moment later the man would pick out the bad loaf and throw it back into the bin. Those chickens, he would say, they might not like that loaf. And the boy would say nothing. He would just smile. It was good bread, not too stale and sometimes very fresh, sometimes still warm, only it was bread that had fallen from the wrapping machine and couldn't be sold to rich people. It was made of the same dough, in the same ovens, only after the loaves fell they were called chicken bread and a whole sackful cost only a quarter. The important man never insulted. Maybe he himself had known hunger once; maybe as a boy he had known how it felt to be hungry for bread. He was very funny, always asking about the chickens. He knew there were no chickens, and he always picked out the best loaves.

Bread to eat, so that he could move through the city and shout. Bread to make him solid, to nourish his anger, to fill his substance with vigor that shouted at the earth. Bread to carry him to death and back again to life, inhaling, exhaling, keeping the flame within him alive. Chicken bread, he used to say, not feeling ashamed. We eat it. Sure, sure. It isn't good enough for the rich. There are many at our house. We eat every bit of it, all the crumbs. We do not mind a little dirt on the crust. We put all of it inside. A sack of chicken bread. We know we're poor. When the wind comes up our house shakes, but we don't tremble. We can eat the bread that isn't good enough for the rich. Throw in the loaves. It is too good for chickens. It is our life. Sure we eat it. We're not ashamed. We're living on the money we earn selling newspapers. The roof of our house leaks and we catch the water in pans, but we are all there, all of us alive, and the floor of our house sags when we walk over it, and it is full of crickets and spiders and mice, but we are in the house, living there. We eat this bread that isn't quite good enough for the rich, this bread that you call chicken bread.

Walking, this boy vanished, and now it is myself, another, no longer the boy, and the moment is now this moment, of my remembrance. The fig tree he loved: of all graceful things it was the most graceful, and in the winter it stood leafless, dancing, sculptural whiteness dancing. In the spring the new leaves appeared on the fig tree and the hard green figs. The sun came closer and closer and the heat grew, and he climbed the tree, eating the soft fat figs, the flowering of the lovely white woman, his lips kissing.

But always he returned to the city, back again to the place of man, the street, the structure, the door and window, the hall, the roof and floor, back again to the corners of dark secrecy, where they were dribbling out their lives, back again to the movement of mobs, to beds and chairs and stoves, away from the tree, away from the meadow and the brook. The tree was of the other earth, the older and lovelier earth, solid and quiet and of godly grace, of earth and water and of sky and of the time that was before, ancient places, quietly in the sun, Rome and Athens, Cairo, the white fig tree dancing. He talked to the tree, his mouth clenched, pulling himself over its smooth limbs, to be of you, he said, to be of your time, to be there, in the old world, and to be here as well, to eat your fruit, to feel your strength, to move with you as you dance, myself, alone in the world, with you only, my tree, that in myself which is of thee.

Dead, dead, the tree and the boy, yet everlastingly alive, the white tree moving slowly in dance, and the boy talking to it in unspoken, unspeakable language; you, loveliness of the earth, the street waits for me, the moment of my time calls me back, and there he was suddenly, running through the streets, shouting that ten thousand Huns had been destroyed. Huns? he asked. What do you mean, Huns? They are men, aren't they? Call me, then, a Hun. Call me a name, if they are to have a name dying. And he saw the people of the city smiling and talking with pleasure about the good news. He himself appreciated the goodness of the news because it helped him sell his papers, but after the shouting was over and he was himself again, he used to think of ten thousand men smashed from life to violent death, one man at a time, each man himself as he, the boy, was himself, bleeding, praying, screaming, weeping, remembering life as dying men remember it, wanting it, grasping for breath, to go on inhaling and exhaling, living and dying, but always living somehow, stunned, horrified, ten thousand faces suddenly amazed at the monstrousness of the war, the beastliness of man, who could be so godly.

There were no words with which to articulate his rage. All that he could do was shout, but even now I cannot see the war as the historians see it. Succeeding moments have carried the germ of myself to this face and form, the one of this moment, now, my being in this small room, alone, as always, remembering the boy, resurrecting him, and I cannot see the war as the historians see it. Those clever fellows study all the facts and they see the war as a large thing, one of the biggest events in the legend of man, something general, involving multitudes. I see it as a large thing too, only I break it into small units of one man at a time, and I see it as a large and monstrous thing for each man involved. I see the war as death in one form or another for men dressed as soldiers, and all the men who survived the war, including myself, I see as men who died with their brothers, dressed as soldiers.

There is no such thing as a soldier. I see death as a private event, the destruction of the universe in the brain and in the senses of one man, and I cannot see any man's death as a contributing factor in the success or failure of a military campaign. The boy had to shout what had happened. Whatever happened, he had to shout it, making the city know. *Ten thousand Huns killed, ten thousand,* one at a time, one, two, three, four, inestimably many, ten thousand, alive, and then dead, killed, shot, mangled, ten thousand Huns, ten thousand men. I blame the historians for the distortion. I remember the coming of the gas mask to the face of man, the proper grimace of the horror of the nightmare we were performing, artfully expressing the monstrousness of the inward face of man. To the boy who is dead the war was the international epilepsy which brought about the systematic destruction of one man at a time until millions of men were destroyed.

There he is suddenly in the street, running, and it is 1917, shouting the most recent crime of man, extra, extra, ten thousand Huns killed, himself alive, inhaling, exhaling, *ten thousand, ten thousand,* all the ugly buildings solid, all the streets solid, the city unmoved by the crime, *ten thousand,* windows opening, doors opening, and the people of the city smiling about it, good, ten thousand of them killed, good. *Johnny, get your gun, get your*

225

gun, *Johnny get your gun: we'll be over, we're coming over, and we won't come back till it's over, over there,* and another trainload of boys in uniforms, going to the war. And the fat man, sleeping in a corner of the Crystal Bar, what of him? Sleeping there, somehow alive in spite of the lewd death in him, but never budging. Pig, he said, ten thousand Huns killed, ten thousand men with solid bodies mangled to death. Does it mean nothing to you? Does it not disturb your fat dream? Boys with loves, men with wives and children. What have you, sleeping? They are all dead, all of them dead. Do you think you are alive? Do you dream you are alive? The fly on your nose is more alive than you.

Sunday would come, *O day of rest and gladness, O day of joy and light, O balm of care and sadness, Most beautiful, most bright,* and he would put on his best shirt and his best trousers, and he would try to comb his hair down, to be neat and clean, meeting God, and he would go to the small church and sit in the shadow of religion: in the beginning, the boy David felling the giant Goliath, beautiful Rebecca, mad Saul, Daniel among lions, Jesus talking quietly to the men, and in the boat shouting at them because they feared, angry at them because they had fear, calm yourselves, boys, calm yourselves, let the storm rage, let the boat sink, do you fear going to God? Ah, that was lovely, that love of death was lovely, Jesus loving it: calm yourselves, boys, God damn you, calm yourselves, why are you afraid? *Still, still with thee, when purple morning breaketh, abide, abide, with me, fast falls the eventide,* ah, lovely. He sat in the basement of the church, among his fellows, singing at the top of his voice. I do not believe, he said. I cannot believe. There cannot be a God. But it is lovely, lovely, these songs we sing, *Saviour, breathe an evening blessing, sun of my soul, begin, my tongue, some heavenly theme, begin, my tongue, begin, begin.* Lovely, lovely, but I cannot believe. The poor and the rich, those who deserve life and those who deserve death, and the ugliness everywhere. Where is God? Big ships sinking at sea, submarines, men in the water, cannon booming, machine guns, men dying, ten thousand, where? But our singing, *Joy to the world, the Lord is come. Let earth receive her King. Silent night, holy night. What grace, O Lord, my dear redeemer. Ride on, ride on, in majesty. Angels, roll the rock away; death, yield up thy mighty prey.*

No, he could not believe. He had seen for himself. It was there, in the city, all the godlessness, the eyes of the whores, the men at cards, the

sleeping fat man, and the mad headlines, it was all there, unbelief, ungod-
liness, everywhere, all the world forgetting. How could he believe? But the
music, so good and clean, so much of the best in man: *lift up, lift up your
voices now. Lo, he comes with clouds descending once for favored sinners
slain. Arise, my soul, arise, shake off thy guilty fears, O for a thousand
tongues to sing. Like a river glorious, holy Bible, book divine, precious
treasure, thou art mine.* And spat, right on the floor of the Crystal Bar. And
into Madam Juliet's Rooms, over the Rex Drug Store, the men buttoning
their clothes, ten thousand Huns killed, madam. *Break thou the bread of
life, dear Lord, to me, as thou didst break the loaves, beside the sea.* And
spat, on the floor, hearing the fat man snoring. Another ship sunk. The
Marne. Ypres. Russia. Poland. Spat. *Art thou weary, art thou languid, art
thou sore distressed?* Zeppelin over Paris. The fat man sleeping. *Haste,
traveler, haste, the night comes on.* Spat. *The storm is gathering in the west.*
Cannon. Hutt! two, three, four! Hutt! two three, four, how many men
marching, how many? Onward, onward, unChristian soldiers. *I was a wandering sheep.* Spat. *I did not love my home.* Your deal, Jim. Spat. *Take me,
O my father, take me.* Spat. *This holy bread, this holy wine. My God, is any
hour so sweet?* Submarine plunging. Spat. *Take my life and let it be con-
secrated, Lord, to thee.* Spat.

He sat in the basement of the little church, deep in the shadow of faith,
and of no faith: I cannot believe: where is the God of whom they speak,
where? *Your harps, ye trembling saints, down from the willows take.*
Where? Cannon. *Lead, oh lead, lead kindly light, amid the encircling
gloom.* Spat. *Jesus, Saviour, pilot me.* Airplane: spat: smash. *Guide me, O
thou great Jehovah. Bread of heaven, feed me till I want no more.* The universal lady of the dark theatre: thy lips, beloved, thy shoulders and thighs,
thy sea-surging blood. The tree, black figs in sunlight. Spat. *Rock of ages,
cleft for me, let me hide myself in thee.* Spat. *Let the water and the blood,
from thy riven side which flowed, be of sin the double cure.* Lady, your arm,
your arm: spat. The mountain of flesh sleeping through the summer. Ten
thousand Huns killed.

Sunday would come, turning him from the outward world to the inward,
to the secrecy of the past, endless as the future, back to Jesus, to God; *when
the weary, seeking rest, to thy goodness flee;* back to the earliest quiet: *He
leadeth me, O blessed thought.* But he did not believe. He could not be-

227

lieve. Jesus was a remarkable fellow: you couldn't figure him out. He had a pious love of death. An heroic fellow. And as for God. Well, he could not believe.

But the songs he loved and he sang them with all his might: *hold thou my hand, O blessed nothingness, I walk with thee. Awake, my soul, stretch every nerve, and press with vigor on. Work, for the night is coming, work, for the day is done.* Spat. Right on the floor of the Crystal Bar. It is Sunday again: O blessed nothingness, we worship thee. Spat. And suddenly the sleeping fat man sneezes. Hallelujah. Amen. Spat. Sleep on, beloved, sleep, and take thy rest. *Lay down thy head upon thy Saviour's breast.* We love thee well, but Jesus loves thee best. Jesus loves thee. For the Bible tells you so. Amen. The fat man sneezes. He could not believe and he could not disbelieve. Sense? There was none. But glory? There was an abundance of it. Everywhere. Madly everywhere. Those crazy birds vomiting song. Those vast trees, solid and quiet. And clouds. And sun. And night. And day. *It is not death to die,* he sang: *to leave this weary road, to be at home with God.* God? The same. Nothingness. Nowhere. Everywhere. The crazy glory, everywhere: Madam Juliet's Rooms, all modern conveniences, including beds. Spat. *I know not, O I know not, what joys await us there.* Where? Heaven? No. Madam Juliet's. In the church, the house of God, the boy singing, remembering the city's lust.

Boom: Sunday morning: and the war still booming: after the singing he would go to the newspaper office and get his Special Sunday Extras and run through the city with them, his hair combed for God, and he would shout the news: amen, *I gave my life for Jesus.* Oh, yeah? Ten thousand Huns killed, and I am the guy, inhaling, exhaling, running through the town, I, myself, seeing, hearing, touching, shouting, smelling, singing, wanting, I, the guy, the latest of the whole lot, alive by the grace of God: ten thousand, two times ten million, by the grace of God dead, by His grace smashed, amen, extra, extra: five cents a copy, extra, ten thousand killed.

I was this boy who is now lost and buried in the succeeding forms of myself, and I am now of this last moment, of this small room, and the night hush, time going, time coming, breathing, this last moment, inhale, exhale, the boy dead and alive. All that I have learned is that we breathe, and remember, and we see the boy moving through a city that has become lost, among people who have become dead, alive among dead moments, crossing a street, the scene thus, or standing by the bread bin in the bakery, a sack of chicken bread please so that we can live and shout about it, and it begins nowhere and it ends nowhere, and all that I know is that we are somehow alive, all of us in the light, making shadows, the sun overhead, space all around us, inhaling, exhaling, the face and form of man everywhere, pleasure and pain, sanity and madness, war and no war, and peace and no peace, the earth solid and unaware of us, unaware of our cities, our dreams, the earth everlastingly itself, and the sea sullen with movement like my breathing, waves coming and going, and all that I know is that I am alive and glad to be, glad to be of this ugliness and this glory, somehow glad that I can remember the boy climbing the fig tree, unpraying but religious with joy, somehow of the earth, of the time of earth, somehow everlastingly of life, nothingness, blessed or unblessed, somehow deathless, insanely glad to be here, and so it is true, there is no death, somehow there is no death, and can never be.

About the Authors

James Baldwin (1924–   ) was born in Harlem, the black ghetto of New York. From his earliest youth, he knew he wanted to be a writer.

As a spokesman in the black citizen's struggle for equality, he supported his early writing career through fellowships. He was in France when he completed his first novel *Go Tell It On the Mountain*, an autobiographical account of his early life in the home of his preacher father. This was followed by *Giovanni's Room* and *Another Country*. Baldwin is skillful in compacting a great deal of emotion in a few sentences. His collections of short stories and essays, *Notes of a Native Son* and *Nobody Knows My Name* reveal clarity of understanding of the black person's plight in the United States. An expatriate for many years, he has recently returned to America.

Konrad Bercovici (1882–1961) was a Rumanian-American novelist, dramatist, short story and essay writer. He was born in Rumania and spent much of his early life among the tents of gypsies who had migrated from Hungary. He learned their language and their culture and felt at home among them. He would say, "There is not a gypsy in the world who cannot tell you who I am. I am a gypsy by choice and not by blood, by temperament and not race."

In 1916 he came to New York and proceeded to add English to the Rumanian, French, German, Greek, Yiddish, Italian and Spanish he already knew. His first book *Crimes of Charity* is an indictment of the indifference of organized charity to the people whom it supposedly helped. He has recorded his life with the gypsies in songs and novels. His work is lively and intimate, filled with intrigue, scandal and gossip—enough to ensure a large reading public both in the United States and abroad. His principal works include *The Crusader*, *A Romantic Biography*, *The Incredible Balkans*, and *It's the Gypsy in Me*.

Daniel Berrigan (1921–   ) was a Jesuit priest who was active in radical political movements in this country in the sixties. He was particularly vocal against American involvement in the Vietnam War action and promoted various acts of civil disobedience which caused him to be jailed on several occasions. Born in 1921, he has been a published poet since 1957 with his book *Time Without Number*, for

231

which he won the Lamont Poetry Award. In 1959 his collection of essays, *Bride: Essays in the Church* followed. Several other poetry collections appeared, two in 1968: *Love, Love at the End,* and *Night Flight to Hanoi.*

Berrigan has been a professor of religion and was also associate director of Cornell University's United Religious Work.

William Browne (1930–   ) was born in New York City. He has led a varied life: he has studied clinical psychology, worked at diverse jobs, and after having had traveled widely, he has returned to the city of his birth. His poetry has been published in the *Pittsburgh Courier, Prëencle Africiane, Phylon,* and in an anthology entitled *Beyond the Blues.*

Witter Bynner (1881–1961) came from a literary family. His grandfather was editor of a newspaper in Worcester, Massachusetts and his uncle was a novelist. While at Harvard, Bynner was on the staff of *The Advocate.* Later he became an assistant editor of *McClure's Magazine* and literary advisor of McClure, Phillips & Co. At one point he conducted a class in verse-writing at the University of California. After this he traveled extensively in the Orient, particularly in China—and Chinese poetry became coupled with Indian poetry, a great influence in his life.

Bynner's translation, with Dr. Kiang Kang-hu, of the poems included in *The Jade Mountains,* 1929, was the first volume of Chinese verse to be translated in full by an American poet.

Melville Cane (1879–   ) a New York lawyer, is also a frequently published poet who has produced enough work for several editions of his own and who has been widely reprinted and anthologized.

He was raised and educated in New York where he received the AB and LLB from Columbia University. He has been a member of Ernst, Cane, Berner and Gitlin, and a director of Harcourt, Brace & World, Inc. In 1948 he received the Columbia University Medal for excellence in law and literature. Among his collected works are: *A Wider Arc,* 1947; *Making a Palm,* 1953; *Bullet-Hunting,* 1960. He was co-editor of *The Man from Main Street,* 1953 and *Golden Years,* 1960.

Willa Cather (1873–1947), brilliant stylist and one of the first American women novelists to be recognized as a substantial artist, grew up in the frontier Nebraska in the latter part of the nineteenth century. The crudeness of existence in the small town of Red Cloud, arid and drab, evoked her deep desire to escape from the grueling mediocrity of her childhood. This escape theme—the need for freedom, the breaking of chains, and the flight into a life of imagination—was to be a major one in much of her fiction. Cather did not start writing seriously until she was into her

232

thirties. Prior to the publication of her first novel *Alexander's Bridge* when she was thirty-nine, she had been a teacher, a journalist and the managing editor of *Mc-Clure's Magazine*. She had earlier published a book of poetry, *April Twilights*, and a collection of short stories, *The Troll Garden*. But the success she felt after publication of *Alexander's Bridge* gave her the impetus to devote all her time for the rest of her life to writing.

She could never rid herself of her childhood experiences. Two of her better known works, *O Pioneers* and *My Antonia*, reflect the deprived adolescent years, the search for self and roots and the struggle for artistic fulfillment.

Cather was a prolific writer. In her seventy-three years she published more than a dozen novels, and several collections of short stories, essays, and literary criticism.

Borden Deal (1922–) is a Southerner, born in Mississippi and educated at the University of Alabama. He beat around the country as a youth, working for a circus, on a showboat, and in the Civilian Conservation Corps. From 1941–42 he worked for the U. S. Department of Labor, where he started writing. He continued to have a varied career—service in the Navy, correspondent for Associated Films, skip tracer for an auto finance company—all jobs which gave him experience for his writing. From 1955 on, he has been a full-time writer; he is a winner of a Guggenheim Fellowship, and recipient of the American Library Association Liberty and Justice Award for *Walk Through The Valley*. Other works include: *Dragon's Wine*, *The Spangled Road*, and *A Long Way To Go*.

John Dos Passos (1896–1970) was born in Chicago and educated at Harvard. He went to France as an ambulance driver at the outset of World War I, and these and other wartime experiences had a vivid impact on his writing. With the publication of *Three Soldiers* in 1921, Dos Passos emerged as a new voice who brilliantly described the struggles of men in the First World War.

He was a man and writer committed to his political values, which are strongly expressed in his most widely recognized work, a social history entitled *U.S.A.*, comprised of *The 42nd Parallel* (1930), *1919* (1932) and *The Big Money* (1936).

He has influenced many 20th century writers and philosophers, including Jean-Paul Sartre, who called him "the greatest American novelist."

Theodore Dreiser (1871–1945), a prolific writer, wrote eight long novels, four collections of short stories, and two volumes of autobiography—in addition to collections of plays, essays and poems. Dreiser is well known for his naturalistic novels, the most praised of which are *Sister Carrie* and *An American Tragedy*. With his intricate and complex style, Dreiser exhibited the literary power to convey compassion for the poor and struggling. He saw people as being shaped by "forces" of nature in which the most ruthless achieved the most success.

Dreiser's father was a German immigrant who did reasonably well at the weaver's trade until a fire destroyed his woolen mill in Sullivan, Indiana. He spent the rest of his life trying to recoup his losses. Supporting the family was left to Dreiser's mother, and the family travelled all over Indiana wherever she could get work. The family's struggles gave him subjects for a lifetime of writing. A sympathetic teacher saw the talent in Dreiser and paid for a year for him at Indiana University, where he discovered the writings of Balzac and began to feel their influence.

Dreiser's work shocked the literary world at the turn of the century because of his complete dedication to unvarnished truth, but enough people were captivated by his work to read it, and he reached material success and visibility as a public figure.

Over the years readers have come to admire *An American Tragedy* as a masterpiece of American art, a shrewdly planned structure of calculated effects, of moral statements about good and evil, and a brilliant portrayal of the nature of "chance" in human existence.

Ralph Ellison (1914–   ) was born in Oklahoma City and studied music at Tuskegee Institute. Early in his youth he changed his career to literature. In 1965 a Book Week poll of critics, authors, and editors called his first novel *Invisible Man* to be "the most distinguished single work" published in America since 1945.

Influenced by Richard Wright, Ellison started writing for the *New Masses,* a black quarterly in the mid-thirties. His writing reflects his interest in the racial identity of the black in America, and he makes great use of irony and fantasy in his work. He is a perennial idealist and has a confident and optimistic attitude toward black American potential. He enjoys the racial and ethnic differences of human beings and encourages respect for those differences.

Ellison has taught at Bard College, at Bennington College and at Rutgers University. He continues to write and lecture.

Edna Ferber (1887–1968) was born in Kalamazoo, Michigan and became a reporter for the *Milwaukee Journal* when she was eighteen—at a time when women reporters were few and far between, and were referred to, rather uncharitably, as "sob sisters." Her own writing is an artful combination of country-girl simplicity and urban sophistication. Not surprisingly, her first novels dealt with the problems of women who sought careers in a man's world.

Ferber won a Pulitzer Prize for her novel *So Big* in 1924; her novel *Show Boat,* which she published in 1926, became a famous operetta. Her versatility was again

234

exhibited when she and the brilliant humorist and playwright George S. Kaufman collaborated to produce *Dinner at Eight, Stage Door, The Royal Family,* and a number of other successful plays. Her journalistic, literary, and dramatic gifts were enormous, and she earned a justly-deserved reputation as one of America's leading women of letters.

Lawrence Ferlinghetti—Born in Yonkers, New York around 1919 (there is some confusion as to the actual date), Ferlinghetti was early deprived of his parents. After his father died and his mother was institutionalized with emotional problems, he was taken to France by an aunt. He remained there for a number of years. Upon his return to America, he lived in an orphanage in Chappaqua, New York. Then he was taken in by the Lawrence family, founders of Sarah Lawrence College in Bronxville, New York, where he spent his most impressionable years.

He was educated at the University of North Carolina and Columbia University, and obtained an advanced degree from the Sorbonne in Paris. He is a founder and editor of City Lights, a bookstore and publishing company in San Francisco, where he now lives. His book of poems *A Coney Island of the Mind* has enjoyed enormous success both here and abroad. He has also written experimental forms of prose in his book *Routines.*

Gerald Green (1922–   ), son of a Brooklyn physician, used his father as protaganist for his first successful novel *The Last Angry Man.* Based on Green's recollections of his early life in Brownsville (Brooklyn), the book pictured the overworked, ill-tempered, non-conforming Dr. Sam Abelman as an ethical life-saver of the slums who refused to compromise his values. The success of this novel gave Green, who had worked as an NBC television writer since his graduation from the Columbia School of Journalism, the opportunity to devote himself entirely to fiction. As a result, there followed several more novels: *The Lotus Eaters,* a satire on the operators, publicists and fixers of Miami Beach; and *The Hidden Light,* a denunciation of the morals and greed of the press. *Portofino PTA,* which was published when Green was living with his family on the Italian Riviera, is a funny memoir of family experiences abroad.

In 1961 Green returned to NBC where he has been writer, director, producer of many well-known programs: Dave Garroway's Today Show, Chet Huntley Reporting, Wide Wide World and a number of documentaries. He has also continued to write novels, always with some humor, always satirically critical of some segment of contemporary society.

In *To Brooklyn, With Love,* he returns as a middle aged suburbanite to visit the scenes of his youth and to remember once more his strong, irrascible but immen-

235

sely honest doctor father. His abiding interest in archeology took him to Israel in 1969 where he visited several digs and recorded his experience in a memoir, *The Stones of Zion*. His 1978 television series of the *Holocaust* won him much praise.

Nancy Hale (1908–   ) bears a distinguished American name. Born in New England, daughter of Philip L. Hale, Boston painter and art critic, granddaughter of Edward Everett Hale, Unitarian minister and author of *The Man Without A Country*, she is also a descendent of Nathan Hale, the famous patriot.

Her first story appeared in the *Boston Herald* when she was eleven. Since then she has published at least a dozen works of fiction: novels and collections of short stories, among them *The Young Die Good* and *Black Summer*.

Donald Hall (1928–   ) grew up in Connecticut and was educated both at Harvard and Oxford Universities. He has been a professor of English at the University of Michigan in Ann Arbor, and now resides in New Hampshire.

Hall is a prolific writer, critic, and poet. His *Exiles and Marriages* won the Newdigate Prize in 1952. *String Too Short To Be Saved*, his autobiography, was published in 1961. He has been an editor of the *Paris Review* and, with Stephen Spender, he edited *The Concise Encyclopedia of English* and *American Poets and Poetry*, 1963. He has recently published a volume of poetry entitled *Kicking the Leaves*.

Ben Hecht's (1894–1964) literary career involved him in a variety of journalistic, theatrical and literary activities. Never one to be placid, he always had several projects going at once. For years he commuted between California—where he wrote, directed and produced many films, among them the famous *Notorious* and *Spellbound*—and Nyack, New York, where he and his collaborator Charles MacArthur wrote plays for Broadway. In 1946 he produced a stirring pageant about the struggle of the Jews for Palestine, *A Flag is Born*, which received much praise. His television series produced in 1953, *Tales of a City*, had a wide audience.

His versatility and dramatic energy led him to publish a philosophical treatise on anti-semites and anti-semitism, *A Guide for the Bedeviled*, which reflected his anger but expressed what Hal Borland called "tart truth."

In 1954 his biography *Child of the Century* was published. Novelist Saul Bellow commented, "His manners are not always nice, but then nice manners do not always make interesting autobiographies and this autobiography has the merit of being intensely interesting. If he is occasionally slick, he is also independent, forthright and original. Among the pussycats who write of social issues today, he roars like an old-fashioned lion."

236

Mark Helprin (1947–   ) spent his youth in New York City, the Hudson River valley, and the British West Indies. He was educated at Harvard College and at the Harvard Center for Middle Eastern Studies, and has served in the British Merchant Navy, and the Israeli infantry and air force.

Many of his stories have appeared in *The New Yorker*, and can also be found in the collection *A Dove of the East*. Helprin is known as an effortless storyteller who reveals clearly the images of the world in which his varied characters live.

Arthur Hoppe (1925–   ) is a syndicated American journalist who has been referred to, by former presidential press secretary Pierre Salinger, as "the best political humorist in the country." He writes for the *San Francisco Chronicle*, and has covered a variety of assignments, which included posing as a Skid Row derelict, before he became a nationally known columnist.

Hoppe's publications include *The Love Everybody Crusade, Dreamboat*, and *The Perfect Solution to Absolutely Everything*. He has been a contributor to *The New Yorker, Harper's, Nation, Yachting*, and other periodicals.

Langston Hughes's (1902–1967) versatility produced many short stories, novels, articles, plays, television scripts, and essays in addition to an autobiography and an enormous quantity of poignant, sensitive poetry. He was born in Joplin, Missouri, but studied at Columbia University at Lincoln University in Pennsylvania, from which he received his degree. His poetry was influenced greatly by Carl Sandburg, and by the rhythms and sounds of jazz. During his career he published nearly thirty volumes of verse and prose.

His mission was to portray Negro life in America, particularly in Harlem where he lived most of his adult life. With poets Claude McKay, Jean Toomer, and Countee Cullen, he was part of the Harlem Renaissance of the 1920s.

Alfred Kazin (1915–   ) was born in Brooklyn. An early and avid reader, his extracurricular high-school activities included writing plays. During his undergraduate years at the City College of New York, he tutored fellow students and worked as a researcher for professors and candidates for advanced degrees. After graduation he taught at CCNY and wrote book reviews for the *New Republic*. His first book *On Native Grounds*, a volume of literary criticism, was published in 1942.

Kazin has been at the center of American intellectual life for the past thirty years. He has told of his experiences in three volumes: *A Walker in the City, Starting Out in the Thirties*, and *New York Jew* (published in 1978). In all of these he paints portraits of the famous literary figures with whom he has had personal relationships: Henry and Clare Luce, Edmund Wilson, Lionel Trilling, Saul Bellow, Sylvia Plath, Hannah Arendt, Randall Jarrell, and Robert Lowell, among them.

237

About the Authors

Kazin has taught at Harvard University, the University of California, the University of Minnesota, and Smith College. In 1963 he was appointed professor of English at the State University of New York at Stonybook.

Bernard Malamud (1914–   ) was brought up in Brooklyn, the son of immigrant parents who had come from Russia in the early 1900s. Although the family lived on the edge of poverty, his youth was not unhappy. He was an avid reader, and was introduced early to the magic of the theatre.

Malamud has taught English and literature in colleges while actively pursuing his writing. He emerged in the 1950s as an urban Jewish writer concerned with the drama of the personality fulfilling itself. His heroes achieve fulfillment only when, after suffering, they learn to love someone more than they love themselves.

Among his many novels are *The Assistant*, *The Fixer*, and, most recently, *Dubin's Lives;* his short story collections include *The Magic Barrel* and *Idiot's First*.

Elva Mangold (E. P. Maxwell) (1923–   ) was born in Newburgh, New York and was educated there at St. Mary's Academy, and later at Russell Sage College. She began writing in the 1940s, selling her first short stories to pulp magazines. A resident of San Francisco, she has worked as a volunteer at San Francisco Airport, with a crippled children's auxiliary, and with the Peninsula Children's Theatre.

Her book *Just Dial A Number* published in 1971 was a Junior Literary Guild selection. She has also edited *The Corral*, the Junior League Magazine.

H. L. Mencken (1880–1956) was born and educated in Baltimore, Maryland. He started his writing career after his father died and he left the family tobacco business to work for the Baltimore *Morning Herald*. He then moved to the Baltimore *Sun* where he worked for many years. He was editor of the *Smart Set* magazine and of *American Mercury*, although he maintained newspaper journalism was his primary loyalty.

In a long literary life, his most successful publication was a treatise *The American Language*, first published in 1919. He had tremendous influence on the most literary-minded artists of his time, Theodore Dreiser and Sinclair Lewis among them.

Lillian Morrison (1917–   ) has been a librarian all during her adult life while at the same time writing poetry. A native of New Jersey, she was educated at Douglass College and Columbia University. She has been young adult librarian at the New York Public Library and was assistant coordinator of young adult services for the Rutgers University Library.

238

Morrison has compiled several volumes of poetry, including *Yours Till Niagara Falls, Black Within and Red Without,* and *Remember Me When This You See.* As a general editor of the Crowell Poets Series, she worked on volumes of poetry by Stephen Crane, Emily Dickinson, Wordsworth, Keats, Whitman, Browning and Blake.

Joyce Carol Oates (1938–   ) was born in Lockport, New York. She has written short stories, novels, poetry, essays, plays, articles, and reviews. Many of her stories are set in Detroit, a city she knows well.

She writes of ordinary people caught up in webs of confusion and horror by society and their own weaknesses. She is noted for her skill in developing tension in her characters; there is a frequent note of terror in her stories, whose dramatic qualities are unforgettable. Oates experiments with parables, allegories, myths, and symbols to explore the inner workings of the human mind. She was awarded a National Book Award for her fiction in 1970.

Carl Sandburg (1878–1967)—The son of poor Swedish immigrants who settled in Galesburg, Illinois, Carl Sandburg held various short-term jobs as a youth—newsboy, janitor, milkman and dishwasher. Driven by a searching spirit of restlessness, he travelled to the wheat fields of Kansas and to the Rocky Mountains for a time. After serving in the Spanish-American War, Sandburg attended Lombard College. During the years that followed, he became an organizer for the Social Democratic party in Wisconsin, secretary to the mayor of Milwaukee, a journalist with the Chicago *Daily News,* and poet laureate of Illinois. In 1926 he was awarded the Pulitzer Prize for his two-volume biography *Abraham Lincoln: The Prairie Years.*

The America Sandburg knew and wrote about was the Midwest—the industrial life of Chicago, the prairie cornfields and agricultural centers, and "the people." In his use of colloquial language, the poet achieved a sense of actuality. Abandoning conventional rhyme and meter, he learned free-verse techniques which included the grammatical paralleling and counterpointing of phrases and clauses. Sandburg also experimented with adapting the Japanese haiku in poems like "Fog" and "Wistful."

Most of Sandburg's verse is collected in his *Complete Poems.* Other major works include his autobiography, *Always the Young Strangers.*

William Saroyan's (1908–   ) imagination and sense of the ironic have captivated the American public for almost fifty years. A Californian by birth, Saroyan inherited his storytelling skill from his Armenian-born father and his grandmother, who later became key figures in many of his tales. He is best known for his short stories which paint sharp, sensitive pictures of characters struggling with the human dilemma in an environment they don't understand. Since 1933, when he emerged with *The Daring Young Man on the Flying Trapeze,* he has published at least a dozen collections of short stories. Among them are *Little Children, Three Times Three, Love, Here is My Hat, Peace It's Wonderful,* and *My name is Aram,* which earned a place as a Book-of-the-Month selection.

His four plays have been both widely acclaimed and loudly denounced. *The Time of Your Life,* produced in 1944, was awarded the Pulitzer Prize (which Saroyan refused) as the best play of the year, and the Critics Circle Prize (which he accepted). *The Time of Your Life* became a film, as did his most famous novel *The Human Comedy.* He later wrote *Laughing Matter* and *Bicycle Rider in Beverly Hills,* both tongue-in-cheek narratives. Saroyan's warmth for people and his gift for expression transform the most ordinary experience into something unique.

Karl (Jay) Shapiro's (1913–) poetry is remarkable for its variety of original styles. His early work expresses concern with the life and customs of modern society. The poetry of his first books is polished, elegant, witty, and conversational, but also contains great compassion and sympathy, as evidenced in such poems as "Auto Wreck" and "Elegy for a Dead Soldier." He explores the ironies, contradictions, prejudices and fantasies of American society while expressing concern for the treatment of Jews and Negroes, as well as about the divisions in this country between rich and poor.

Born in Baltimore, Maryland in 1913 and educated at the University of Virginia, Johns Hopkins and Pratt Library School, Shapiro has taught at several universities, including Loyola of Chicago, the University of Nebraska, and the University of Illinois. He has won several prestigious awards, including a Guggenheim Fellowship and the Pulitzer Prize. He is a member of the Bollingen Prize Committee and a Fellow in the American Letters of the Library of Congress.

John Updike (1932–), novelist, short story writer and poet, was born in 1932 and raised in Shillington, Pennsylvania. The son of poor school teachers, he managed to go to Harvard University and the Ruskin School of Drawing and Fine Art in Oxford, England.

In 1955 he joined the staff of *The New Yorker* as "Talk of the Town" reporter, and was a prolific contributor of parodies, essays, verse, and stories. Many of his early works relate to the small-town life of his boyhood. *Poorhouse Fair* is set in a home for the old in New Jersey. *Rabbit Run,* his most famous work, considered by many to be his best, is a grotesque allegory of American life. In *The Centaur,* Updike based his story of a school teacher father who sacrifices his life for his son on the myth of Chiron, the Centaur who died to atone for Prometheus's theft of fire from the gods. It received the National Book Award for fiction.

240

Lew Welch (1926–1971) was born in Phoenix, Arizona and educated at the College of the Pacific, Reed College, and the University of Chicago.

His poetry was greatly affected by his contact with William Carlos Williams, who influenced three collections of poetry: *Wobbly Rock*, 1960, *Hermit Poems*, 1965, and *On Out*, 1965.

While at Reed College, he wrote his thesis on Gertrude Stein whom he admired greatly. He had a lifelong interest in structural linguistics and did a considerable amount of advertising writing. His army experience in World War II led to a bout with amnesia which his poetry writing helped him overcome.

E. B. White (1899–   )—Born in Mount Vernon, New York, White graduated from Cornell University after having served as a private in the U.S. Army. After college, he went West and worked as a reporter on the *Seattle Times;* from there he went to Alaska as a mess boy in a ship, and then to New York where he became production assistant in an advertising agency before joining the staff of *The New Yorker.* For eleven years, he wrote most of the "Notes and Comment" columns in that magazine.

White's literary talents are vast indeed. His style is highly individual—a critic in *Time* magazine called it "a kind of precocious off-hand humming." He and William Strunk collaborated on the highly successful writing guide, *Elements of Style.* His books *Charlotte's Web* and *Stuart Little* are classics in children's literature, beloved by young readers around the world.

He is the recipient of many awards and honors, both in and out of the literary world. In 1963 President John F. Kennedy awarded him the Presidential Medal of Freedom, the highest honor a civilian can receive from his government in peacetime.

William Carlos Williams (1883–1963) was born and raised in Rutherford, New Jersey where he wrote and practiced medicine until his death.

He said, "I've been writing, trying to get a few things said, ever since I started to study medicine. One feeds the other, in a manner of speaking. Both seem necessary to me. One gets me out among the neighbors, the other permits me to express what I've been turning over in my mind as I go along."

Williams attended preparatory school in Geneva and received his MD from the University of Pennsylvania. He did graduate work in pediatrics at the University of Leipzig. In 1926 he received the Dial Award of $2,000 for "Services to American Literature," and is considered one of America's major poets.

The subject of **Thomas Wolfe**'s (1900–1938) work was always Thomas Wolfe. All of his novels tell of his life in great detail, his youth in *Look Homeward Angel* in Asheville, North Carolina and his adult life in *Of Time and the River, The*

241

About the Authors

Web and the Rock, and *You Can't Go Home Again*. Wolfe set down in realistic, exact descriptions everything he thought or experienced, and the result was brilliant fiction.

As an author, he was unsure of himself and agonized over everything he wrote. He was a prolific writer, but he lacked artistic control and the ability to pare his fiction into form suitable for publication. His work needed considerable editing, and this, for many years, the famous editor Maxwell Perkins did for him.

Richard Wright (1908–1960) started his career as a writer in the Federal Writers' Project during the Depression. Born near Natchez, Mississippi in 1908, he worked during his youth at menial jobs. In 1939 he won *Story Magazine*'s prize for "Uncle Tom's Children," written while working for the WPA. *Native Son*, his second novel, has become a classic in American literature, as has his autobiography *Black Boy* published in 1945.

Wright grew up in a world of harsh racial discrimination. He was enraged by the impotence of his people and the inequities in American society: "Watching the white people eat would make my empty stomach churn and I would grow vaguely angry. Why could I not eat when I was hungry?"

He became an expatriate writer in Europe after World War II and continued to write there until his death in 1960.

(Continued from page iv)

ELVA MANGOLD, "The Land of Room Enough" from *The First Story of Job* by Elva Mangold, Pilot Industries, Inc., 1960. Reprinted by permission of Pilot Books.

RICHARD WRIGHT, "Hunger." From pp. 13–16 (under the title "Hunger") from *Black Boy* by Richard Wright. Copyright, 1937, 1942, 1944, 1945 by Richard Wright. By permission of Harper & Row, Publishers, Inc.

NANCY HALE, "The Copley-Plaza." Reprinted by permission of Charles Scribner's Sons from *The Emperor's Ring* by Nancy Hale. Copyright 1954 by Nancy Hale. First published in *The New Yorker*.

CARL SANDBURG, "Good Morning, America." From *Good Morning, America*, copyright 1928, 1956 by Carl Sandburg. Reprinted by permission of Harcourt Brace Jovanovich, Inc.

EDNA FERBER, selection from *A Peculiar Treasure*. Based on *A Peculiar Treasure* by Edna Ferber Copyright © 1938, 1939 by Edna Ferber; Copyright © 1960 by Morris L. Ernst, et al., Trustees; Copyright © Renewed 1966 by Edna Ferber All Rights Reserved.

LEW WELCH, "After Anacreon," selection from *Ring of Bone* by Lew Welch. Copyright © 1973 by Donald Allen, Literary Executor of the Estate of Lew Welch. Reprinted by permission of Grey Fox Press.

DANIEL BERRIGAN, "The News Stand." Reprinted with permission of Macmillan Publishing Co., Inc. from *No One Walks Waters* by Daniel Berrigan. Copyright © 1964, 1966 by Daniel Berrigan. Originally appeared in *Ave Maria* magazine.

BERNARD MALAMUD, "The Prison" from *The Magic Barrel* by Bernard Malamud. Copyright © 1950, 1958 by Bernard Malamud. Copyright renewed © 1978 by Bernard Malamud. Reprinted with permission of Farrar, Straus & Giroux, Inc.

BEN HECHT, "Chicago" from *A Child of the Century* by Ben Hecht. Copyright © 1954 by Ben Hecht. Reprinted by permission of Simon & Schuster, a Division of Gulf & Western Corporation.

KONRAD BERCOVICI, "The Newly Rich Goldsteins." "The Newly Rich Goldsteins" is reprinted from *The Dust of New York* by Konrad Bercovici, with the permission of Liveright Publishing Corporation. Copyright 1919 by Boni & Liveright. Copyright Renewed 1947 by Konrad Bercovici.

JOYCE CAROL OATES, "How I Contemplated the World from the Detroit House of Correction and Began My Life All Over Again." Reprinted from *The Wheel of Love* by Joyce Carol Oates by permission of the publisher, Vanguard Press, Inc. Copyright, ©, 1970, 1969, 1968, 1967, 1966, 1965, by Joyce Carol Oates.

KARL SHAPIRO, "D.C." Copyright 1947 by Karl Shapiro. Reprinted from *Collected Poems 1940–1978*, by Karl Shapiro, by permission of Random House, Inc. Originally appeared in *The New Yorker*.

WILLA CATHER, "Paul's Case." Reprinted from *Willa Cather's Collected Short Fiction, 1892–1912* (rev. ed.) with introduction by Mildred R. Bennett. Edited by Virginia Faulkner by permission of the University of Nebraska Press. Copyright © 1965, 1970 by the University of Nebraska Press.

MARK HELPRIN, "Back Bay Conservatory." Copyright © 1975 by Mark Helprin. Reprinted from *A Dove of the East and Other Stories*, by Mark Helprin, by permission of Alfred A. Knopf, Inc.

LANGSTON HUGHES, "Ballad of the Landlord" from *Montage of a Dream Deferred* by Langston Hughes. Reprinted by permission of Harold Ober Associates Incorporated. Copyright 1951 by Langston Hughes.

THOMAS WOLFE, "Only the Dead Know Brooklyn." Reprinted by permission of Charles Scribner's Sons. Copyright 1935 Charles Scribner's Sons.

Acknowledgments

E. B. WHITE, selection from *Here Is New York*. Abridged from *Here Is New York* from *Essays of E. B. White*. Copyright 1949 by E. B. White. Reprinted by Permission of Harper & Row, Publishers, Inc.

WILLIAM BROWNE, "Harlem Sounds" from *American Negro Poetry* edited by Anna Bontemps.

JAMES BALDWIN, "Fifth Avenue, Uptown: A Letter from Harlem" excerpted from the book *Nobody Knows My Name* by James Baldwin Copyright © 1960 by James Baldwin. Originally published in *Esquire*. Reprinted by permission of The Dial Press.

WILLIAM CARLOS WILLIAMS, "Approach to a City" from *Collected Later Poems* by William Carlos Williams. Copyright 1950 by William Carlos Williams. Reprinted by permission of New Directions.

WITTER BYNNER, "Pittsburgh," from *A Cantical of Pan*. Reprinted by permission of The Witter Bynner Foundation for Poetry, Inc.

ARTHUR HOPPE, "Interesting Native Customs in Washington and Other Savage Lands." Copyright 1962 Chronicle Publishing Company, reprinted by permission of the author.

DONALD HALL, "Detroit." First published in the *Hudson Review*, Vol. XIII, #4, winter 1960–61. Reprinted by permission of the author.

MELVILLE CANE, "Park Pigeons." Copyright 1930, 1958 by Melville Cane. Reprinted from his volume *So That It Flower* by permission of Harcourt Brace Jovanovich, Inc.

BORDON DEAL, "Antaeus." Copyright © 1961 by Southern Methodist University Press. Used by permission of The Bordon Deal Family Trust (Bordon Deal, Trustee).

JOHN UPDIKE, "Scenic." From *The Carpentered Hen and Other Tame Creatures* by John Updike. Copyright © 1957 by John Updike. Originally appeared in *The New Yorker* and reprinted by permission of Harper & Row, Publishers, Inc.

H. L. MENCKEN, selection from *Happy Days*. Copyright 1939 by Alfred A. Knopf, Inc. and renewed 1967 by August Mencken and Mercantile Safe Deposit and Trust Co. Reprinted from *Happy Days,* by H. L. Mencken, by permission of Alfred A. Knopf, Inc. Originally appeared in *The New Yorker*.

GERALD GREEN, selection from *To Brooklyn With Love* by Gerald Green. Copyright © 1967 by Gerald Green. Reprinted by permission of Simon & Schuster, a Division of Gulf & Western Corporation.

RALPH ELLISON, selection from *Shadow and Act*, by Ralph Ellison. Copyright © 1964 by Ralph Ellison. Reprinted by permission of Random House, Inc.

MARK HELPRIN, "Willis Avenue." Copyright © 1975 by Mark Helprin. Reprinted from *A Dove of the East and Other Stories*, by Mark Helprin, by permission of Alfred A. Knopf, Inc. Originally appeared in *The New Yorker*.

JOHN DOS PASSOS, "San Francisco Looks West" from *State of the Nation* by John Dos Passos. Reprinted by permission of Elizabeth H. Dos Passos.

WILLIAM SAROYAN, "Resurrection of A Life" from *The Daring Young Men on the Flying Trapeze*. Reprinted with kind permission of the author.

PICTURE CREDITS

Page 2: *A City of Fantasy*, American School, Mid-Nineteenth Century. Courtesy of the National Gallery of Art. Gift of Edgar William and Bernice Chrysler Garbisch, 1967.

Page 6: *Tug of War*. Courtesy of the National Archives.

244

Acknowledgments

Page 23: *Chalk Games.* Photograph by Arthur Leipzig. Used with permission.

Page 25: *Mullen's Alley, ca. 1888−9.* Photograph by Jacob Riis, Jacob Riis Collection. Courtesy of the Museum of the City of New York.

Page 60: Courtesy of the New York Times.

Page 67: *Hester Street from Clinton Street, New York.* Courtesy of the Museum of the City of New York.

Page 84: Courtesy of American Airlines.

Page 139: David A. Krathwohl, Stock, Boston, Inc.

Page 148: *View of St. Louis, ca. 1939,* by Joe Jones. Courtesy of the St. Louis Art Museum. Gift of Mrs. Robert Elman.

Page 152: Harry Wilks, Stock, Boston, Inc.

Page 155: *Skating in Central Park, 1894.* Photograph by Byron, the Byron Collection. Courtesy of the Museum of the City of New York.

Page 170: Rick Stafford, Stock, Boston, Inc.

Page 189: Owen Franken, Stock, Boston, Inc.

Page 189: Jan Lukas, Photo Researchers, Inc.

Page 212: *Willis Avenue Bridge,* by Ben Shahn. Courtesy of the Museum of Modern Art, New York. Gift of Lincoln Kirstein.

Index

Index